A GENERAL THEORY (
AND JUS

Intro, 1-5, 6.1-6.3, 7.3

A General Theory of
Domination and Justice

FRANK LOVETT

OXFORD

UNIVERSITY PRESS

OXFORD
UNIVERSITY PRESS

Great Clarendon Street, Oxford OX2 6DP
United Kingdom

Oxford University Press is a department of the University of Oxford.
It furthers the University's objective of excellence in research, scholarship,
and education by publishing worldwide.

Oxford is a registered trade mark of Oxford University Press
in the UK and in certain other countries

British Library Cataloguing in Publication Data
Data available

Library of Congress Cataloging in Publication Data
Library of Congress Control Number: 2009943745

ISBN 978–0–19–957941–9
ISBN 978–0–19–967299–8 (pbk)

Printed in the United Kingdom by
Lightning Source UK Ltd., Milton Keynes

This book is dedicated to the memory of
Brian M. Barry (1936–2008)
whose passion for social justice inspired generations of students.

Contents

Acknowledgments

This book owes its genesis to a conversation over coffee with Philip Pettit, to whom I must first give thanks for support, advice, and friendship during the ten years or so that it has been in progress. Whatever the merits of this work, they owe a great deal to Philip's inspiration; whatever its mistakes, they are my own. Having worked on this project for so long, however, I have naturally accumulated many other debts. With respect to the earliest version of the book, I must give pride of place to my sponsors and mentors at Columbia University—Brian Barry, Jon Elster, and David Johnston especially—whose warm counsel and support during my time in graduate school was simply invaluable. I was also extremely fortunate to have had an exceptional dissertation committee that included not only David, Brian, and Philip, but also Jeremy Waldron and Nadia Urbinati. Julian Franklin, Paul MacDonald, Scott Morrison, Murat Akan, and Mehmet Tabak also read the earlier version in whole or in part, and provided many suggestions and recommendations. A significantly revised and improved version, written in 2007, was first presented at two-day intensive workshop organized by Kit Wellman under the auspices of the Center for the Study of Ethics and Human Values at Washington University; in addition to Kit, the participants in this workshop were Jack Knight, Andrew Rehfeld, Clarissa Hayward, Ian MacMullen, Larry May, Marilyn Friedman, Jim Bohman, and Richard Dagger. I was honored and humbled by their willingness to devote such time and energy to reading and discussing my ideas, and the final version of this book owes a great deal to their searching critiques. The final manuscript, prepared in the spring of 2008, was read comprehensively by Cécile Laborde, José Martí, and Peter Morriss, among others. Their extremely helpful comments have led, I hope, to many further improvements. Throughout this process, I have additionally had the benefit of many exceptional editors. First, my editors at Oxford University Press, Dominic Byatt, Elizabeth Suffling, and Louise Sprake, who have been indispensable in bringing my work to print. The second version of the manuscript was meticulously edited by my wife Elizabeth Vickerman, and the final version by Melissa Cook. The expression "copy-editing" significantly understates their contribution, as both have saved me from countless embarrassing errors and conceptual confusions. Elizabeth also provided invaluable assistance in constructing the book's index.

I have presented parts of my work many times, in talks at New York University, Yale, Princeton, Massachusetts Institute of Technology, Chicago, and San Diego; at the annual meetings of the Northeastern Political Science Association, the Midwestern Political Science Association, and the American Political Science Association; and at numerous workshops at Columbia University and Washington University. In each case, the participants (too numerous to mention) made comments and posed questions that have provoked reflection, and often led to changes in my views. Parts of Chapter 3 were published earlier in my article on "Power" in the *Companion to Contemporary Political Philosophy*, Vol. 2, Robert E. Goodin, Philip Pettit, and Thomas Pogge, eds. (Blackwell Publishing, 2007). Parts of Chapters 5 and 7 were published earlier in my article on "Domination and Distributive Justice" in the *Journal of Politics*, vol. 71, no. 3 (2009), and a part of Chapter 7 is appearing simultaneously in my article on "Cultural Accommodation and Domination" in *Political Theory* this spring. I am grateful to Blackwell Publishing, Cambridge University Press, and Sage Publications for their permission to reuse these materials. I should also thank the Core Curriculum at Columbia University, which provided financial support during the summers in which I wrote the earliest version of this book; the Department of Political Science at Washington University, which provided a congenial home while I wrote the second version; and the Princeton University Center for Human Values, which provided the opportunity to write the final version during my sabbatical.

Finally, I must thank my family, friends, and loved ones for their enduring support and encouragement, without which I would never have succeeded in completing this work.

1

Introduction

In all societies, past and present, many persons and groups have been subject to domination. Properly understood, domination is a great evil, the suffering of which ought to be minimized so far as this is possible. Indeed, it is a grave objection to any political theory or doctrine that it would ignore, permit, or even encourage the avoidable domination of any person or group.

Many, I think, would agree with these or similar assertions. This being so, one might expect the subject of domination to constitute a central topic of debate among contemporary political and social theorists and philosophers. In one respect, this expectation is duly satisfied, for many situations or states of affairs are described in the relevant literatures as involving domination. For example:[1]

- The practice of slavery, wherever and whenever it has appeared, has been described as a form of domination.

- Regimes of systematic discrimination against minority groups—as, for example, those regimes certainly in the past, and to some extent perhaps today, disadvantaging European Jews, African Americans, and homosexuals nearly everywhere—have been described as forms of domination.

- Despotic, totalitarian, and colonial political regimes have all, at various times, been described as forms of domination.

- Entire modes of production—feudal, capitalist, and so forth—have been described as forms of domination, as have more narrowly defined methods of economic organization (e.g., unregulated wage–labor in the nineteenth century).

- Institutional structures, such as the criminal incarceration or mental health systems—especially in the form that these institutions have taken over the past century or two in the West—have been described as forms of domination.

---

[1] Many specific examples of each could easily, if tediously, be recited; this will only be done in the course of discussion so far as it is appropriate and useful.

- Some intra-familial relations (between husband and wife, parent and child, etc.), especially when actually or potentially abusive, have been described as forms of domination.

For the moment, I do not mean to claim that any or all of these are genuine instances of domination. Whether they are or not remains to be seen. Rather, I mean only to suggest the wide range of situations or states of affairs to which the concept has been applied.

Given this diverse and widespread usage, it stands to reason that political and social theorists must have attempted something like a general analysis of the concept of domination—much as they have with power, equality, autonomy, community, and other basic concepts in social and political theory. In this second respect, however, our expectations are disappointed. General accounts of domination are, to say the least, few and far between. Those that can be found are, for the most part, brief, ad hoc, restricted to one or another aspect or form of domination, hopelessly vague, or some combination of the above. None, to my knowledge, discusses the relative advantages or disadvantages of two or more competing conceptions (as do discussions of negative versus positive liberty, causal versus dispositional accounts of power, and so on). This lacuna is striking, if perhaps understandable, as we shall see. The present study aims to redress it.

1.1 THE PROJECT AND ITS AIMS

Domination should be understood as a condition experienced by persons or groups to the extent that they are dependent on a social relationship in which some other person or group wields arbitrary power over them; furthermore, it is terribly wrong for persons or groups to be subject to avoidable domination and thus, as a matter of justice, the political and social institutions and practices of any society should be organized so as to minimize domination, to the extent that this is possible.

The first half of the above statement briefly describes what I refer to as the *arbitrary power* conception of domination. Part I develops this conception, and argues for its merits as against several possible alternatives. Nearly every aspect of the arbitrary power conception might be considered controversial, and yet nowhere in the literature can one find even a clear list of alternatives, much less a rigorous discussion of their relative merits and demerits. The presentation of alternatives in Part I should be interesting and useful, I hope, even to those who, in the end, remain unconvinced by my arguments for the arbitrary power conception in particular.

The second half of the above statement briefly describes the main idea of *justice as minimizing domination*, a conception of social justice. Part II outlines justice as minimizing domination, and argues that it offers a better account of distributive justice, multicultural accommodation, and constitutional democracy than do some other well-known theories of social justice. Part II is, if anything, more controversial than Part I. At a minimum, however, I hope to convince the reader that a rigorous conception of domination might contribute something of value to these (and other) debates central to the contemporary political theory and philosophy.

Parts I and II together constitute a complete theory of domination. By describing my goal as the development of a *theory* of domination, I mean to emphasize that this study covers not only a descriptive account of what domination is, but also a normative account of what should be done about it. In other words, by a theory of domination, I mean a theory that is relevant and useful for moral or political philosophy.

Of course, not every meaningful use of the English word "domination" is covered by this theory: I do not have in mind Pete Sampras's domination of the Wimbledon Championship in the 1990s, for instance. The precise scope of my discussion will become clear as the theory itself develops, but the examples cataloged earlier in this introduction may serve as a rough preliminary guide. In other words, my interest concerns domination in its original meaning as a sort of personal rule or mastery. The term domination ultimately derives from *dominus*, the primitive Latin word for the master of a house. Eventually, the Romans came to understand domination generally as the opposite of freedom—a free person (*liber*) was someone not subject to the domination (*dominatio*) of another, and vice versa.[2] My aim is to develop a theory of domination in roughly this original sense. Much later, of course, the word "domination" accumulated various subsidiary meanings, in English and other languages, derived from this original. Presumably, to describe athletic preeminence as domination, or to say that "pennies dominate her coin collection," and so forth, was first to engage in metaphor, and only later to use the term in a semantically literal sense.

What would constitute a successful theory of domination, so understood? In my view, success should be assessed according to three principal criteria.

---

[2] Further details on the evolution of the term domination can be found in Appendix I.

First, a successful theory of domination should be a *general* theory. In other words, its application should not be limited to this or that particular case or finite set of cases. Rather, it should be open in the sense that it would enable us to say of new and unanticipated situations or states of affairs whether they count as genuine instances of domination, and, if so, what should be done about them. A discussion of, say, nineteenth-century European colonial domination—while certainly interesting (or not) on its own merits—would fail to be general in the required sense. So too would a theory that excluded from consideration possible instances of domination in the so-called private sphere, as opposed to the public or political sphere—as, for example, the domination that may occur within familial relationships. Indeed, one underlying theme of this study is that *all* forms of domination should be considered unjust, and that domination should be reduced whenever and wherever it occurs, at least so far as this is feasible. If one assumes that theories are general by definition, this criterion may seem a mere formality; nevertheless, it serves as the chief grounds (in Chapter 4) for rejecting a view that I refer to as the hegemony conception of domination.

Second, a successful theory of domination should be both descriptively and normatively *useful*. A descriptively useful theory is one capable of discriminating among real-world situations or states of affairs according to the level or degree of domination—it should be "descriptively contoured," one might say.[3] A normatively useful theory is one that supplies clear goals or aims for political action that are neither infeasible on the one hand, nor too easily achieved on the other. Thus, a theory asserting that domination is everywhere inescapable, and resisting it utopian, would fail to be useful on both descriptive and normative grounds. So too would a theory characterizing domination so vaguely or loosely that many decidedly different experiences, inciting contradictory political responses, would be lumped together under a single heading. It is primarily this criterion of utility that, in Chapters 3 and 4, drive us from the imbalance of power conception to the revised imbalance of power conception and, finally, to my preferred arbitrary power conception. (In order to be normatively useful, a theory of domination must also satisfy something called the separation thesis, as explained in Section 1.4.)

And third, a successful theory should sit reasonably well with our relevant pre-existing intuitions concerning the concept of domination. Of course, it is not necessary that the theory vindicates all of our intuitions exactly as they presently are, and in any case people's intuitions often differ; but a successful theory must respect them at least to the extent that it is recognizably a theory

---

[3] For the notion of a contoured theory, I am indebted to Millgram (2000).

of domination and not something else. Thus, a theory that did not include slavery as an instance of domination would, it seems to me, clearly be inadequate. What we want is something along the lines of what John Rawls calls a "reflective equilibrium" in our understanding on domination: the idea here being, roughly, that our intuitions retained after due consideration and reflection should match our theory, and vice versa. (This is explained further in Chapter 2.)

At various stages in this study, I elaborate on these criteria as necessary, but I do not offer any justification of them as the *right* criteria. This is partly because I think their appropriateness is reasonably obvious, and partly because an adequate justification would, in any case, take us too far afield.

Some readers may want to know whether the theory developed here purports to be a universal theory—applicable to all societies and all historical circumstances. The answer depends on what one means by universality. As discussed later, it is not my view that theories about social phenomena are natural artifacts, so to speak, waiting to be uncovered through diligent and careful research. When it comes to social phenomena, there is no truth in definition. On the contrary, definitions can be judged as better or worse only in light of the work we want them to do. Thus, we cannot claim that a particular theory of domination is objectively true in the sense that, say, many believe the law of gravity is objectively true. If this is what one means by universality, then of course my theory is not universal (because no such theory could be).

However, there is another sense in which a theory might be regarded as universal. Suppose that a theory of domination could, at least in principle, be usefully put to work in any society, or in any historical context. By way of a parallel, consider Amartya Sen's view that poverty should be understood as lacking the basic capabilities to function in one's local culture: in principle, at any rate, we can employ his conception of poverty universally, once the variable substantive content of "basic capabilities" has been filled in on a case-by-case basis.[4]

The general theory of domination developed here aspires to be universal in this second sense. Whether it succeeds or not, individual readers must judge for themselves. Note that universality in the second sense does not follow from generality, since an appropriately general theory might be open to new cases only within some culturally or historically restricted domain. In other words, universality is much stronger than generality. However, since a general,

---

[4] Sen (1983, 1992, pp. 115–16) drawing on a passage in Smith (1776, V.2.2, pp. 938–9). I am indebted to Pettit (1997, p. 158) for suggesting this idea and its relevance here.

though not fully universal, theory might nevertheless be very useful, universality should not be viewed as a criterion of the theory's success or failure.

1.2 WHY A THEORY OF DOMINATION?

Before considering what sort of methodological approach would be appropriate for a study of this sort, we might reasonably ask: Why bother developing a theory of domination at all? One answer could be, because no one else has. For some, this would be sufficient. In my case, however, there are broader motivations, which I ought to make explicit at the outset.

For some time, I have been dissatisfied with the liberal-contractualist doctrine that is pre-eminent in contemporary (Western) political theory and philosophy. The term *liberal contractualism* here refers to a loose tradition encompassing the ideas of figures such as John Locke, Jean-Jacques Rousseau, and Immanuel Kant, and in our own day John Rawls, Brian Barry, Thomas Nagel, T. M. Scanlon, and others. Roughly speaking, liberal contractualists contend that just political and social institutions and practices are those that reasonable people in a diverse or pluralistic society would agree can serve as the impartial basis for a fair system of cooperation.[5] Admittedly, this is an extremely attractive political doctrine in many respects. For one thing, it is "political, not metaphysical," as the slogan goes, because it does not appear to depend on the truth of any particular conception of the good or comprehensive doctrine. For another, it holds out the powerful vision of a perfectly voluntaristic society—that is, a society in which no one is forced to live under political and social institutions that they do not accept as reasonable and fair. Thus, in Rousseau's famous words, despite "uniting with all" in a single political community, each person "nevertheless obeys only himself and remains as free as before."[6]

Despite these important strengths, however, liberal contractualism has come under increasing criticism in recent years. Feminists have attacked the liberal-contractualist strategy of shielding the private sphere from public or political interference, which, they argue, masks considerable gender domination in the family and obstructs efforts to redress this persistent injustice.

---

[5] With some caveats, we might substitute "political liberalism" (as distinct from ethical or perfectionist liberalism on the one hand, and minimalist or modus vivendi liberalism on the other) for the term liberal contractualism. The associated conception of social justice is variously referred to as justice as fairness, justice as impartiality, or justice as reciprocity. I discuss liberal contractualism further in Chapter 6.

[6] Rousseau (1762, I.6.4, p. 148).

Deliberative democrats have attacked liberal contractualism for valuing individual rights too highly over the need for robust democratic participation, and for providing no more than weak, instrumental arguments on behalf of minimal representative democracy. Multiculturalists have attacked liberal contractualism for failing to perceive the various cultural injuries inflicted by liberal institutions, and for being unable or unwilling to do anything about them. There is some truth, in my view, to these (and other) criticisms. Each strikes at the very core of liberal-contractualist doctrine, for the difficulty in each case arises (albeit, in somewhat different ways) from the aspiration to achieve a voluntary consensus on shared political and social institutions and practices through the consignment of important moral and ethical disagreements to the private sphere of civil society.

These critiques arise mainly in debates among professional political theorists and philosophers, of course. Outside the academy, liberal contractualism faces a different set of challenges. In particular, an extremely important and perhaps underrated challenge is presented by what one might call common-sense libertarianism.[7] The need for a progressive political doctrine that can effectively compete with common-sense libertarianism has become especially pressing with the collapse of radical theories such as Marxism and socialism. So long as the latter were taken seriously, liberalism served as a sort of moderately progressive middle way between the far right and the far left. For many people, however, it is no longer possible to view liberalism in this way. The effect of this can be seen, for example, in the growing difficulty liberals now have in articulating the case for redistributive policies that would combat severe poverty and inequality. There is undoubtedly a variety of reasons for this rhetorical weakness in the face of common-sense libertarianism. One might be that it is increasingly difficult for people to view their society as a system of mutual cooperation, given the importance now placed on privacy, individualism, personal autonomy, and so on (values which, ironically, liberalism itself has partly been responsible for promoting). Certainly, there are others as well, but it is not important to elaborate. What is important is that justice as minimizing domination represents a possible progressive alternative—one that might better answer these challenges, both inside and outside the academy. The inspiration for this idea has a surprising origin, which I explain briefly.

---

[7] Boaz (1997) or Murray (1997) can be taken as examples here. Naturally, more sophisticated libertarian theories have been developed, but the general consensus among professionals is that libertarianism faces insurmountable objections. For a good overview of this consensus, see Kymlicka (1990, ch. 4).

In recent years, there has been a remarkable resurgence of interest in the republican tradition of Western political thought. This tradition includes the writings of Machiavelli and his fifteenth-century Italian predecessors; the English republicans Milton, Harrington, Sidney, and others; Montesquieu and Blackstone; the eighteenth-century English commonwealthmen; and many Americans of the founding era such as Jefferson and Madison. These writers emphasize many common ideas and concerns, such as the importance of civic virtue and political participation, the dangers of corruption, the benefits of a mixed constitution, the rule of law, and so on. Often, they are called the "classical republican" (or sometimes, "neo-Roman") political writers because they characteristically draw on classical examples—from Cicero and the Latin historians especially—in making their various arguments.

One group of contemporary theorists, represented by Quentin Skinner, Philip Pettit, Maurizio Viroli, and others, has aimed to develop insights from this tradition into an attractive civic republican (or neo-republican) political doctrine. On their view, what ties together the classical republican writings is a deep commitment to the core value of political liberty or freedom, where this last idea is crucially understood, not as the absence of interference (as on the standard negative liberty view), but rather as the absence of domination. Political liberty, in other words, is a sort of independence—from slavery, from despotic or autocratic government, from colonial subjugation, and from other sorts of mastery or domination.[8] Once understood in this light, it is clear that robust civic virtues, active political participation, a mixed constitution, the rule of law, etc., are cherished by the classical republicans as instrumental goods, useful in securing and maintaining political liberty so understood.[9] What is more, their writings can thus be seen as contributing— admittedly in an often haphazard and inchoate manner—to the development of an attractive political doctrine that is independent and distinct from the mainstream liberal tradition that eventually supplanted it.

What would a contemporary civic republican political doctrine, if fully worked out, look like? To date, the most comprehensive attempt to explore this question is represented by Pettit's *Republicanism: A Theory of Freedom and*

---

[8]   See, for example, Skinner (1991, 1998); Pettit (1989, 1997, 1999); Viroli (2002); and Maynor (2003).

[9]   This civic republican interpretation of classical republican tradition should thus be carefully distinguished from an earlier, and competing, civic humanist interpretation, as found for example in the work of Arendt (1990, 1993); Wood (1969); Pocock (1975); or Rahe (1992). On the civic humanist view, active political participation and civic virtue are understood to be constitutive of the best human life, and thus are valued intrinsically (not instrumentally). This is not my view, nor is it the view of Skinner, Pettit, Viroli, and the other civic republicans. For further discussion, see Lovett (2005).

Government.[10] The rough idea is to define political liberty or freedom as non-domination, and then to adopt the general advancement of liberty, so understood, as our chief political aim.

The mutual affinity between Pettit's project and the conception of social justice as minimizing domination advanced in this study should be obvious. From one point of view, the latter could be seen as merely a redescribed and systematized version of the former. There are also, however, significant differences between the two—for instance, my inclusion of dependency in the conception of domination, our differing accounts of arbitrariness, and the different connections we draw between freedom from domination and democracy. Also, this study addresses in detail topics such as distributive justice and multicultural accommodation that have been given scant attention in the civic republican literature until recently. That said, the inspiration for this study lies firmly in the intrinsic appeal of civic republicanism, and in the possibility that it might offer an attractive alternative to liberal contractualism.

This story might be surprising because many are not in the habit of regarding republicanism as an especially *progressive* political doctrine.[11] While I agree with Pettit that the progressive potential can be found in the classical republican writings, it is important to emphasize that—unlike Pettit—I am not interested in squaring my conclusions here with anything that one can find in the classical republican tradition. Indeed, the discussions that follow will often seem wholly detached from what many readers would regard as the typical concerns of the contemporary civic republicans. This does not strike me as a problem. The best theory of domination is whatever the best theory turns out to be. Whether or not the aim of minimizing domination, so understood, generates institutions or policies the classical republicans would have endorsed is, in my view, beside the point. To borrow a phrase from Wittgenstein, civic republicanism is, for me, a ladder to be thrown away once it has been climbed.

A thorough discussion of the strengths of justice as minimizing domination can be found in Chapter 6, but one advantage it might have over some competing political doctrines is worth mentioning here. In defining social justice as the minimization of domination, we exploit an asymmetry (noticed by others) in our moral intuitions with respect to the good and just on the one hand, and the evil and unjust on the other. We may be able to find normative propositions nearly everyone would agree with in either category, but whereas in the former category these propositions tend to be vague and empty (such as "democracy is good" or "justice is giving each their due"), while in the

---

[10] Pettit (1997).

[11] This is largely, in my view, due to continuing influence of the civic humanist interpretation of classical republicanism, which offers the picture of an (often, frankly) elitist political doctrine.

latter category they tend to be specific and concrete (such as "rape and torture are wrong" or "slavery is unjust"). Why this asymmetry in our intuitions exists (since it does not, in my view, correspond to a genuine asymmetry in fully worked-out moral or political philosophies) is not clear, but we ought to take full advantage of the opportunity it provides in constructing a political doctrine from the ground up, so to speak. As Judith Shklar would say, we are on more solid ground when we begin with some concrete *summum malum* such as domination rather than some vague and hypothetical *summum bonum*.[12] A less romantic path, perhaps, but also one less fraught with the dangers particular to political theory and philosophy.

Though important for contemporary civic republicans, a study of domination may also interest a much broader audience. Its value does not depend on one's commitment to a specific view of political liberty, or to the civic republican political doctrine more generally. As noted earlier, the concept of domination is employed in a wide range of political and social theory literature. Therefore, a robust theory of domination will be valuable even to those not particularly interested in or sympathetic with the contemporary civic republican agenda.

Working out such a theory proves no easy task. Along the way, we must grapple with a remarkable diversity of complex issues—some obvious and perennial, others unexpected and arcane. The fact that working out a general theory of domination involves so many interrelated and deep conceptual problems could itself be a sufficient reason for undertaking this study. In my case, however, it is not the only reason.

1.3 EXISTING ACCOUNTS OF DOMINATION

Suppose that, for these reasons or others, one is interested in developing a theory of domination. Naturally, it would make sense to begin by considering those accounts that are presently available, and the extent to which they meet the desiderata mentioned earlier for a successful theory.

The best-known and most often referred to discussions of domination are probably those found in the famous "lordship-bondage" passages of G. W. F. Hegel's *Phenomenology* on the one hand, and in the sections of Max Weber's

---

[12] Shklar (1998). Of course, any completely elaborated conception of social justice will have to be sophisticated and complex: the point is rather that it should be grounded directly on a core of concrete, straightforward, and powerful intuitions.

Economy and Society concerned with legitimate authority on the other.[13]
Unfortunately, neither supplies what is looked for here. The first amounts
to an analysis of only one aspect of the generic domination experience—the
dynamic by which, Hegel argues, domination will tend to be self-defeating.
The second considers in detail only one type of domination—namely, domination maintained through legitimation beliefs; Weber's general definition of
domination is stated only briefly, without elaboration, justification, or any
consideration of alternatives. (It seems to be an example of the revised
imbalance of power conception, discussed in Chapters 3 and 4, though one
cannot be certain on the basis of the text alone.)

The only reasonably sustained analyses of domination are commonly attributed to Karl Marx and Michel
Foucault as well, though neither uses the expression with much frequency.
Although the former has much to say about exploitation, alienation, and
ideology of obvious relevance for any respectable theory of domination, this
does not itself amount to his necessarily *having* such a theory. Foucault's
theory of domination is usually found by glossing the discussions of power in
his writings as discussions of domination, which two expressions he does
indeed use interchangeably at times. Though disputable, this glossing
implies his commitment also to some version of the imbalance of power
conception.[14]

The only reasonably sustained analyses of domination to be found in the
contemporary literature are those in Chapter 6 of Thomas Wartenberg's *The
Forms of Power* and Chapter 2 of Pettit's aforementioned *Republicanism*.[15]
Both offer versions of the arbitrary power conception that in some respects
are similar to mine (Pettit's account in particular is discussed in Chapter 4),
but neither provides any systematic treatment of that conception's advantages
over the alternatives; nor, for that matter, do the contributors (other than
Pettit) to the considerable civic republican literature.[16] The term "domination" does not merit an entry in *The Social Science Encyclopedia* (1996), *The
Blackwell Encyclopedia of Political Science* (1991), the *Dictionary of Political*

---

[13] Hegel (1807, §§178–96, pp. 111–19) and Weber (1922, esp. pp. 53–4, 212–301, 941–55). In
both, the discussion is of *Herrschaft*, which in the former case is usually translated as "lordship"
and in the latter case as "domination." Some discussion of Weber can be found in Chapter 4 and
of Hegel in Chapter 5.

[14] See, for example, Foucault (1980, pp. 92, 95–6, 98, and *passim*). In a late interview
(Foucault 1988, p. 3ff.), he refers to domination as "congealed power," but he does not expand
much on this comment.

[15] Wartenberg (1990); Pettit (1997).

[16] Wartenberg discusses two "techniques" of domination, but under the same general
conception, which is not contrasted with alternatives. Pettit and the other civic republicans
consider in detail the advantages of liberty as non-domination over liberty as non-interference,
but the definition of domination employed in the former is always more or less stipulated.

Thought (1996), the *Encyclopedia of Sociology* (2000), nor any other comparable reference work of which I am aware.[17]

The remaining diverse and scattered discussions of domination fall roughly into four groups. First, there are a small number of works entirely devoted to the discussion of one or more instances or aspects of domination, but which nevertheless fail to provide anything more than a brief ad hoc analysis of the concept itself. Good examples include Albert Memmi's *Dominated Man*, Barry Adam's *The Survival of Domination*, and James Scott's *Domination and the Arts of Resistance*.[18] These are interesting and valuable works, whose lack of the sought-after analysis should not be regarded as a serious flaw. Their authors' interests are different from mine. For example, Adam's book is not about developing a theory of domination per se, but rather about the ways in which dominated groups cope with that condition in everyday life. To this end, he can easily make do with a rough-and-ready notion of domination, elaborated only to the point where it becomes possible to identify with some confidence a few persons or groups suffering under domination. The same goes for Scott's book, which is primarily concerned with bringing to light what he calls the "hidden transcripts" of the domination experience, and Memmi's book, which is a collection of essays on a variety topics, linked only in that each concerns historically dominated groups. Other than these, there appear to be no book-length treatments of domination.

Second, there are a number of relatively short—consisting of a few paragraphs at most—typically un-detailed, and often vague accounts of domination appearing in the course of work mainly concerned with some other topic. Not all of these are well known, and none is particularly illuminating. To pick two examples more or less at random, Amy Allen offers a short analysis of domination in her book, *The Power of Feminist Theory*. She concludes this discussion by offering the following definition: "Domination entails the ability of an actor or set of actors to constrain the choices of another actor or set of actors in a non-trivial way, and in a way that works to the others' disadvantage."[19] Based on the context, this may be an example of what I call an outcome-based conception of domination; outcome-based

---

[17] *The Blackwell Dictionary of Twentieth-Century Social Thought* (1992) has an entry under the heading domination referring the reader to the entry on authority, but apart from defining authority as "legitimate domination," no discussion of domination can be found there. Other reference works without entries under the heading domination include: the *Reader's Guide to the Social Sciences* (2001), *The Blackwell Dictionary of Political Science* (1999), *The Blackwell Companion to Political Philosophy* (1993), and the *International Encyclopedia of the Social Sciences* (1968).

[18] Memmi (1971); Adam (1978); Scott (1990).

[19] Allen (1999, pp. 124–25).

conceptions are discussed and rejected in Chapter 2. Similarly, after a short discussion, Iris Young in *Justice and the Politics of Difference* defines domination as "institutional conditions that inhibit or prevent people from participating in determining their actions or the conditions of their actions." She adds, by way of clarification, that "thorough social and political democracy is the opposite of domination."[20] This identification of non-domination and democracy has become popular recently, but it is puzzling in a way. If the idea is to define democracy as non-domination, then of course a conception of domination remains wanting; but if the idea is to define domination as a lack of democracy, then are we not defining one complex and controversial idea with reference to another even more complex and controversial idea? At any rate, supposing the latter is intended, this seems to be an example of what I call form-restricted conceptions of domination (the hegemony conception being another). Form-restricted conceptions are discussed and rejected in Chapter 4.

Third, there are writings in which an author holds out the promise of an extended discussion of political domination and then fails to deliver. For example, one might expect a book titled *Domination and Power* to offer a theory of domination, but in fact it is about something else entirely, namely, an attack on critical theory's approach to the problem of how the individual agent is historically constituted.[21] Similarly, we may consider Timo Airaksinen's essay, titled "The Rhetoric of Domination." Its first sentence reads, "The crudest mechanism of interpersonal domination is *coercion*" (emphasis in original), and a discussion of the latter concept, not the former, and its relation to rhetoric ensues.[22] Or again, consider Angus Stewart's *Theories of Domination and Power*, which is really an attempt to revive an Arendtian conception of power, and has next to nothing to say about domination.[23] These and other similar works are obviously irrelevant for our purposes.

Finally, there are innumerable works, on almost every conceivable topic, in which the term domination appears here and there in the general course of discussion, sometimes even in the work's title, without any apparent concern to establish its meaning. Perhaps its meaning is thought to be obvious and unproblematic—though, of course, it does not appear so to me. Examples of this last sort are far too numerous to cite in any comprehensive manner and, in any case, their very lack of concern for analyzing the concept of domination renders them useless from the point of view of this study.

Given the failure of contemporary political and social theorists to reflect on the different possible accounts of domination, and to argue clearly for their

---

[20] Young (1990, p. 28). [21] Miller (1987).
[22] Airaksinen (1992). [23] Stewart (2001).

respective merits or demerits, I generally find it more useful simply to refer to the arguments for and against different possible *conceptions* without much concern for whose conceptions those happen to be. Most of the important contenders have already been mentioned: apart from the arbitrary power conception, there are outcome-based conceptions, various imbalance of power conceptions, and form-restricted conceptions (including the hegemony conception). Chapters 2–4 argue that each of the alternatives to the arbitrary power conception fall short with respect to the desiderata proposed above. Whether one is convinced by this argument or not, simply specifying and naming the alternatives represents an advance over the literature as it presently stands.

Why has the concept of domination almost completely escaped the sustained analysis in political and social theory? One reason could be that many people believe that great, and perhaps insurmountable, difficulties stand in the way of success.

There are many ways in which the attempt to produce a general theory of domination might be expected to fail. For starters, there is the obvious possibility that domination is not a coherent concept at all. That is, one might find on close examination that the situations or states of affairs taken to be examples of domination are so individually diverse that one cannot reasonably consider them instances of a single social phenomenon at all. In this case, the term "domination" might turn out to be empty rhetoric—just a sloppy, shorthand way of saying some situation or state of affairs is bad without specifying why. It is my contention, of course, that this is not the case, and that there exists a distinct felt experience to which we may appropriately refer by using the term domination. To be sure, the term itself may often be employed rhetorically, but its very rhetorical force derives from some hazy notion of the experience the term is meant to capture. It is this distinct felt experience—to which people loosely refer by using the word "domination"—that is ultimately of interest to me.

Even supposing that domination does exist as a discrete social phenomenon, however, a second possibility is that it might turn out to be a strictly subjective experience, not an objectively definable situation or state of affairs. Domination might be something that persons or groups can experience themselves, but not something that can be adequately described from the perspective of an external observer. An analogous problem might arise if the various forms domination takes are so historically mutable that no single objective description can hope to capture more than a single form present at one particular time and place.[24] In either case, while the aim of this study

---

[24] Versions of the latter objection appear in Adam (1978, pp. 6–8) and Miller (1987, pp. 9–10).

would remain sound, the particular approach adopted (more on this shortly) certainly would not. The best approach to understanding domination would rather consist in something quite different—say, in the exploration of domination narratives.

Even if these first two problems are surmounted, there remains a third: while domination may be a discrete and objectively definable situation or state of affairs, it might turn out that various problems of measurement or interpersonal comparison render the concept useless for political and social theory. Naturally, this third problem represents somewhat less of a threat to this study than the first two. Though less satisfying, perhaps, a study concluding that some particular avenue of thought will in the end bear no useful fruit can still be regarded successful. One important implication of such a conclusion would be that, whatever else its merits, a civic republican political doctrine as envisioned by Pettit and others cannot realistically be put into practice. My hope is that this will not turn out to be the case, but it is a real possibility nevertheless.

These problems represent the null hypotheses, so to speak, of my study. The best way to overcome such obstacles is to do the very thing that they suggest may not be possible: that is, construct a persuasive theory of domination that refers to a discrete and externally definable state of affairs and that can contribute to current debates in political theory and philosophy. How, then, should we go about doing this?

1.4 THE GENERAL APPROACH

The various social phenomena designated by the term domination might be studied in different ways.

A social scientist interested in domination would typically begin by choosing some empirical puzzle to serve as the focus of investigation. For instance, one might study the economic, historical, or cultural *causes* of domination: Why do systems of domination arise, when and where they do? What supports or maintains them? What explains variations in the forms of domination that exist? What ultimately causes the decline and fall of systems of domination? and so on. Alternatively, one might study the economic, historical, or cultural *effects* of domination: How do systems of domination influence the distribution of various social goods? What are the psychological effects of domination on those who suffer under it (or on those who inflict it)? Does domination alter the historical and political dynamics of a society? What are people's opinions or attitudes regarding systems of political domination (in general, or with respect to some system of domination in particular)? and so on.

Questions like these are certainly worthy subjects of research, but they will not be addressed here, or at least not directly.[25] From both a conceptual and a motivational point of view, the aims of this study precede such empirical research. With respect to the former, before studying the causes and effects of domination (or anything else, for that matter), one should have a clear idea of the thing itself whose causes and effects one intends to research. With respect to the latter, one would presumably be motivated to undertake such research precisely because it is unjust for persons and groups to be subject to avoidable domination, and thus relevant determining what are its causes and effects.

Political theorists will easily grant this conceptual and motivational priority. Nevertheless, they too may be surprised by my approach. A political theorist interested in domination might typically begin with a historical–linguistic analysis of the concept. For example, one might trace the usage of the term domination in detail from its roots in early Roman law, through the concept's role in the *Corpus iuris* of Justinian, to how it was understood by the medieval glossators, and so on, down to its modern usage in English and other languages. Alternatively, a political theorist might identify a few signal theorists of particular interest from the point of view of an account of domination, and study their respective reflections on the concept in detail, carefully tracing out the part it plays within each of their broader theoretical systems, and so on.[26]

Neither approach is taken here (though Appendix I offers some notes regarding the linguistic history of the term "domination"). Again, this is not because such discussions of domination cannot be interesting in their own way, but rather because the aims of my study are different. From the point of view of developing a conception of social justice as minimizing domination, we want to know not what some particular writer *means* in using the concept, but rather what the best available understanding of the concept is and why—specifically, the best understanding according to the three desiderata proposed earlier.

In contrast to these more familiar methods, my approach might be described as constructivist, on a presently less common, but perhaps more straightforward, understanding of this term. Roughly speaking, I attempt to build or construct a conception of domination out of simpler and more

[25] At various points in the argument, of course, I will have to make assumptions regarding the correct answer to empirical questions of this sort. Ideally, these assumptions should be as weak and uncontroversial as possible, and explicitly expressed rather than implied.

[26] In conversation, a friend jocularly referred to the latter as the "time-travel" method of political theory—"Thucydides, Hobbes, and Foucault on Domination," etc.; I share his view that political theory in this mode is of dubious value.

primitive ideas in social and moral theory that, presumably, we are generally more comfortable with—the less familiar thus being explained with reference to the more familiar.[27]

The constructivist metaphor is usefully active rather than passive. It is not my view that the underlying field of social experience is naturally differentiated into concepts, classes, or categories, such that we might, through diligent and careful research, "discover" the true meaning of a term like domination. There is no objective truth in definitions per se. Thus, the decision to section off a particular segment from the continuous mass of social phenomena must necessarily be an evaluative decision (implicitly, if not explicitly).[28] This is not to say there are not better or worse ways to construct our conceptions of social phenomena, but rather that our constructions will be better or worse depending on the specific purposes we want them to serve. Among the most important of these purposes is simply facilitating agreement concerning how to cut up the undifferentiated mass of social phenomena into discrete concepts, classes, and categories. Only having done this can we begin to advance our knowledge of the social world: only having agreed on what counts as an instance of domination, say, can we begin to productively investigate its causes, its characteristic effects, what should be done about it, and so forth. The descriptive account of domination in Part I aims to construct a conception of domination that can be useful in these sorts of investigations.

Of course, like many social phenomena, domination has normative as well as purely descriptive features—in other words, features that give us reasons for performing or not performing certain actions. Many people, for example, will want to say that being subject to domination is bad for various reasons, and that we should, therefore, aim to reduce or eliminate domination whenever we can, other things being equal.[29] Part II analyzes the normative features of those social phenomena that count, according to the descriptive account developed in Part I, as genuine instances of domination; and indeed I argue that domination, so described, generates precisely the sorts of reasons for practical action suggested. But the descriptive account itself makes no reference to those normative features of domination. Throughout this study, in

[handwritten margin notes: acknowledges interest/ evaluative decision]

---

[27] This sense of constructivism should be distinguished from *social constructionism*—that is, the view that knowledge is created through the social interaction of human beings. The constructivism I have in mind is agnostic with respect to the deep ontological character of the primitive ideas in social and moral theory employed in the constructive process.

[28] Something like this view is articulated in Weber (1904).

[29] Note that, strictly speaking, I regard evaluative statements that something is good or bad as reducible to (or shorthand for) normative statements about things we should do or not do. More on this in Chapter 5.

other words, a strict separation is maintained between descriptive and normative analysis.

Many readers will regard this separation as, to say the least, controversial, and perhaps even disingenuous.[30] In my view, however, such a separation is absolutely essential—both in this study, and indeed to political theory more generally. Let me explain.

I have said that a successful theory of domination should be a useful one. That is to say, we want our theory, however it turns out, to make a *practical difference*—to give us reasons for doing or not doing certain things. Few, presumably, would object to this. Nevertheless, agreeing to this basic desideratum entails some striking methodological commitments. This can easily be seen in a simple parallel example. Suppose, for the sake of argument, we want to argue:

> Wilderness areas ought to be preserved for reasons x, y, and z.

Further suppose that our argument, whatever it happens to be, is sound (i.e., that x, y, and z are indeed good reasons for preserving wilderness areas). Does it follow that we have practical reasons for doing or not doing certain things in particular? Not necessarily.

For our argument to make a practical difference, we would need to show that a specific tract of land counts as an instance of wilderness in the relevant sense. Even if we agree that wilderness areas ought to be preserved, we will not know what to do in the case of the Mojave Desert, for example, unless we further agree whether it counts as a wilderness area or not. What then counts as wilderness? Whatever our criteria are, they must be descriptive, not normative. This is not simply because, as some believe, people are more apt to agree on descriptive than they are on normative criteria (often this is true, though not always). Rather, it is because normative criteria cannot as such supply the traction or anchoring needed to make a practical difference. Suppose, for example, we defined wilderness as any tract of land having intrinsic value. Among other things, what it means for something to have intrinsic value is for that thing to be worthy of special promotion or protection. If wilderness areas do indeed have intrinsic value, then we can add this attribute to the list of our reasons for preserving them, but we are no closer to determining whether the Mojave Desert specifically counts as one. A normative theory of wilderness preservation (or anything else) will not touch down

---

[30] It may seem to be disingenuous insofar as it will turn out that, on my view, domination is *always* bad. How can it always be bad, one might ask, unless badness has been built into the definition? My reply, discussed in Chapter 5, is that the necessity in question is empirical, not analytical: domination is necessarily bad given the sorts of creatures human beings happen to be.

in the realm of actual experience until it incorporates at least some strictly descriptive components. Only then can it make a practical difference.

When it comes to theories of domination, this problem plagues many well-known discussions. For example, in recent work, Ian Shapiro argues that deliberative institutions should be judged according to their efficacy in reducing domination (on which point, I agree). Searching for his definition of domination, however, we discover that he regards it as "the illegitimate exercise of power."[31] In other words, a criterion of something's counting as domination, according to his view, is that it be illegitimate. Now to say that an imbalance of power is illegitimate is to say, among other things, that it is something we have good reasons for reducing, and vice versa. Thus, Shaprio's argument proves ineffective: it amounts to the circular claim that deliberative institutions ought to be judged according to their efficacy in reducing the sorts of imbalances of power that we ought to reduce. A theory of domination can only make a practical difference if our descriptive account of what counts as an instance of domination is held strictly separate from our normative account of what we should do about it.

This does not mean, of course, that our *selection* of a particular descriptive account of domination must—or even could—be based on strictly non-normative criteria. Quite the contrary; as I have already said, there is no objective truth in definitions. Rather, it means that with respect to whatever account of domination we do settle on ultimately, it ought to be true of that account that real-world situations or states of affairs can be identified or described as instances (or not) of domination without reference to whatever normative features those situations or states of affairs in question happen to have. Wrongness or badness should not be a part of our definition of domination. It is not necessary that *all* concepts in political theory or philosophy have strictly descriptive definitions like this, of course. Different concepts serve different roles in a theoretical system. But for a complete argument in moral or political philosophy to work—for it to make a practical difference—at least *some* of the concepts employed in that argument must be strictly descriptive.

These issues have been discussed extensively in legal philosophy, where the methodological position I have advanced often goes by the name of the *separation thesis*. In that context, the question is whether we can identify laws with reference to specific descriptive social facts alone, separate from our evaluation of those facts as good or bad from a normative point of view. Many legal positivists argue that we must, if the law is going to make a practical difference (and, presumably, the law does indeed make a practical

---

[31] Shapiro (2003, p. 4).

difference).[32] The importance of the separation thesis is by no means limited to the province of analytic jurisprudence, however. It is of general importance to social and political theory, and indeed it crops up repeatedly in this study.

Thus, it is perhaps important to emphasize that, although I repeatedly insist in Part I on excluding normative questions from the discussion, in no sense do I mean to depreciate the role of normative theory. On the contrary, as I have argued, it is my view that holding firmly to the separation thesis is necessary precisely in order to develop a successful normative argument—an argument that makes a practical difference—regarding domination. There would be little point in undertaking our descriptive labors in the first place if we did not have strong normative feelings about domination. In a motivational sense, normative analysis is the *raison d'être* for descriptive analysis.

*   *   *

The most important organizational principle of this study, of course, lies in the separation maintained between the descriptive analysis in Part I and the normative analysis in Part II. The remaining details can be reviewed briefly.

According to the descriptive analysis of Part I, domination should be understood as a condition suffered by persons or groups whenever they are dependent on a social relationship in which some other person or group wields arbitrary powers over them: this is the arbitrary power conception of domination. The arbitrary power conception naturally divides into three primitive building blocks: the idea of being dependent on a social relationship, the idea of having social power over another person or group, and the idea of being able to exercise such power arbitrarily. These are the topics of Chapters 2, 3, and 4, respectively.

According to the normative analysis in Part II, we should regard it as unjust for a person or group to be subject to avoidable domination, and thus the political and social institutions and practices of any society should be arranged so as to minimize domination. This part of the argument can also be divided into three stages: first, an account of why non-domination should be regarded as an important human good; second, an account of how a conception of social justice based on this idea is best structured; and third,

---

[32] This conceptual claim about the separation of law and morality is advanced most strongly by Kelsen (1967), Raz (1979; 1985), and Shapiro (2000). On some interpretations, it is also the view of Hart (1994), though others believe that he held a somewhat weaker *separability* thesis. Legal positivism is, of course, perfectly consistent with the claim that our selection of one account of law rather than another might be—indeed, almost certainly is—normatively motivated; and also with the claim that there might well be contingent, empirical connections between the law, as defined by our selected account and morality. These are parallel with the claims I have made here about an account of domination.

examples of how this conception would operate in practice. These are the topics of Chapters 5, 6, and 7, respectively. Chapter 7 argues, among other things, that justice as minimizing domination supports the public provision of an unconditional basic income, the extension of special cultural accommodations under some conditions, and constitutionally restrained democracy as the optimal form of government.

The study ends with a short conclusion (Chapter 8) and two appendices: the first relating the linguistic history of the term domination and the second experimenting with various formal models of domination.

Part I

Descriptive Analysis

2

Social Relationships and Dependency

My aim in Part I of this study is to lay out a rigorous, general conception of domination. As discussed in Chapter 1, however, a complete theory of domination should include not only a descriptive conception of domination, but also a normative account of what (if anything) we ought to do about it. By itself, a descriptive conception of domination—without some broader normative theory of which it is a part—would be of limited interest. Thus, my aim is specifically to develop a conception of domination that can serve as the basis for a discussion, in Part II, of a normative account of justice as minimizing domination. For important reasons discussed in Chapter 1, it is essential to this purpose that the conception of domination itself remains strictly descriptive.

In this chapter, I argue that domination should be defined *structurally*, according to a specific understanding of that term. I reject the idea that domination should be characterized in terms of the contingent outcomes or results of certain actions or events—as, for example, that one group dominates another when the former benefits at the latter's expense.[1] Rather, I argue that whenever persons or groups are structurally related to one another in a particular way, this situation in itself constitutes domination, regardless of the outcomes or results we happen to observe in any particular case. But at the same time, I reject the view that structures themselves dominate people, as if there can be subjects of domination without there also being agents. In other words, in my view, domination is always a relationship among different persons or groups, never a relationship between people and structures as such.

No doubt this is somewhat obscure as it stands, but exactly what I mean and why it is important should, I hope, be clear by the end of this chapter.

---

[1] Outcome-based conceptions of domination like this can be found, for example, in Adam (1978, p. 8), Miller (1987, p. 2), Allen (1999, p. 125), Kittay (1999, pp. 33–5), and Lukes (2005, pp. 85–6). Friedman (2008, p. 252) proposes an outcome-based conception as an alternative to Pettit's arbitrary power conception.

2.1 THE OBJECT AND METHOD OF
DESCRIPTIVE ANALYSIS

Before commencing the main discussion, let me say a few words concerning the object and method of descriptive analysis in general, as this may be useful for understanding the overall approach in Part I.

2.1.1 Reflective equilibrium and the case method

Often it is helpful to distinguish between concepts and conceptions. A conception of domination is an account of what would have to be true of a particular situation or state of affairs for it to count as a genuine instance of domination. Or, put in another way, a conception is a rule or principle for sorting patterns of facts (real or hypothetical) into two sets: those that are instances of domination on the one hand, and those that are not on the other. By contrast, the concept of domination is the abstract notion of domination as such—a merely formal, dictionary definition, if you like.

Ideally, one might say, there is only one concept of domination. Necessarily, however, there are many competing conceptions of domination, each of which can be thought of as a particular substantive construction or interpretation of that concept. When two people argue over the meaning of domination, their disagreement concerns these differing conceptions—specifically, which of them constitutes the best interpretation of the underlying concept that, we must assume, they already share. If they did not already share the same underlying concept, it would be difficult to say what their disagreement was about. It would be as if one person were insisting that 24th June was a Sunday and another that it was a Tuesday, when the first is thinking of June 2007 and the second person of June 2008. The shared concept of domination is the thing that competing conceptions of domination constitute arguments about.[2]

But how, we might ask, are such disputes to be carried out and resolved in a reasonable manner? That is the question.

---

[2] Further elaboration of the concept–conception distinction can be found in Rawls (1971, pp. 5–6, 8–11) and Dworkin (1986, pp. 70–1). Rawls derived the distinction from Hart (1994, pp. 159–63). Dworkin (1986, p. 44) uses a similar example of two persons agreeing that there are many banks in North America, when one is thinking of river banks and the other of savings banks: since they do not share the same concept, their agreement is illusory.

Domination comes in many forms. The forms of domination are the various fact patterns (real or hypothetical) that count, according to various conceptions, as instances of domination. Thus, the domination of slaves by slave masters, assuming it counts under our current conception, would be one particular form of domination; antebellum slavery in the American South would be a specific historical instantiation of this form, as would slavery in ancient Rome or colonial Brazil. A dispute between two competing conceptions of domination can be thought of as a dispute regarding which fact patterns should count as forms of domination. Now, if it were simply a question of my list versus yours, it would indeed be difficult to see how our dispute could ever be resolved in a reasonable manner. Of course, we often have fairly strong intuitions concerning what should count as domination, and these intuitions may serve as the basis for drawing up an initially plausible list of its forms. But when our intuitions differ—as often they do—there would seem to be no good reason for preferring one list to another as such.

This is why we should think of a conception of domination as a rule or principle for sorting real or hypothetical fact patterns into sets. The conception is the sorting principle itself, whereas a list of domination's various forms is merely the by-product of applying that principle to a range of possible examples.

This important distinction, between a sorting principle and the list of forms that is its by-product, makes possible an answer to the question of how disputes concerning different conceptions can be resolved in a reasonable manner. The idea is to first propose a sorting principle, and then to test it against a range of cases. Assuming that our intuitions regarding some of those cases (specifically, whether they should count as genuine instances of domination) do not correspond with the results generated by the proposed sorting principle, we will have to make revisions in the former, the latter, or both. In making these revisions, our judgments are guided by the relative strength of our various intuitions, and by the power and utility of alternate sorting principles: roughly speaking, one sorting principle is better than another if it captures more of our stronger intuitions with greater conceptual efficiency. After an iterated process of testing and revising, we eventually arrive at a conclusion we are happy with—in other words, we end up with a sorting principle that sits well with the intuitions we have decided, after reflection, to keep. This approach is sometimes called the case method of analysis. When successful, it results in what John Rawls calls a "reflective equilibrium" with respect to the concept at issue.[3]

---

[3] Rawls (1951, 1971, pp. 46–53); see also Daniels (1979).

Let me emphasize that this sort of conceptual analysis is only the starting point for developing a complete theory of domination (and arriving at a reflective equilibrium only one of the three criteria for success outlined in Chapter 1). We should not be under any illusions regarding what the case method alone conclusively demonstrates, and the actual carrying out of such an analysis is bound to seem, at times, gratuitously meticulous. Done well, however, it renders transparent the different meanings we might assign to a complicated concept such as domination: this in itself is valuable, in that it forces us to choose one conception in particular, and demands that we be absolutely clear regarding which we have chosen and why.

2.1.2 Some initial examples

With this in mind, let us begin by considering a few examples of how the concept of domination is commonly used. Now, of course, as I have just finished saying, it is controversial which uses are appropriate and which are not, so we must proceed with an open mind.

Initially, at least, we can suppose that some uses are more central, and others more peripheral, to our intuitions. The many derivative uses of the term, some noted in Chapter 1, are obviously irrelevant to our interests, and thus can be set aside: "Pete Sampras dominated tennis in the 1990s," "pennies dominate her coin collection," "a mountain dominates the view from our valley," and so forth. Other common uses of the term, however, are not so easily dismissed. Sometimes people refer to a particular idea or theory dominating its field, as, for example, "The particle theory of light dominated physics until the nineteenth century"; or similarly, with reference to the work of an author, "His new book is dominated by a concern with thus and such." Somewhat differently, the term can be used in business, "The XYZ Firm dominates the widget production market"; or in politics, "The republican party dominated American politics in the 1920s." Depending on one's preferred conception, some of these might be regarded as genuine instances of domination. Suppose we adopt a conception defining domination in terms of ideological hegemony (Chapter 4 discusses this view), then it might be difficult deciding whether the particle theory of light should or should not count as a genuine instance of domination. Under some other conceptions, however, this use of the term might easily be set aside as metaphorical.

Let us put these sorts of borderline cases aside, for the moment, and concentrate on examples lying at the core, rather than the periphery, of our intuitions. The best examples are presumably those referring to the not too distant, historical past: on the one hand, our intuitions are liable to be clouded or biased concerning what is currently relevant for us; but on the other hand, our intuitions are liable to be weak and uncertain concerning what is historically and culturally very distant from us. Consider, therefore, the following reasonably typical passages:[4]

[1] Absolutism was essentially just this: a redeployed and recharged apparatus of feudal <u>domination</u>, designed to clamp the peasant masses back into their traditional social position—despite and against the gains they had won by the widespread commutation of dues.

[2] Slavery is one of the most extreme forms of the relation of <u>domination</u>, approaching the limits of total power from the viewpoint of the master, and of total powerlessness from the viewpoint of the slave.

[3] As a little economy and a little state, ruled by a father-king, the family has long been a setting for the <u>domination</u> of wives and daughters (sons, too). It isn't difficult to collect stories of physical brutality or to describe customary practices and religious rites that seem designed, above all, to break the spirits of young women.

[4] Up to now, we know only two authentic forms of totalitarian <u>domination</u>: the dictatorship of National Socialism after 1938, and the dictatorship of Bolshevism since 1930. These forms of <u>domination</u> differ basically from other kinds of dictatorial, despotic, or tyrannical rule.

Passages like these are quite common, and the particular ones selected here were chosen more or less arbitrarily; they have been singled out merely because they will prove useful in the later discussion. For the time being, we need not take any position on the question of whether, for example, traditional families really were instances of domination or not. Moreover, we should not be distracted by empirical details such as whether absolutism was indeed "redeployed and recharged" feudalism or not—an interesting historical question in itself, of course, but neither here nor there for our purposes. The relevant issue is how the concept of domination is being used.

In the first passage above, the author refers to a specific historical instantiation of domination—the domination of the European peasantry by feudal nobility in the early modern period. This might be regarded as falling under some general form of what might be called class domination. In the second excerpt, the author refers directly to a general form of domination, that is, slavery. In the course of Patterson's book, many historical instantiations of this form are compared and contrasted. The third quote also refers to a general form of domination, and family relations in nineteenth-century

---

[4] The passages can be found in Anderson (1974, p. 18), Patterson (1982, p. 1), Walzer (1983, p. 239), and Arendt (1968, p. 117), respectively.

England, for example, might constitute one historical instantiation of this form. The fourth passage is somewhat ambiguous but appears to suggest the following: that although totalitarianism, dictatorship, despotism, and tyranny are all instances of domination, the first presents some new and special features.[5] If so, we might loosely group all four of these instances under a single general form of domination termed "autocratic government."

While these uses of the concept of domination are not uncontroversial, they represent fairly central cases of what one would intuitively expect an acceptable conception of domination to cover. One thing we might gather from these passages is that the authors seem to think of domination as a sort of relationship between persons or groups. The instances of domination we have include: the apparatus of feudalism, the institution of slavery, certain sorts of familial arrangements, and totalitarianism. In each case, what is being described as domination is a particular manner in which persons or groups might stand in relation to one another.

I will argue that this view is fundamentally correct, and that our conception of domination should indeed be based on this idea. In order to argue this, however, I first need to explain the general idea of a social relationship, and this turns out to be not as simple as one might expect. Thus, some distinctions are in order.

2.2 PURPOSEFUL, RATIONAL, AND REASONABLE ACTION

Sometimes, things happen to people; other times, people do things. When a person does something, we call it an *action*. Let us say that an action is *purposeful* if it can be described, at least on our ordinary understanding of things, as (directly or indirectly) intentionally motivated by some goals or aims of the actor's. Of course, the action need not succeed in attaining its intended goal or aim for it to count as purposeful, provided that some goal or aim of the actor intentionally motivated it. Also, purposeful action need not be instrumental in the narrow sense: when one plays recreational tennis, for instance, one's aim might be the enjoyment of the activity itself. This counts as purposeful action.[6]

---

[5] Alternatively, Arendt might mean that whereas dictatorship, despotism, and tyranny are *not* instances of domination, totalitarianism is, and that is precisely what makes it distinct. The context of the passage, however, suggests the former interpretation: Arendt repeatedly refers to "total domination," as if to distinguish the features of totalitarianism from ordinary domination.

[6] This was observed by Aristotle, *N. Ethics*, 1094a3.

To describe an action as purposeful is not necessarily to (causally) explain it in such terms. Whether we believe it is even possible to explain actions with respect to intentional motivations may depend on our view of free will and determinism. If strict determinism is true, then the purposeful descriptions of human action we commonly use might not, interpreted literally, be the correct explanations of those actions. As it happens, I do not believe that strict determinism is true, but that is a topic for another time.[7] It is enough for our purposes here that we generally *describe* much human action as if it were intentionally motivated by goals or aims; this can be taken as shorthand for whatever turns out to be the correct explanation.

Human action can be either directly or indirectly purposeful. Suppose a person decides to eat a sandwich because she is hungry: her action, in this case, is purposeful in the direct sense. Much of what we do is directly purposeful, but some of it is purposeful only indirectly. For example, people sometimes act out of habit without reflecting on what they are doing or why. Habitual behavior can nevertheless usually be described as purposeful in an indirect sense. While it is true that I brush my teeth each morning out of habit and without conscious reflection, it is also true that I adopted this habit to begin with so as to prevent cavities, and that, were I to read a convincing study showing that some other procedure were better suited to that end, I would drop the former habit in favor of the latter. Habitual or rule-following activities, in general, are often purposeful in this indirect sense. Indeed, this is sometimes true even of habits or rule-following behaviors that were not originally adopted on the basis of reflective choice. Suppose a person, without any deliberate reflection, observes some traditional rule from a very early age (perhaps unconsciously imitating the behavior of her parents). Later in life she might reflect on this tradition and decide for some reason or other to deliberately maintain it: from that moment, at least, her tradition-observing action counts as purposeful. Deliberate reflection, together with the opportunity to do something different, is sufficient.

Most human actions can be described as purposeful, at least in the sense I have just explained. There are, however, exceptions. Involuntary actions, such as reflex responses, the beating of one's heart, or actions directed under hypnosis, are obviously not purposeful. Moreover, it is not enough to have options, unless one is also aware of them. If I am not aware that I may put my savings into a money market, then we cannot describe my failing to do so as purposeful. Finally, at least sometimes, people act in a purely spontaneous

That's inaction

---

[7] See Searle (2001) for an excellent recent discussion, however.

manner, without any sort of goal or aim in mind, even when they have, and are aware of, the opportunity to make a deliberate choice.

Purposeful action is *rational* when two additional conditions are met—consistency and efficiency. The first is met when purposeful action is intentionally motivated by goals or aims that are mutually consistent; the second when the particular actions chosen are, to the best knowledge of the actor, the most efficient means of realizing those goals or aims.[8] Either or both conditions might fail. Suppose a person desires to be both famous and to be left alone. These goals might turn out (at least in societies like ours) to conflict with each other. If so, actions intentionally motivated by these conflicting aims would be purposeful but not rational. Or suppose a person is made suddenly very angry, and in the heat of the moment strikes out in revenge. Her action is purposeful, but if it turns out that her aim (revenge) might have been more efficiently achieved by biding her time and waiting for the most opportune moment, her action would not be described as rational.[9]

This is a strictly descriptive conception of rationality. In principle, we can determine whether a person's goals or aims are mutually consistent without evaluating their substantive content; and likewise, whether particular actions are the most efficient means for attaining given goals or aims without evaluating the rightness or wrongness of those actions in any normative sense.[10] In this connection, it is important not to confuse the term "rational" with the terms "selfish" or "egoistic." For example, suppose a person has the altruistic aims of reducing hate speech and respecting the right of free speech. If these aims are not consistent, then her endeavors to achieve them simultaneously will not be rational. Understood in a certain way, however, her goals might be consistent: for example, if she regards the latter as a side constraint on her efforts to achieve the former. Supposing that she endeavors to achieve her two aims on this (or some other) consistent interpretation of their content, then her action might count as rational. Similarly, despite having altruistic aims, she might pursue them inefficiently, and this would not be rational; efficient action in pursuit of those same altruistic aims, however,

---

[8] Efficiency must, of course, be interpreted broadly. Suppose a person wants a higher income, but is too lazy to work hard enough to get one. He is not necessarily acting irrationally; rather, he might simply place a high value on leisure relative to income. Working less, thus, represents for him an efficient optimization of two goods, income and leisure. It is not irrational to wish the trade-offs were different than they are.

[9] For further discussion of rational and irrational action, see Davidson (1980), Elster (1979, 1983*a*, ch. 3, 1983*b*, 1986, 2000, 2007, chs. 11–13), Hastie and Dawes (2001), Searle (2001), and Sen (2002).

[10] Sometimes, a distinction is drawn between "thin" and "broad" conceptions of rationality (e.g., Elster [1983*b*, ch. 1]). This is the thin conception.

would be rational. The important point here is that, in determining the rationality of her actions, it is irrelevant that her aims happen to be altruistic, just as it would be irrelevant if her aims happened instead to be egoistic.[11] Rationality is a descriptive concept.

We should further distinguish rational action on the one hand, from *reasonable* action on the other. Purposeful action counts as reasonable if it is intentionally motivated by goals or aims that it is ethically or morally reasonable to have.[12] Generally speaking, it is better to do more good than less, and better to pursue the good consistently rather than inconsistently. In this sense, our criteria for reasonable action will include the criteria for rational action.[13] It does not follow, however, that all rational action will be reasonable. For example, suppose that it is morally unreasonable to have the aim of getting rich by theft. In this case, a crafty embezzler who succeeds in robbing millions of dollars from his company's shareholders might be acting rationally (in that his aims are consistent, and his means efficient), but not reasonably. Of course, it is disputed what goals or aims it is reasonable to have. On one theory—what is called *ethical egoism*—it is only reasonable to have self-regarding or egoistic goals and aims. If ethical egoism were the correct view, then our altruist who aimed to reduce hate speech while respecting the right of free speech might (like the embezzler) be acting rationally, but not reasonably. Fortunately, in my view, ethical egoism is almost certainly false.[14] *but he may disagree on less extreme terms*

Since, by definition, we cannot determine whether purposeful action is reasonable without substantively evaluating its goals or aims on normative grounds, reasonableness is not a descriptive concept. This is, of course, precisely the point. The rational and the reasonable serve different conceptual roles.

---

[11] Rational action as defined here thus includes both what Weber (1922, pp. 24–6) terms "instrumentally rational" and "value rational" purposeful action.

[12] The use of these terms stems from Rawls (1993, pp. 48–54), but is now common. Rawls attributes the distinction to Kant. Note that Rawls's official definition of reasonableness is narrower than this, because it incorporates some substantive ethical assumptions; the definition given here is intended to be ethically agnostic, and thus more general.

[13] This is not to say that a person who aims to do the right thing, but through clumsiness does so inefficiently, thereby does something unethical or immoral. It is to say, however, that his actions are less reasonable than they might otherwise be.

[14] Ethical egoism should not be confused with *psychological egoism*. The latter is not a theory about what sorts of goals or aims it is reasonable to have, but rather about what sorts of goals or aims human beings do in fact have. Roughly speaking, it is the view that all people are, in fact, motivated only by self-regarding egoistic goals and aims. Rationality is also often confused with psychological egoism. The former, however, is agnostic toward the goals or aims people might have, provided they are consistent, while the latter is not. Like ethical egoism, psychological egoism is almost certainly false. These terms derive from Sidgwick (1907, pp. 39–42). See also Gert (1972), Kavka (1986, ch. 2), and Feinberg (1993).

2.3 SOCIAL RELATIONSHIPS

Sometimes, we need not consider what other people might do. Whether we achieve our goals or aims in such cases is determined simply by what we decide to do—or, at any rate, by what we decide to do plus (some degree of) luck. Other times, our fates are out of our hands, determined entirely by the decisions of others, by luck, or by some combination of these. Most of the time, however, whether we achieve our goals or aims will depend jointly on what we decide to do together with what others decide to do (and, perhaps, luck).

This, quite naturally, makes us interested in what others might or might not do. In many cases, indeed, what we will want to do *depends* on what others are likely to do, and vice versa. This is especially the case when we are acting rationally: the most efficient means for realizing our goals or aims might vary according to what sorts of actions others are themselves likely to take. A person who aims to reduce hate speech, say, might be more successful adopting one course of action if people are more likely to respond to incentives, and another if people are more likely to respond to argument. Whenever what we want to do, if we are going to be rational, depends in part on what others are likely to do, this is called a *strategic situation*. Of course, we might choose to ignore the actions of others in such cases. This does not mean the situation is no longer strategic, but only that we are (irrationally) ignoring that fact.

2.3.1 A definition

Situations can be fully or partially strategic. A situation might be partially strategic, for example, if one person or group must anticipate the purposeful action of another in deciding what to do, but not vice versa. Interpreted strictly, this will be rare.[15] A situation might be partially strategic in a different way, if one (or more) of the persons or groups involved is unaware of the strategic nature of the situation; until they become aware of this fact, they might behave as if the situation were not strategic.[16] In fully strategic situations, what two or more persons or groups will each want to do depends in part on what the others are likely to do, and everyone is aware of this fact.

---

[15] Even an all-powerful slave master, who has nothing, in particular, to fear from his slave, might nevertheless prefer not to go to the trouble of beating him provided he is obedient. In this case, what the slave master wants to do depends (in a small way, perhaps) on what his slave does.

[16] This is not the same as my knowing, but ignoring, the strategic nature of a situation. In the former case, but not the latter, other parties to the relationship can safely expect that I will not act strategically.

Whenever two or more persons or groups are, in some significant respect, fully related to one another strategically, let us say they are engaged in a *social relationship*. Or, in Max Weber's words:

> The term "social relationship" will be used to denote the behavior of a plurality of actors insofar as, in its meaningful content, the action of each takes into account that of the others and is oriented in these terms.[17]

Not all relations among people are social relationships, so defined. Sometimes, this is simply because our actions have no significant effect on other people. Even when some significant outcome is the joint product of many people's actions, however, the individuals involved still might not be engaged in a social relationship. A classic example is the so-called tragedy of the commons scenario. Imagine a group of families sharing a common lake. Each family can, with some degree of effort, properly dispose of their waste, or else, with no effort, merely dump it in the lake. In the former case, each family must bear the entire cost of proper disposal themselves; in the latter case, since their waste is dissipated throughout the lake, each family hardly notices its marginal contribution to lake pollution. Every family faces exactly the same trade-offs in favor of dumping. In such scenarios, the outcome (a level of lake pollution) will be the joint product of the actions of all. But from each individual family's point of view, it does not matter what the other families do: regardless of whether the others pollute the lake or not, the trade-offs facing each family individually favor polluting. This, of course, is ultimately worse for everyone (hence the tragedy). But the relevant observation here is a narrow one. Since the preferred course of action for each individual in such scenarios does not depend on what the others do, they are not engaged in a social relationship.[18]

More importantly, the interactions among buyers and sellers in a fully competitive market are, in an approximate sense, not strategic. This is because each individual buyer or seller can safely regard equilibrium prices as determined by the market as a whole, and decide what to do on the assumption that neither they, nor anyone else, can affect those prices unilaterally. Situations that are non-strategic in this way are sometimes called *parametric*.[19] In a parametric situation, even if what I want to do is, in a technical sense, dependent on what others do, for the most part I need not

---

[17] Weber (1922, p. 26).

[18] This assumes, of course, that there are no reputation effects to consider, and that everyone does indeed have the preferences assumed. If either condition does not hold, the scenario is not a genuine tragedy of the commons, and so it might constitute a social relationship after all.

[19] Following Elster (1979, pp. 18–28, 117–23 and 1983a, pp. 74–83).

take this into account, since the relevant aggregate outcomes of their actions are highly predictable and unaffected by my own decisions. Thus, when I am related to others parametrically, I need not worry how their decisions will strategically interact with my decisions. It follows that many of the economic relations between persons or groups in a fully competitive market would not count as social relationships, so defined.[20]

Many other situations would, however. Relations of domination provide a notable example. Consider one of the core cases mentioned earlier in this chapter—early modern European feudalism. Peasants must anticipate the punishments nobles are likely to dish out if they do not receive their feudal dues, and the former must plan their purposeful action accordingly. Nobles, for their part, must consider what peasants are likely to do if excessive demands are imposed on them. This is true even if the peasants are too weak as a class to seriously threaten the social position of the nobility: if the nobles' demands are too great, for example, the peasants might plausibly believe that they will be punished no matter what they do, and thus the threat of punishment will no longer have its desired incentive effect. This is a fully strategic situation, and so the imagined peasants and nobles are engaged in a social relationship. Similar stories could be told in each of the other core cases of domination mentioned earlier.

Indeed, all relations of domination constitute social relationships. If two or more persons or groups need not take into consideration what the other(s) are likely to do in formulating their respective plans for purposeful action, then their relations to one another cannot be relations of domination. This is a strong claim, and I have certainly not shown yet that it is true in all cases. To do so, however, requires fully explaining what it means for one person or group to have arbitrary power over another. This I discuss in Chapters 3 and 4. For now, my claim can be regarded as provisional.

2.3.2 Membership

Let us call the various parties to a social relationship its *members*. Suppose that the members can be given on a list 1, 2, ..., n, and that the complete set of members can be designated N. Nothing important, in my view, hinges on whether we imagine these members to be individuals or groups, provided that

---

[20] Even in a fully competitive market, however, people might enter into arrangements that would count as social relationships: labor contracts, for instance. Thus, not all economic relations between persons or groups are parametric. This will be discussed later.

the groups in question are indeed capable of undertaking rational, purposeful action.[21] For ease of exposition, I sometimes write as if members are individual persons, but this should not be taken to mean that they could not be groups as well, or at least under the right conditions.

If we are considering a social relationship of domination, we may suppose that some of these members are the *agents* of that domination, and at least some of the others are *subjects*. How do we determine who is an agent and who is a subject of domination? The answer to this question, of course, hinges on what the best conception of domination turns out to be, and so must be deferred. In the meantime, the terms agent and subject can be regarded as convenient placeholders.

Might there be subjects of domination without there being agents? In my view, the best answer is no—or, at any rate, not unless we want to use the term domination metaphorically. Some apparently disagree. Their view is considered in Section 2.4.3.

It is important to emphasize here, however, that relations of domination are not always—indeed, perhaps rarely are—strictly dyadic.[22] Often, 1 maintains domination over 2 only with the (perhaps tacit) assistance of 3. In this case, 3 might herself be a member of the social relationship, even if she herself neither actively dominates, nor is dominated by, the others. But if the purposeful action of 3 will remain unchanged regardless of whatever 1 and 2 happen to do, then 3 is not herself a member of the social relationship in question; in this case, 1 and 2 stand in a strictly parametric relation with her. Nevertheless, her actions may partly constitute the background conditions for the social relationship of which 1 and 2 are members. In slave societies, for instance, many people who are neither slave owners nor slaves themselves act in certain predicable ways—upholding a system of property law that recognizes slaves as legitimate objects of ownership, say. These people may continue to uphold the law of property as they always do, regardless of the actions of slave owners and their slaves. Their predictable purposeful action constitutes a part of the background conditions for the social relationships of domination existing between slave owners and their slaves, and indeed partially makes the institution of slavery itself possible. But, strictly speaking, they are not themselves members of those relationships, and thus not themselves agents of that domination.

This last point might be taken to imply that the upholders of property law bear none of the moral responsibility for the institution of slavery. Nothing

---

[21] This, of course, is open to dispute, but it would be tedious to rehearse this well-known debate here, and its resolution either way would not change the argument of this study.

[22] This point is emphasized in Wartenberg (1990, ch. 7) and Hayward (2000).

could be further from my view. But who is morally responsible for domination, and who has obligations to do something about it, are not presently at issue (these questions being reserved for Part II of this study). The present issue is simply that of defining and descriptively characterizing the experience of domination. Just as we can define what it means to be punched in the face without deciding whether bystanders are wrong not to restrain would-be pugilists, so too we can define what it means to be subject to domination without determining who is (normatively speaking) responsible for that domination.

From this point of view, two related considerations weigh against our counting all persons having some causally efficacious role in making domination possible among the agents of that domination. First, the role of these external enablers is descriptively and experientially different from that of genuine agents. The experience of a slave in facing his master, for example, is fundamentally distinct from his experience in facing a potential juror he happens to meet on the street. If we expand the meaning of domination to cover both experiences, simply on the ground that the latter would indeed uphold the master's right of property in the slave, then we will only want a new term corresponding to the first experience alone, so as to pick out its special and distinctive features.[23] Second, as discussed in Chapter 5, the wrongness of domination is specifically related to some features of the first sort of experience, not necessarily present in the second. Since the moral position of external enablers will thus be different from that of the direct agents, conceptual clarity and utility are best served by matching the one term with a single, distinct experience.

2.3.3 Exit costs and dependency

To some extent, people can enter and exit social relationships voluntarily; this being the case, the membership of a social relationship is not absolutely fixed. The relative ease of entry and exit can vary tremendously, however, depending on circumstances. Exiting a friendship is (usually) much easier than exiting a marriage, and exiting a marriage today is (usually) much easier than exiting a marriage that was in the nineteenth century. Exit was nearly

---

[23] Note that I assume here the relations between the slave and the potential juror are not otherwise characterized by domination—that is, independently of the condition of slavery itself. In many slave societies, this is not the case. In the antebellum American South, for example, general race relations were such that, apart from slavery itself, all whites to some extent directly subjected all blacks to domination. The issue here is narrower: whether a particular non-slave-owning white *qua* potential juror, etc., should be considered a member of the particular relations of domination obtaining between slaves and their particular masters.

impossible for the slaves in the antebellum American South—their only hope being a dangerous attempt at flight; by contrast, slavery in ancient Rome was somewhat more open, insofar as slaves could sometimes earn their own manumission.

Let us call the degree to which a person or a group's continued membership in some social relationship is not voluntary their level of *dependency* on that social relationship. Dependency should be thought of as a sliding scale, varying according to the net expected costs (i.e., expected costs less any expected gains) of exiting, or attempting to exit, a social relationship.[24] It should go without saying that dependency on a given social relationship need not be symmetric (my dependency is not necessarily high just because yours is), nor zero-sum (my dependency is not necessarily low just because yours is high). From the degree of dependency of one member in a given social relationship, nothing can be inferred about the extent of the dependency of the other members.

To forestall any confusion later on, let me emphasize that I will not distinguish between an exit attempt's being (relatively) costly and its being (relatively) involuntary. On some conceptions of what is voluntary and involuntary, these might not be the same. For example, suppose a border patrolman points his gun at someone trying to flee her country, and shouts "Stop right there, or I'll shoot!" Clearly, continuing in her exit attempt should be regarded as costly, but if she decides to stop this might nevertheless be thought a voluntary decision in the sense that, strictly speaking, it remains within her power to assume the risk. I do not regard this as a useful conception of what it means for something to be voluntary or involuntary.[25] Accordingly, I will simply define the degree to which membership in a social relationship is involuntary as equivalent to the relative expected costs (less the relative expected gains) of attempting to exit.

Exit costs must be understood broadly here. They are not limited to material costs alone. Quite the contrary, exit costs are often to some extent psychological, and thus subjective. The dependency of a person on a particular social relationship depends on her (true or false) beliefs about the dangers of an exit attempt, together with her (true or false) beliefs about the merits of any

---

[24] See Weber (1922, pp. 28, 43–6), Emerson (1962), Okin (1989, ch. 7), Barry (2001, pp. 146–54), and Shapiro (2003, pp. 43–6). Note that this definition is considerably broader than that of Kittay (1999, pp. 30–1 and *passim*), who restricts the meaning of dependency to cases in which one party depends on another for his or her essential basic needs. More on this point will be explained shortly.

[25] But it would seem to be the view of Hobbes (1651, I.14.2, p. 86 and II.21.1–3, pp. 139–40). He argues that a man who must throw cargo overboard to prevent his ship from sinking is nevertheless free not to do so.

outside options relative to the merits of her present situation. Sometimes, it is in the interest of some members of a social relationship that others in the same relationship not attempt to exit: in such cases, the former have every reason to increase the dependency of the latter. This they might do simply by explicitly raising the direct costs of exit—making the punishment for attempted flight more severe, say. Alternatively (or in addition), they might propagate the belief that the current arrangement is beneficial and natural, that the alternatives are much worse than they seem, or even that the (apparent) alternatives do not exist at all. Any of these strategies, to the extent that they succeed, would increase levels of dependency on the social relationship. In short, what determines dependency is the cost of exit from the subjective point of view of the person or the group in question.

Imagine that a person is engaged in a social relationship she regards as exceptionally valuable. Perhaps she is the personal advisor of a powerful king, or she holds an unusually lucrative job. If she values her current position highly enough, she might subjectively regard her exit costs as severe, even if her next best option is—at least by objective standards—not bad at all. (We must factor in diminishing marginal returns here, of course: in order to generate equivalent exit costs, the absolute difference between two relatively good options must usually be greater than the absolute difference between two relatively bad options.) She is "bound by golden fetters," so to speak. Should we regard her dependency as correspondingly high? For the purposes of developing a conception of domination, the best answer is yes.[26] The reason for this will be clear from the discussion in Section 2.5.1. But it is worth pointing out here that dependency as such is not necessarily a bad thing. Many of the most valuable connections among human beings—partnerships of friendship or love, parental relationships, and so on—are unavoidably relationships of dependency. Dependency is a problem, however, when conjoined with certain other factors that, taken together, constitute domination. From this point of view, what matters is a person's subjective exit costs, not the objective value of her next best option. This, at any rate, is what I attempt to argue.

2.4 DOMINATION AS STRUCTURE

Consider again our core cases of domination. What makes these sorts of social relationships, and not others, instances of domination? In particular, does this

---

[26] Barry (2001, pp. 149–50) and Shapiro (2003, pp. 44–6) take something of a contrary view, but they are putting the idea of exit costs to other uses.

have something to do with outcomes or results of those relationships? Or does it have something to do with the structure of the relationships themselves?

This is a significant question, and it gets at the heart of my main substantive argument in this chapter. In order to answer this question, it helps to first have a more precise notion of what is meant by the structure of a social relationship.

2.4.1 Opportunity sets

Persons and groups engaged in purposeful action within a social relationship always decide what to do within some finite range of feasible options. Let us call the range of options practically available at a given time to a given member of some social relationship his or her *opportunity set*.[27]

What determines the shape of an opportunity set? Purposeful action is, obviously, limited by physical constraints and the laws of nature. Human beings cannot fly unassisted, but they can (normally) choose to walk, run, or stand still. We cannot pass through solid objects, but we can pass around them in the direction we choose. Our options are also clearly affected by our natural endowments and capabilities such as strength, health, native intelligence, and so forth; and by our artificial or social endowments such as wealth, status or reputation, position or title, and so on. Other things being equal, presumably the greater one's natural and social endowments, the wider one's opportunity set is likely to be.

But this is far from the whole story. To a large extent, the range of purposeful action available to us depends less on our endowments than it does on the organizational features of the society in which we live. Having a great deal of money, for example, expands our opportunities because we live in a society in which money can buy many things. Rules and conventions govern not only what money can buy, but also how money can be obtained, and indeed what counts as money in the first place. These sorts of organizational features correspond to what Rawls calls the "basic structure of society"—that is, all the political and social institutions and practices that constitute the relatively stable background conditions or expectations against which the members of a given society live out their lives.[28]

The basic structure of society is both constraining and enabling at the same time. Consider, for example, the system of private property. Notice that, to begin with, its existence in a given society is a social fact: it exists (to the extent

---

[27] The language here roughly follows that of Elster (2007, p. 165 and *passim*).
[28] Rawls (1971, pp. 7–11, 54–8, 1993, pp. 257–88).

that it does) insofar as the members of that society can generally be relied on to behave in the various ways that having such a system requires. This includes not only in the main respecting the rules governing one another's property holdings, but also (depending on the situation and one's particular social role) sometimes acting so as to enforce those rules against others who do not. There would be no private property as we know it if people did not generally act as if there were.

A system of private property in many ways constrains our opportunity sets. It closes the option of simply taking from others whatever we might happen to want or need—or, more precisely, doing so without risk of punishment. On the other hand, the system is also enabling, adding to our opportunity sets paths of purposeful action that would not have been there otherwise. For example, only within a functioning system of private property can we save and invest our earnings. If someone dispossesses me of my property, I can summon the community's aid in reclaiming it. And so on. The same is true of all aspects of the basic structure of society: they are both constraining and enabling at the same time. This should be obvious, but at times structure and opportunity are referred to as strict opposites—as if human behavior were either structurally determined or else completely unconstrained. Structure and opportunity are not opposites. Rather, they are flip sides of a coin: to describe the opportunities available to a person or group *is* to describe the structure of their immediate environment, and vice versa.[29]

Insofar as the basic structure of society constitutes a relatively stable set of background conditions and expectations that will not be significantly affected by the unilateral decisions of individuals (which is most often, but not always, the case), its rules can be safely regarded as artificial laws of nature, exogenous to any decisions made within a given social relationship. Let us, then, say that the structure of a social relationship is the complete description of its members' opportunity sets, as determined by their respective natural and social endowments and, more significantly, by the relevant features of the basic structure of the society in which that relationship is embedded. Included in these opportunity sets will be the exit options (with their attached prospective costs and benefits) available to each member.

Of course, the structure of a social relationship is, in truth, only relatively fixed. In the long run, external or internal events might cause the structure to change (i.e., add or subtract options from the opportunity sets of the social relationship's members). Sometimes, the events in question might even be the

---

[29] Only in the extreme case where a person is limited to a single option can we accurately speak of structure as determining (and not merely influencing) the outcome. See Elster (2007, pp. 165–71).

actions taken by the members of that social relationship themselves. It is important in this connection, however, to distinguish between objective and subjective opportunity sets—that is, between the options for purposeful action that are (in fact) available to a person or group, and the options for purposeful action that persons or groups happen to be aware of at a given time. The latter are often significantly smaller than the former. People are not always aware of the possibilities for changing their structural environment. This may be because they have failed to reflect on such questions, or because they have been deliberately confused by others, or because it is too complicated to work out how to make changes. It is also important not to underestimate the collective-action problems (difficulties in coordination, the prevention of free riding, and so on) that might present additional barriers to change, even when people know that structural change is, in principle, both possible and desirable. For these reasons, from an external descriptive point of view, we can often regard structural environments as being relatively more fixed than they perhaps really are. *⌐ appears/seems*

What is left, once the structural environment of a social relationship has been fully described, is the purposeful action of the members themselves— what they decide to do, given the choices they believe (at least in the short run) they happen to have. Thus, the system of private property partially *as does* constitutes the structural environment of the relationship between master *the punish-* and slave, just as the rules of feudal obligation partially constitute the structural environment of the relationship between noble and peasant. Particular *ment* masters and slaves, nobles and peasants decide what to do within that *system* framework, and while their respective decisions clearly affect one another, those interactions and their particular results (at least so far as they leave the framework generally unchanged) are not, by definition, themselves a part of the social relationship's structure. *✓ what about chattel slavery*

2.4.2 Structure-based conceptions

Now let us return to the question posed earlier: What makes a social relationship a relationship of domination? To make the discussion more concrete, I will focus on two of our core examples: slavery and traditional family relations.

Each of the particular relationships of slavery in a given society might, as a group, share many characteristics. In particular, they might all have quite similar structural environments—for example, they may share similar rules regarding how masters can treat their slaves, whether or not slaves can own property of their own, what will happen to slaves who attempt to escape, and so on. To fully describe these common structural features is to characterize the institution of slavery in that society. I will not bother to do this, since it is not important for the argument here.

Despite this structural similarity, however, each particular relationship of slavery will no doubt play out differently. This is for the obvious reason that particular masters and slaves will make different choices within their respective opportunity sets. For example, one master might be unusually harsh in the treatment of his slaves, whereas another (who faces, by assumption, more or less the same opportunity set) is comparatively lenient. It follows that even when two social relationships have roughly the same structure, the outcomes or results of each might differ substantially. Something similar, of course, can be said of marriages in nineteenth-century England or America. While the structural environment defined by traditional Anglo-American family law and custom was broadly similar for all marriages, each individual marriage played itself out very differently. Many husbands treated their wives with respect, even if they were not constrained to do so by traditional law and custom; others did not.

Certainly, slavery counts as an instance of domination, if anything does. Many would also say (rightly, in my view) that women were subject to domination at the hands of their husbands under traditional family law and custom. Now suppose we thought that domination had something to do with the outcomes or results of a particular social relationship. In this case, we would have to examine how each social relationship happens to play itself out in order to determine whether anyone is actually subject to domination or not. For example, if we define domination as one person or group benefiting at the expense of another, then to determine whether a particular slave is subject to domination, we must determine whether that slave's master has actually benefited at his expense. Likewise, we would have to look and see whether a particular husband benefited at the expense of his wife in order to determine whether she was subject to domination. Since different people, even when faced with similar opportunity sets, will make different choices, the results will vary from case to case, and so too will our findings of domination. Let us call this an *outcome-based* conception of domination.

Of course, I have been talking about specific individuals here—particular masters and slaves, particular husbands and wives. One might interpret the outcome-based conception somewhat differently, on the level of groups. We might say, for instance, that one group (e.g., women) is subject to domination if another group (men) generally benefits at the former's expense through a particular institution (traditional marriage). This would not alter the main point. On this revised definition, we must still examine the aggregate results of the institution, and not its internal structure, in order to determine whether it constitutes domination or not. If it should turn out that women on the whole benefited from the traditional institution of marriage, then it would follow—whatever structure traditional marriage relationships happened to have—that women were not, by definition, the subjects of domination.

Now suppose we take a different view, according to which domination refers not to any specific pattern of outcomes or results, but rather to the structure of social relationships as such. From this viewpoint, it would not matter how a particular relationship happened to play out: we would be committed to saying that, other things being equal, the slave of a lenient master is a subject of domination no less than the slave of a harsh master (though, of course, their situations may certainly differ in other respects, such as in their respective levels of health, happiness, and so forth). Likewise, on this view, we would be inclined to agree with J. S. Mill, who complains that merely because

> men in general do not inflict, nor women suffer, all the misery which could be inflicted and suffered if the full power of tyranny with which the man is legally invested were acted on; the defenders of the existing form of the institution think that all its iniquity is justified . . . But the mitigations in practice, which are compatible with maintaining in full force this or any other kind of tyranny, instead of being any apology for despotism, only serve to prove what power human nature possesses of reacting against the vilest institutions.[30]

Let us call this second view a *structure-based* conception of domination. Which of these two views is better? Different readers may have different intuitions.

My view, however, and the view probably of a majority of those who have reflected on this question, is that the second is better. In other words, on the best view, domination should be understood to refer to the structure of a social relationship itself, and not to the specific ways in which it happens to play out in some particular case.[31] This is also the opinion, I might note, of many people formerly subject to severe domination themselves. Frederick Douglass, for example, writes:

> My feelings [towards slave masters] were not the result of any marked cruelty in the treatment I received; they sprung from the consideration of

---

[30] Mill (1869, II.2, p. 506).
[31] This is the view taken by Scott (1990), Wartenberg (1990, ch. 6), Isaac (1987*a*), with the caveat that he ultimately defines domination differently than I will), and Pettit (1997, ch. 2). On some interpretations, it is also the view of Hegel; see Wartenberg (1990, pp. 121–6).

> my being a slave at all. It was slavery—not its mere incidents—that
> I hated.[32]

Now, apart from our intuitions here (and, perhaps, the testimony of persons subject to domination themselves), are there any other compelling reasons for favoring the structure-based view over the outcome-based view?

One such reason might stem from the pragmatic worry that observable results are not always a good indicator of what is really going on in a given social relationship. This is because persons and groups subject to domination sensibly adjust many of their actions to minimize its ill effects. For example, they might adopt a public persona that does not challenge the established system of domination. Consider, in this light, the testimony of another former slave, Lunsford Lane:

> I had endeavored so to conduct myself as not to become obnoxious to the
> white inhabitants, knowing as I did their power, and their hostility to the
> colored people . . . First, I had made no display of the little property or
> money I possessed, but in every way I wore as much as possible the aspect
> of slavery. Second, I had never appeared to be even so intelligent as
> I really was. This all colored people at the south, free and slaves, find it
> particularly necessary for their own comfort and safety to observe.[33]

To the extent that such strategies succeed, the slave might seem not much worse off than some free persons. Indeed, the outcome-based view would seem to commit us to saying that, as a slave comes to understand his master's psychological dispositions better and better, and thereby increasingly succeeds in avoiding overt abuse, he is less and less subject to domination. This does not seem right. The same point holds in other cases. For example, when traditional family law grants husbands excessive power over their wives, it will often be difficult to say whether a particular husband has failed to exercise his powers out of self-restraint, or merely because his wife (sensibly) has avoided challenging them. "There would be infinitely more" women complaining of ill usage, Mill points out, if complaint "were not the greatest of all provocatives to a repetition and increase of the ill usage."[34] James Scott's *Domination and the Arts of Resistance* is essentially an extended catalog of these sorts of anticipatory moves on the part of persons and groups who are subject to

---

[32] Douglass (1855, p. 161).

[33] Quoted in Osofsky (1969, p. 9); cf. Genovese (1974, pp. 597–611).

[34] And what is worse, even women who could demonstrate abuse in court would subsequently be "replaced under the physical power of the culprit who inflicted it." Thus, "even in the most extreme and protracted cases of bodily ill usage," women "hardly ever dare avail themselves of the laws made for their protection" (Mill 1869, I.11, p. 486).

domination.[35] In focusing on outcomes and results, therefore, we often misunderstand the real character of these social relationships.

Of course, it might theoretically be possible to refine our measure of outcomes so as to pick up on these subtle differences. Presumably, deference itself takes some effort, and so the person who undertakes such deference will, to that extent, be worse off than the person who does not.[36] But in a sense, this is precisely the point. To be subject to domination is, among other things, to be engaged in a social relationship structured in such a way that one must often employ the arts of deference in order to secure reasonably good outcomes or results. Whether particular slaves or wives, for example, choose to avail themselves of those tactics is neither here nor there; and, by the same logic, whether particular masters or husbands act benevolently because they are intrinsically good-natured, or rather because they have been suitably ingratiated, is irrelevant. The domination lies in the structure of the relationship itself, not in its results or outcomes.

2.4.3 Domination without agents

As suggested earlier, it is important to understand what precisely is meant by a structure-based conception of domination. Specifically, to say that domination refers to the structure of a social relationship is not to say that those structures themselves subject persons or groups to domination, and thus, by implication, that there could be domination without agents. This latter possibility should be distinguished from the observation that domination sometimes arises unintentionally, without anyone having deliberately set out to subject others to domination: the question of how domination might arise, and whether anyone can be blamed for its having arisen, is beside the point when it comes to defining domination and describing its character.[37] Our present issue is strictly a definitional and descriptive one. Am I correct to assume, as I have, that it is not possible for structures as such to dominate persons or groups, and thus for there to be subjects of domination without there being any agents?

It is easy to find examples of the claim that structures themselves subject persons or groups to domination. Michel Foucault's studies of disciplinary institutions, and of sexual and other cultural norms, are often interpreted in

---

[35] Scott (1990). Analogous arguments on this point can be found in Wartenberg (1990, p. 124) and Pettit (1997, pp. 60–1).

[36] I am grateful to Ian MacMullen for pointing this out.

[37] Young (1990, pp. 40–2), for example, seems to confuse these two, inferring from instances of the latter the existence of the former.

this way. Critical theorists such as Marcuse and Habermas sometimes describe their project as, in part, an attempt to liberate people from the domination of consumerist or rationalist ideologies (Chapter 4 discusses theories of ideological hegemony in more detail). Václav Havel describes the situation under late east-European communism as one in which everyone is mutually dominated by the system itself.[38] Prosaic versions of this notion pervade many people's thinking about domination. It is often said, for example, that traditional family law dominated women, that Jim Crow and segregation dominated American blacks, that laissez-faire ideology dominates economic thinking under capitalism, and so on—as if laws, policies, or ideas themselves could be regarded as social agents.

Of course, we might use the term domination, in such contexts, as a sort of shorthand: "American blacks were dominated by Jim Crow" might be taken as shorthand for "under the institutions of Jim Crow, American blacks were frequently subject to domination at the hands of whites." Let us put this possibility aside. Here I am interested in the claim that structures themselves literally dominate persons or groups, where this is not merely being used as shorthand.

Surely, this claim is false. Imagine an island populated by a small group of slave masters and a large group of slaves. On my view, relations between these groups are relations of domination because they are structured in some particular way, and not because the slave masters happen to be cruel and abusive (if indeed they are). But suppose the slave masters come to see the wickedness of slavery, perhaps under the influence of a visiting priest. One night, they abandon the island, never to be seen again. Would we want to say that the slaves left behind remain subject to domination the next day? We would not. This is not to deny that there might be after-effects of their having been slaves. They might have been deprived of nutrition, education, and so on, and it may take some time for them to learn how to govern themselves and make their own way in the world. This would certainly be hard for them, but hardship does not, as such, constitute domination. Once their masters have fled, there is no longer anyone present to order them around, to whip and beat them, and (on the other side) no one for them to bow and scrape before and curry favor with. When there are no agents, there is no domination.

If this example is too fanciful, consider another somewhat closer to our experience. Imagine a society in which the law of property recognizes the possibility of ownership in human beings, but in which it just happens that there are as yet no slaves. After some time, however, slaves are imported, and the law duly supports their masters' rights of ownership. Later still, the

---

[38] Havel (1992).

masters repent, and manumit their slaves. The laws, however, remain unchanged throughout these events. Only in the middle period is it accurate to
say that anyone is subject to domination. During that middle period, while it
is absolutely correct to say that the institution of property played a significant
role in *enabling* domination, it is not correct to say that the slaves were
dominated *by* that institution. The actual experience of domination here is
the experience of particular slaves, facing their particular masters.

Thus, it is important not to confuse the sensible claim that persons or
groups dominate one another under certain structural conditions with the
obscure and dubious claim that structures themselves dominate persons or
groups. Structures define the respective roles of agent and subject in all
relations of domination, but real persons or groups must occupy those roles
for the experience of domination to exist. Domination is always a relationship
among persons or groups, never a relationship between persons or groups
and structures as such.

2.5 DOMINATION AND DEPENDENCY

I have not yet specified what sort of structural environment makes a given
social relationship an instance of domination, only that domination has
something to do with structure. In the remainder of this chapter, I give only
a partial answer to this question, related to the idea of dependency introduced
earlier. A complete answer is developed in Chapters 3 and 4.

2.5.1 The dependency condition

Suppose that a person or a group is subject to domination to the extent that
they are a member of some social relationship structured in a particular way
(which, for the moment, we have not yet specified). What is to prevent them
from leaving the scene of their domination? Assuming that, other things being
equal, most people prefer not to be subject to domination (more on this is
discussed in Chapter 5), it would seem that something must hold them in
place. What holds them in place is, presumably, the cost of exit. Whatever else
we will want to say, then, domination requires at a minimum some degree of
dependency on the part of the subject person or the group. In other words,

dependency is a necessary, though (as we shall see) not a sufficient, condition of domination.

Furthermore, supposing all the necessary and sufficient conditions of domination (whatever these turn out to be) are met, it is plausible to think that the greater the dependency of subject persons or groups, the more severe their domination will be, other things being equal. Let me explain.

Consider the overall prospects a person places on remaining in some social relationship G in which she is subject to domination. Suppose we compare these with her prospects in G', representing the best outside option of which she is aware, all things considered. Further suppose there are some costs and risks associated with leaving or attempting to leave G for G'. The overall value of the former from her point of view, less the overall value of the latter, plus the costs and risks of undertaking the move itself, represents a rough measure of her dependency on social relationship G. (Naturally, if this value is zero or less than zero, there is no dependency.) As her dependency increases, so too does the leeway of the agents of her domination—they can treat her with greater severity in rough proportion to their confidence that she will not leave. Notice that it does not matter, in this respect, whether we as external observers happen to regard her best outside option G' as pretty good, and her exit costs as reasonably low. What matters is whether or not she is likely to leave, and this is strictly a function of her subjective perception of the exit costs, whatever their basis happens to be. <u>Persons bound with golden fetters are as much at the mercy of their masters as persons bound with iron.</u> The former might be better off in other respects, to be sure, but our aim is not to assess a person's overall level of well-being: it is only to assess the degree to which he or she experiences domination specifically.

Let us test this thinking with our core examples of domination. The grave dangers of attempting escape made the exit costs for typical slaves in the antebellum American South extremely high, even relative to the benefits they might hope for in escape.[39] Since their dependency was very high, so too—by my argument—was the severity of their domination. Comparatively speaking, we would expect the domination of American slaves to be greatest in those states where escape was most difficult—in the Deep South—and somewhat less great where it was less difficult—in the Border States. And indeed, this seems to have been the case.[40] Likewise, we might note that slavery was generally much less severe in ancient communities that observed

---

[39] Douglass (1855, p. 45), writes that "I was a slave—born a slave—and though the fact was incomprehensible to me, it conveyed to my mind a sense of my entire dependence on the will of somebody I had never seen."

[40] Douglass (1855, ch. 4).

the practice of manumission and other means of exit.[41] This example is straightforward.

What about domination in the family? Under traditional family law and custom, a woman's prospects outside marriage were generally low in England and the United States (and elsewhere, both then and, to some extent, today). Moreover, the legal and cultural difficulties of divorce made exit extremely costly for most women. Together, these factors contributed to a moderately high level of dependency on the marriage one was already in, thus supporting the domination of women.[42] Of course, husbands were also dependent on their wives, if not to the same degree. Dependency is not zero-sum. But, as will be discussed in Chapter 3, this had less effect because of the imbalance of power between husbands and wives: to repeat, dependency is a necessary but not sufficient condition of domination. Here we may also see the importance of our focus on subjective, rather than objective, exit costs. Compare the wives of one society, which presents them no options outside marriage, with the wives of another, which does. Suppose, however, that women in the second society have been thoroughly convinced that their highest possible calling is motherhood within a traditional family. Subjectively speaking, their exit costs from marriage will be high, but from an objective point of view, their outside options seem perfectly good. It would be a mistake to think that husbands in the second society are not thereby afforded considerable leeway in the treatment of their wives, and thus (other things being equal) that their wives' domination might be as great or greater.

Another core example of domination is autocratic government. All things considered, it is far from easy for most people to leave one society for another. This means that the dependency of a society's members is quite high, and it follows that any domination they suffer at the hands of their government will be rather severe indeed. As we would expect, totalitarian and despotic states often deliberately attempt to raise the costs of attempted emigration, precisely in order to strengthen the grip of their domination.

Finally, similar evidence can be drawn from the history of feudalism: serfs were bound to the land, and thereby suffered even worse domination at the hands of their lords than they might have otherwise.

Let me emphasize again that the level of dependency does not fully determine the severity of domination. As we shall see, several different aspects of a

---

[41] In Roman law, for instance, an abused slave could theoretically demand sale to a less abusive master: see *Institutes*, I.8.2. For a comparative discussion of manumission, see Patterson (1982, chs. 8–10).

[42] This, of course, is the general drift of Mill (1869). Similar arguments can be found in Okin (1989, ch. 7, 2002) and Vaughan-Evans and Wood (1989, esp. p. 151).

social relationship's structural environment contribute to its being a relationship of domination. The claim here is only that given two social relationships with otherwise equivalent structural environments, the domination suffered will be worse in the one where the dependency of the subjects is higher. To put it formally, if the level of domination D in a given social relationship is a function f of dependency d and several other variables we have not yet specified, that is, if $D = f(d, \cdot)$, then the first-order partial derivative of f with respect to d will be greater than zero: $\partial f / \partial d > 0$.[43]

2.5.2 Decentralized domination

The examples we have discussed are reasonably straightforward. Other cases are less obvious because it is not always clear how to define the membership of the appropriate social relationship.

Suppose a person has her choice among a wide range of different masters in alternative social relationships $G_1, G_2, \ldots, G_n$. Further suppose that the costs and risks of leaving one for another are quite low, but that her prospects with any are more or less equally dismal. Now it might seem that, despite her poor prospects with the master she does eventually select, her dependency on him in particular is nevertheless low, for she is always free to exchange him for another. It might then seem to follow (by my argument) that she cannot suffer much by way of domination.

But this conclusion is too hasty. Perhaps the masters have successfully colluded to keep the prospects of servants low in general. In this case the relevant choice is not among $G_1, G_2, \ldots, G_n$, which should be regarded a single social relationship G including all the masters as members, but rather between G and H—say, where H is not having a master at all. Her prospects under H might be very low indeed (perhaps starvation). If so, then we have an instance of what might be called decentralized domination, the nature of which is partially obscured until our analysis comprehends how the membership of the relevant social relationship is defined. One might easily imagine a Marxist analysis of the wage–labor system along these lines.[44] Sometimes, decentralized domination of this sort is described as impersonal, in the sense that no individual servant or worker is dependent on any one master or employer in particular, and thus it is mistakenly thought to be an instance of agent-less domination. Once the relevant social relationship has been

---

[43] In Appendix II, I try to support this conclusion further in a formal model.

[44] See, for example, the discussion in Cohen (1983); I am grateful to Jon Elster for pointing out this reference and its significance here.

properly defined, however, we see this is not the case. The agents of domination in this case are properly defined as the complete set of masters.

In a perfectly free market, however, there would theoretically be no dependency, for all entries and exits would presumably be costless. (In economics lingo, at a Walrasian competitive equilibrium, all buyers and sellers are indifferent between their current transactions and their next-best options.) Scenarios like the one described above, for example, would not arise, because free entry into any market would make attempts at employer collusion impossible. If employers had to compete for workers as much as workers had to compete for jobs, the latter would not be dependent on the former: workers unhappy with their current employers would always be able to find others ready to hire them at an equivalent wage. Since at least some degree of dependency is a necessary condition for domination, in a perfectly free market there would be none.

Markets are rarely perfect, however. To begin with, there will always be *aka never* deviations from the ideal competitive situation due to monopolistic practices, pricing externalities, government interventions, and so on. Theoretically, perhaps, some of these deviations could be eliminated with properly designed institutions. Others cannot. For example, the standard general market equilibrium model assumes that all exchanges can be perfectly enforced exogenously in the courts, but this is clearly not the case. Many contracts necessarily have vague or complicated terms that, being open to interpretation, create opportunities for shirking. The need of the contracting parties to endogenously enforce such exchanges themselves distorts prices, thus producing deviations from the perfectly free market in which there would be no dependency.[45]

This last discussion leads us to the general observation that it will be impossible to eliminate all dependencies. What is more, it is far from clear that we would want to, were it in our power to do so. Dependency on one's family, on one's friends and loved ones, on one's job, and so on is an irreducible and not always lamentable fact of everyday social life. As suggested earlier, dependency in itself is not necessarily a bad thing. Nevertheless, to the extent that it does contribute in maintaining relations of domination, easing dependency can be one tool among others for reducing domination,

---

[45] See Shapiro and Stiglitz (1984); the application of this finding to the discussion here can be seen clearly in Bowles and Gintis (1992, 1993). The rough idea is this: since an employer cannot rely on the exogenous enforcement of all the provisions in a labor contract, he will have to offer above-equilibrium wages to induce the optimal effort–wage ratio. It follows that labor markets will not clear (i.e., there will be involuntary unemployment), and those persons who do get hired will not necessarily be indifferent between their current job and their next-best alternative—either another job or unemployment. What Bowles and Gintis call the "enforcement rent" is roughly equivalent to dependency as defined in this study.

supposing we want to reduce it (more on this in Part II). For example, a public provision of unemployment benefits reduces the dependency of workers, and thus reduces any domination they might suffer at the hands of their employers. Employers, for their part, have historically tried to increase the dependency of their workers artificially, for instance by collusive practices such as blacklisting. Restricting these practices might further reduce worker dependency. Similarly, as Mill observed, opening employment opportunities for women reduces their dependency on their husbands, thus reducing domination in the family. Precisely in order to maintain their domination over women, it was necessary for men to prevent this from happening, which they did both formally (by creating legal barriers to women's employment) and informally (by propagating the ideology that women were naturally unsuited to anything other than the duties of motherhood).[46] And so on. Reducing dependency, in most cases, reduces domination. Since it will not always be possible or desirable to do so, however, there are (fortunately) other strategies for accomplishing this aim as well, as we shall see.

Supposing the general idea of dependency is now reasonably clear, we may conclude this chapter by reiterating its main claim: namely, that the domination of one person or group by another is constituted by the structural environment of their social relationship, and that this environment must include, as a minimum, some degree of dependency on the part of the former. (Note that any dependency of the *agent* of that domination on the same social relationship is not at issue. Indeed, it is entirely possible that the agent's dependency will turn out to be greater than the subject's in some cases: slave masters might, for example, greatly prefer keeping their slaves to giving them up, and a given husband in nineteenth-century England might be even more averse to divorce than his wife. This, however, is beside the point. It is dependency on the part of the subject that constitutes a necessary condition of domination.) Characterizing the remaining structural features of domination requires a richer account of the goals or aims of a social relationship's members, and of the opportunity sets available to them. Chapter 3 begins the task of developing that account.

---

[46] Mill (1869, esp. ch. 1).

3

The Imbalance of Power
Conception

Chapter 2 argued that domination should be understood structurally—in other words, that we should regard the domination of one person or group by another as consisting in particular features of their social relationship's structural environment. With this in mind, let us consider again Orlando Patterson's use of the concept, quoted earlier:

> Slavery is one of the most extreme forms of the relation of domination, approaching the limits of total power from the viewpoint of the master, and of total powerlessness from the viewpoint of the slave.

What I wish to draw attention to here is the close association drawn between domination and power. This is a perfectly natural association. Indeed, the most common view of domination may be that it simply *is* power—or, to be more precise, that it is any social relationship structured such that one person or group in that relationship has more power than another. Patterson himself says precisely this:

> Relations of inequality or domination, which exist whenever one person has more power than another, range on a continuum from those of marginal asymmetry to those in which one person is capable of exercising, with impunity, total power over another.[1]

Nor need we single out Patterson in particular. For example, in earlier work such as his well-known "Two Lectures" on power, Michel Foucault seems to more or less use the terms "domination" and "power" interchangeably.[2] It is true, as we shall see, that near the end of his life Foucault proposed a somewhat more refined definition, but this merely demonstrates the usual pattern: before thinking about it more carefully, one's natural and relatively unreflective view seems to be that domination simply amounts to one person

---

[1] Patterson (1982, p. 1).
[2] See Foucault (1980, pp. 92, 95–6, 98, *passim*). Similar identifications of domination and power can be found in Isaac (1987*a*, pp. 5, 23) and Stewart (2001, pp. 49–53).

or group having more power than another. In the discussion that follows, I refer to this as the *imbalance of power conception* of domination.

My aim is to show that the imbalance of power conception is inadequate, and that it ought to be rejected. The main part of this argument must wait until Chapter 4. For the moment, my goal is to define what it means for one person or group to have power over another. This requires that we back up for a moment, and further develop some ideas introduced in Chapter 2.

3.1 STRATEGIES, PREFERENCES, AND EXPECTATIONS

In Chapter 2, I discussed the idea of opportunity sets. The opportunity set of a person or a group is the range of feasible options available to them at a given time. As a preliminary to our discussion of power, it is necessary to discuss in somewhat greater detail the content of these opportunity sets.

3.1.1 Actions and strategies

Opportunity sets, one might suppose, are composed of (possible) actions. This, however, is not quite correct. More precisely, opportunity sets are composed of (possible) *plans for action*. The significance of this difference can be seen with the help of a simple example. Imagine a military general anticipating an attack. He can either face his army to the left or to the right: these are the possible actions available to him. But suppose that he has carefully posted scouts that will inform him of the direction of his enemy's march in advance. In this case, he can wait to see what his enemy does first, before deciding which way to face his own army. His opportunity set is thus composed of a number of possible plans, some of which might respond contingently to what his enemy does. One plan might be "always face left," but another might be "face left if the enemy advances from the left, otherwise face right." (Other, more fanciful, plans might be "face left if it rains, otherwise face right," "face left on Tuesdays, otherwise face right," and so on.) Strictly speaking, what the general chooses from his opportunity set is a plan, not merely an action.

The plans in our example above are relatively simple. In complex situations, we might imagine more elaborate plans involving sequential steps that take into account multiple contingencies—for instance, "first do A, and then B; if x happens, then do C, and then, if y happens, D and E, but otherwise nothing; if x does not happen, do F, then G, and finally H." The relevant contingencies here could be the observed future actions of other people, or they could be future natural events, or events of chance. Plans can also be open-ended or indefinite rules of thumb, as for example "always take an umbrella if it is cloudy or raining; otherwise, do not."

Let us call a complete plan of action, however simple or elaborate, a *strategy*. In technical terms, a strategy can be described as a function mapping sets of possible histories into sets of possible actions. In our simple example of the general awaiting an attack, the set of possible histories has two elements, $H = \{$enemy advances from the left, enemy advances from the right$\}$, as does the set of possible actions, $A = \{$face left, face right$\}$. The strategy "always face left" simply maps both possible histories into the same action, like so (Figure 3.1).

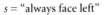

$s = $ "always face left"

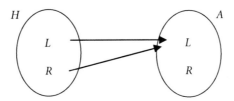

Figure 3.1

Any strategy, no matter how complex, can be described as a mapping like this—as a function that takes histories as inputs and generates action as outputs. Strategy functions are formally notated as either $s: H \rightarrow A$ or $s(h) = a$, where $h_1, h_2, \ldots, h_n$ represent possible histories in the set H, and $a_1, a_2, \ldots, a_n$ represent possible actions in the set A.

Of course, as more contingencies and more possible actions are taken into consideration, the number of possible strategies expands exponentially. It follows that some of the strategies theoretically available to a person or group will be incredibly complex—indeed, beyond the cognitive capacity, or at any rate the patience, of ordinary people. Recall from Chapter 2 that a subjective opportunity set is the set of options both available and *known* to be available to a person or group. A possible strategy might not be known either because its existence has been deliberately obscured, because it has not occurred to the potential actor, or because it is too complex to work out in detail (given the cognitive abilities of the actor, the cost and effort of working it out, or the limited time available for doing so). When real people engage in purposeful action, they select strategies from their subjective opportunity set only.

3.1.2 Outcomes and preferences

At least on our ordinary understanding of things, persons, or groups engaged in a purposeful action select (directly or indirectly) strategies from their subjective opportunity sets with an eye toward achieving their goals or aims.

Often, this is fairly easy to do. Imagine a very simple situation in which one needs to consider neither the actions of others nor the element of luck. In such situations, each possible strategy corresponds directly to a particular outcome. For example, if we have a fruit basket with both apples and oranges, the strategy "eat an apple" corresponds directly with the outcome that we eat an apple, and the strategy "eat an orange" corresponds directly with the outcome that we eat an orange. Let us call a set of possible outcomes X an *outcome space*. Suppose that a person, when given an opportunity set with these two options, generally selects the strategy "eat an apple." One way to describe this is to say that she *prefers* to eat apples. This preference can be formally represented as a subjective ranking over the outcome space in question.[3] (Indifference—liking apples and oranges equally—counts as a ranking for this purpose.) Presumably, this subjective ranking reflects the degree to which each of the possible strategies realizes whatever goals or aims the person happens to have. Notice, however, that we need not know the content of these goals or aims in order to know what her ranking is. For example, she might prefer eating apples because she thinks they taste better, or because she believes them to be farmed in a more environmentally sustainable manner, or for some other reason. Whatever her goals or aims happen to be, we can usually deduce her formal preference ranking simply from the evidence of our observation that she selects certain strategies ("eat an apple") over others ("eat an orange") from a given opportunity set. Hence, these are often called "revealed preferences," in the sense that the decisions people make reveal their subjective preference rankings over possible outcomes.

The goals or aims underlying a subjective preference ranking might be self-regarding or other regarding, and they might be altruistic or egoistic. I have deliberately defined preference here in such a way as to be agnostic toward a person or a group's substantive goals or aims. This allows us to employ preference as a strictly descriptive term.

Also note that we need not suppose subjective preferences are fixed. People often change their mind, or have their minds changed, for a wide variety of reasons. Indeed, decisions made at one time, on the basis of one set of

---

[3] This preference need not be absolute, of course. If she prefers a mix of fruit, she might rank the outcome in which she has eaten two apples and one orange over the outcome in which she has eaten three apples. For ease of exposition, I will keep the examples very simple.

preferences, may themselves lead a person or group to adopt a different set of preferences in the future. For example, I might want to learn more about what goes on in an emergency room because I intend to go to medical school. Later, however, having volunteered at an emergency room with that purpose in view, I realize I do not want to be a doctor after all. Even if, at this later stage, I am glad to have had the experience of volunteering, insofar as it discouraged me from pursuing a career I did not actually want, this later preference cannot itself be the reason for my earlier decision to volunteer. At any given time, we can only make decisions on the basis of the preferences (and information) we happen to have at that time. This is trivially true.

One last point: for each possible strategy, there exists, in a technical sense, a different possible outcome. The difference need not be, however, any material difference in the ordinary sense. For example, one might eat an apple as it is, or else cook it to make apple sauce first. These alternate strategies might seem to have the same outcome (the apple is eaten, one way or another), but they must nevertheless be assigned different outcomes in the outcome space. This is so that, if a person prefers to follow one path toward eating an apple rather than another, this fact can be represented in her subjective ranking of the possible outcomes. People often care quite a bit not only about *what* happens, but *how* it happens—what process gets them there. Suppose a doctor has two patients in need of a kidney transplant. It might matter quite a bit—both to the doctor, and possibly to her patients—that she decides to give the first available kidney to one patient rather than the other because his need is greater, say, and not because he wins a coin toss. Analogously, I might like to eat the last apple in a fruit basket, but strongly prefer that, rather than take it for myself, it be offered to me by my host. So long as every possible strategy corresponds to a formally (even if not materially) different outcome, we can take process considerations like these into account when describing subjective preference rankings.[4]

3.1.3 Rational preferences

In Chapter 2, I discussed rational and reasonable purposeful action; we can now formally represent these as conceptions of rational and reasonable subjective preferences. Let us say that persons or groups act rationally if the decisions they make reveal a subjective preference ranking over outcomes satisfying two conditions:

---

[4] The various technical difficulties that arise when we associate outcomes with material results, neglecting the *paths* to those results, are discussed in Sen (2002, esp. chs. 3–4).

(C) The ranking is *complete*, in the sense that for any two possible outcomes x_1 and x_2 in a given outcome space, it is the case that the person or group either prefers x_1 to x_2, or prefers x_2 to x_1, or is indifferent between them.

(T) The ranking is *transitive*, in the sense that for any three possible outcomes x_1, x_2, and x_3 in a given outcome space, it is the case that if the person or group prefers x_1 to x_2, and also prefers x_2 to x_3, then it is also the case that they prefer x_1 to x_3.

The first condition is so weak as to appear trivial. What about the second? Suppose I acted as if I strongly prefer apples to oranges, oranges to pears, and pears to apples. This would be irrational. It might lead me to "improve myself to death": if I had ten oranges, I might agree to trade them for nine apples (because apples are better than oranges); I might then trade these for eight pears (because pears are better than apples), and these in turn for seven oranges (because oranges are better than pears); and so on, until I have only a single piece of fruit left.

People do sometimes have irrational preferences like this—usually, no doubt, because they have failed to notice the irrationality. This does not, in itself, mean that rationality is not being used as a descriptive term here. It is a descriptive fact whether or not a person or group makes decisions revealing rational preferences. If we went on to suggest that it is *good* for a person to have rational preferences, then we would indeed be making a normative claim about the sorts of preferences it is *reasonable* for them to have. As noted in Chapter 2 (with respect to goals and aims), it is presumably reasonable to have rational preferences, other things being equal. It is also, presumably, reasonable to prefer helping others to hurting them, to prefer not discriminating on the basis of race or gender, and so on. In this part of the study, however, I am putting such normative considerations aside.

In many cases, strategies do not deterministically lead to particular outcomes. This might be due to the intervention of luck. For example, one option in my opportunity set might be to keep my dollar, while another might be to spend it on a lottery ticket. In this case, while there are only two available strategies (to play or not to play the lottery), there are three possible outcomes: $0 (if I play and lose), $1 (if I do not play), and the lottery prize less $1 (if I play and win). This too can easily be captured in descriptive subjective preference rankings. Indeed, it permits us to considerably enrich our account of subjective preference. Suppose a person strongly prefers apples to oranges. Given the choice of getting an orange for certain, or a one-third chance of getting an apple, however, suppose she is indifferent. Now we can imagine that this person is acting so as to maximize a *utility function* according to which oranges have a utility value of 1 and apples a utility value of 3 (or 7 and

21, or 0.2 and 0.6, or indeed any multiples of this ratio). With the help of a few additional technical assumptions and some clever proofs, in fact, it can be mathematically shown that *whatever* people are doing—and whatever their reasons for doing it may happen to be—provided that they act rationally their purposeful action can be summarized, so to speak, as if it were an attempt to maximize a cardinal utility function *u* in which each possible outcome in the outcome space *X* is assigned a positive real number (in the notation described earlier, a subjective utility function for person *i* would be formally represented as $u_i: X \to R_+$).[5]

This is an extremely useful fact, as we shall see. It is very important, however, not to imagine that utility functions represent anything more than an artificial summary of observed purposeful action. Considerable confusion has been caused by the mistaken view that there exists—or that it is claimed that there exists—some real and measurable property called "utility" that subjectively or objectively adheres to actual or possible states of the world; and (even worse) that actual persons or groups consciously aim to maximize this imaginary property. There is clearly no such thing as utility in this sense. Utility functions are merely useful mathematical representations of what persons or groups happen to do, and nothing more.

3.1.4 Rationality and expectations

So far, I have assumed that outcomes are determined simply by what a person or a group decides to do (together, perhaps, with luck). Things get more complicated when outcomes are the joint effect of the actions of two or more persons or groups (together, perhaps, with luck).

The military general anticipating an attack, described earlier, provides a simple example. The enemy, we might suppose, has an opportunity set with two strategies: advance from the left or advance from the right. The general, since he can make his action contingent on what the enemy does, has an opportunity set with four strategies: always face left; always face right; face left if the enemy advances from the left, otherwise face right; and face right if the enemy advances from the left, otherwise face left (recall that people choose strategies, or plans for action, not actions). Since there are $2 \times 4 = 8$ possible

---

[5] The original approach is due to von Neumann and Morgenstern (1944). Restatements can be found in Luce and Raiffa (1957, ch. 2), Savage (1972, ch. 5), and Hastie and Dawes (2001, ch. 12). With one exception, the additional assumptions needed are arcane and mathematical. The exception is a continuity assumption, which would be violated by persons having strictly lexical preferences (but see Posner [2000, ch. 11] for good reasons to doubt the existence of bona fide lexical preferences).

pairings of their respective strategy options, we have in principle eight possible outcomes. These can be represented in a table (Table 3.1). In general, if $S_1, S_2, \ldots, S_n$ represent the opportunity sets for persons or groups $1, 2, \ldots, n$, then the outcome space X must in principle include $|S_1| \times |S_2| \times \ldots \times |S_n|$ possible outcomes. Each outcome represents what happens when the various parties adopt some particular combination of strategies from their respective opportunity sets—what is called a *strategy profile*. These outcomes will not always be different in any obvious material sense. Thus, x_{13} and x_{14} in Table 3.1 might seem to be identical, insofar as both result in the enemy advancing from the left and the general's forces facing the right. Nevertheless, as discussed earlier, it is important to keep each formal outcome distinct, since people might care not only what happens, but also *how* it happens (i.e., what profile of strategies ultimately led to a given outcome).

Table 3.1

The enemy's strategy	The general's strategy			
	Always face left	Face left if advance from left	Face right if advance from left	Always face right
Advance from left	x_{11}	x_{12}	x_{13}	x_{14}
Advance from right	x_{21}	x_{22}	x_{23}	x_{24}

Situations like these, in which outcomes are the joint effect of the actions taken by two or more persons or groups, are often called *game-theoretic* situations. In a game-theoretic situation, we are naturally interested in what others are likely to do. Often, indeed, what we will want to do in a game-theoretic situation depends on what others are likely to do, and vice versa; in Chapter 2, this was called a strategic situation. Not all game-theoretic situations are (fully or partially) strategic, however. Broadly speaking, there might be two reasons for this.

In some game-theoretic situations, we might happen to have what is called a *dominant strategy*. A dominant strategy is a plan for action we will want to adopt regardless of what others might happen to do. This can be illustrated as follows. Suppose that each time the general's forces face in the direction of the enemy's advance, he repels the attack, but when his forces face the other way, the enemy dislodges his army and gains territory. In this case, the general presumably has a dominant strategy: "face left if the enemy advances from the left, otherwise face right." Of the four plans for action available to him, this one always serves him well, regardless of what the enemy decides to do. The enemy, by contrast, does not have a dominant strategy. If the general's strategy was "always face left," then the enemy would want to advance from the right, whereas if the general's strategy was "always face right," then the enemy would want to advance from the left. If the general adopts his dominant strategy, the enemy might want to flip a coin. The enemy's best strategy, in other words, depends on the strategy adopted by the general. Thus, our imagined scenario is an example of a partially strategic situation—strategic from the enemy's point of view, but not from the general's.[6] When all the participants in a game-theoretic situation have a dominant strategy, their relations are not strategic at all. This is the case in a pure tragedy of the commons. As discussed in Chapter 2, a tragedy of the commons does not constitute a social relationship.

Game-theoretic situations might also fail to be strategic by virtue of their being parametric. In a fully competitive market, the outcome (an equilibrium price) is the joint product of the actions taken by many people—countless individual decisions to buy or sell. Obviously, each is interested in what the other buyers and sellers are likely to do, insofar as each is interested in what the equilibrium market price turns out to be. Thus, a fully competitive market is a game-theoretic situation. Nevertheless, its participants are not related to one another strategically. This is because no individual buyer or seller in a fully competitive market can affect prices unilaterally—each is a price-taker, and none a price-maker. It follows that each market participant can, from his or her own point of view, regard the equilibrium market price as exogenously fixed and decide what to do on that basis, without taking into consideration what the other market participants are likely to do. Though game theoretic, this situation is parametric, not strategic.

In non-strategic situations, we can simply choose the strategy in our subjective opportunity set that best realizes our goals or aims, without worrying about what other people are likely to do. When we are related to other people strategically, however—i.e., when we are engaged in a social relationship as defined in Chapter 2—we are compelled to make assumptions regarding what they are likely to do. How should we assume other people will behave? On what basis should we form our expectations? Naturally, we can and do use many different methods. Sometimes we make assumptions on the basis of what we wish another person would do; sometimes, on the basis of what we ourselves would do in that person's position; sometimes, randomly; sometimes on the basis of astrological charts; and so on. Most often, however, we assume that others will act rationally. This does not mean that we expect others will act egoistically, necessarily; rather, it is only to say that we usually expect others to do what, in fact, they would prefer to do, given the

---

[6] If the general did not have scouts, however, this would be a fully strategic scenario.

preferences they happen to have. This seems trivial. Nevertheless, it is an important assumption, as we shall see in later discussion. Indeed, let us say that it is *rational for* a person or group to base their expectations regarding the behavior of other persons or groups on the assumption that they also will act rationally. (Thus, if the enemy in our running example is rational, he will assume that the general, acting rationally, will adopt his dominant strategy, "face left if the enemy advances from the left, otherwise face right.") This somewhat expands our conception of rationality.

Most people, most of the time, act rationally, at least so far as they are able. This is an empirical generalization, and I do not attempt to defend it. Supposing that I am right, however, it follows that the assumption that people will act rationally is very reliable. This is a part of the argument for regarding rationality as the basis for our expectations, but only a part. The deeper argument is that, at some level, we usually cannot help but rely on this assumption: to try to understand the voluntary behavior of others is, in effect, to try to explain it in terms of its being rational, i.e., in terms of the goals or aims that seem to motivate it.[7] When others do not act as we expect, we usually take this to mean we are mistaken about their goals or aims, not that they are being irrational in failing to advance the goals or aims we have attributed to them. Accordingly, we generally adjust our beliefs about the goals or aims of others so as to make rational sense of whatever behavior we actually observe. When we cannot do this—when a person's behavior appears thoroughly chaotic or unmotivated (and not just occasionally so)—we simply cannot understand it as rational, and thus we cannot form expectations about what they are likely to do. There is no alternative assumption we can turn to instead. Fortunately, however, this is the exception, and not the rule. For the most part, when we must decide what to do, and when this depends to some extent on what others are likely to do, our usual assumption that they will act rationally is very reliable.

3.2 POWER IN GENERAL

With these preliminaries out of the way, we are now in a position to define the centrally important concept of power. Some believe this cannot be done. Before proceeding, I should briefly explain why I think they are wrong.

---

[7] This argument was most famously elaborated by Davidson (1980).

3.2.1 Essentially contested concepts

The standard explanation for why we cannot define power is the claim that it is an essentially contested concept.[8] Obviously, by "essentially contested" one does not simply mean that political and social theorists have in fact contested all the conceptions of power put forward so far, as this by no means demonstrates that agreement is not possible in the future. Nor can one simply mean that power is an essentially complex or messy concept (unlike, say, the concepts of mass or velocity). It may well turn out that power is a complex phenomenon, not always easy to observe and perhaps impossible to measure precisely. This does not, however, preclude agreement on a relatively precise definition, provided that it is formulated at a sufficient level of abstraction. Rather, to say that the concept of power is essentially contested, one must mean that there is something about the nature or essence of the concept of power as such that necessarily precludes agreement on a single conception or, at any rate, makes agreement extremely unlikely. But depending on how we interpret this last claim, it is either trivial, or else false.[9]

perhaps agreement is not desirable

Why might something about the concept of power as such preclude agreement on a single conception? One view might be that agreement on a conception of power is impossible because there is no truth in definitions per se—at least, or especially, when it comes to defining social phenomena. I made this very claim in Chapter 1. It would be philosophically naive, I think, to seriously believe that settling on any particular definition of power (or domination, or other similar terms) is a matter of discovering the natural demarcations inherent in social phenomena themselves. Any particular definition, it follows, is always contestable in the sense that it cannot be verified by empirical observation. Indeed, empirical observation can only settle a dispute when the disputants are already agreed on the conceptions they are using. If *this* is the claim, then it is (trivially) true, but unenlightening. We would still want to know why political and social theorists have not in fact settled on some conception of power as a matter of theoretical convenience or convention.

This leads us to a stronger version of the claim that there is something about the concept of power itself (and perhaps other political concepts) that renders even an agreement of convenience or convention impossible. Roughly, the

I concede the desirability of this

[8] The idea of essentially contested concepts derives from Gallie (1956). The claim that power is an instance of this is made by Connolly (1983, pp. 93–101), Lukes (2005, pp. 29–38), and others.

[9] The essential contestability of the concept of power has also been challenged by Wartenberg (1990, pp. 12–17), Dowding (1991, pp. 167–73), and Morriss (2002, pp. 199–206). My argument here roughly follows that of Dowding.

argument is that any attempt to advance a particular conception of power must itself be a sort of exercise of power—an attempt to exclude competing conceptions for political reasons. In general, we may suppose that people will fail to agree on definitions whenever different interests are served by competing interpretations of a concept. As Thomas Hobbes says, if it were contrary to "the interest of men that have dominion that the three angles of a triangle should be equal to two angles of square," then the notion would not only be "disputed," but "suppressed as far as he whom it concerned was able."[10] Different political views underlie different conceptions of power, we might suppose, and thus, advancing one conception in particular will itself always be an act of political rhetoric.

No doubt, attempts to advance political interests by rhetorical definition have frequently been made. But does essential contestability follow from this fact? In my view, it does not. Consider an example, drawn from Hobbes himself. By his definition, a "commonwealth" is a sovereign "whose acts a great multitude, by mutual covenants one with another, have made themselves every one the author," so that the sovereign "may use the strength and means of them all as he shall think expedient for their peace and common defense." The liberty or freedom of subjects in a commonwealth, he later adds, is the "silence of the law."[11] Now this is not at all how many of his seventeenth-century English readers would have used these terms. Most would have understood the term "commonwealth" to mean roughly an independent political community not organized as a monarchy, and "liberty" to mean a citizen's enjoyment of that condition. Hobbes deliberately defines these terms polemically. He hopes to convince his readers that, contrary to a common but (in his view) entirely mistaken claim, deposing an absolute monarch would not necessarily lead to greater political liberty.

Clearly, the terms commonwealth and liberty are here subject to political contestation, and important interests underlie each interpretation. Does it follow, however, that either must be an *essentially* contested concept? It does not. Surely, no intelligent republican reader of Hobbes could have been fooled by such a rhetorical sleight of hand. The slightest reflection would show that little of substance hinges on how these terms are defined. The real issues concern where the sovereign power ought to be located (in a monarch or in the people); whether it can be delegated, limited, or divided; and so on—regardless of which terms are used to designate which concepts. It is entirely open to a reader of Hobbes to say, "If that's what you mean by a

---

[10] Hobbes (1651, I.12.21, p. 70). I am grateful to David Johnston for pointing out the relevance of Hobbes for this discussion.

[11] Hobbes (1651, II.17.13, p. 114) and (1651, II.21.18, p. 146), respectively.

'commonwealth,' then that's not the issue. In your language what I want is limited, democratic sovereignty."

Attempting to advance political interests by rhetorical definition is futile, precisely because of the ease with which linguistic conventions can be co-opted by the opposition. Indeed, the very notion of a concept's being essentially contested is nearly self-defeating, for the possibility of contestation depends on the fact that there is no truth to definitions, and it is this very fact that makes co-opting linguistic conventions so easy.

Appearances to the contrary, there is, in my view, something of a convergence in the literature on power.[12] One reason disagreement seems to persist is because social and political theorists have often directed their sights at different levels of analysis. Many have tried to explicate not power as such, but rather one or another *form* of power. By a form of power I mean a particular technique or method by which a person or group exercises power. For example, one way of exercising power is through authority, another is through the control of valued resources, another is through personal charm, and so on. Obviously, power comes in many forms. Indeed, it would not be possible to catalog them all, since people are ingenious at discovering new forms. This does not, however, preclude agreement on a general conception of power as such.

Some political and social theorists have perhaps resisted the effort to develop a conception of power at the appropriate level of generality because power is so closely associated with the concept of domination. For the most part, people regard domination as a bad thing, and if domination were simply an imbalance of power, then it would follow that an imbalance of power must be a bad thing. But once power is defined at the appropriate level of generality, as we shall see, it is by no means clear that imbalances of power are necessarily bad. This difficulty can be eliminated, however, by carefully distinguishing domination from power as such, as I will do.

3.2.2 A General conception of power

In defining power, it turns out, it is difficult to improve on Hobbes himself. "The power of a man (to take it universally)," he writes, is simply "his present means, to obtain some future apparent good."[13] Notice that this is a strictly descriptive conception of power, not to be confused with *authority*, which

---

[12] In particular, the view explicated here is very nearly the same as that of Barry (1980, 2002), Wartenberg (1990), Dowding (1991, 1996), and Morriss (2002). Indeed, Lukes himself has more or less come round to the same view; see Lukes (2005, pp. 69–74).

[13] Hobbes (1651, I.10.1, p. 58).

Hobbes defines as "the right of doing any action."[14] To have or not have power is a descriptive fact, whereas to have or not have authority is a normative fact. When John Locke defines political power as "a right of making laws," he should have said this was the definition of political authority.[15] Of course, if (as a matter of descriptive fact) many people believe that their government has the authority to rule them, this may in turn increase the power of that government. But this is only to say—which is obvious—that to be believed to hold authority is to have, other things being equal, additional means to obtain future apparent goods.

Hobbes describes power as the ability to obtain "future apparent goods." By this he does not mean, however, things that are in fact (objectively or normatively speaking) good for the person or group in question. On the contrary, by "good" Hobbes means merely "whatsoever is the object of any man's appetite or desire"—or, in other words, something a person or group happens to want subjectively.[16] This is an important observation. We may believe that martyring oneself in a suicide bombing is not, on the whole, good for one; and, indeed, we may be correct. (Hobbes, certainly, would have thought so.) But this is neither here nor there when it comes to power: if a person has the requisite means and opportunity to obtain something, then it follows that she has the power to obtain it.[17]

In other words, we must be careful to understand power in desire-independent terms. Power is not the ability to obtain what we actually happen to want, but rather the ability to obtain whatever we might happen to want. If power were not understood to be desire-independent in this way, a person could become more powerful merely by tailoring what she wants to fit what she can already accomplish. I have the power to jump off a bridge, even if I do not want to, but I do not have the power to fly, nor can I make myself more powerful merely by convincing myself that I do not want to. Whatever its merits as an ethical doctrine, this is clearly not the notion of power we are interested in.

Using the terminology of this study, we may express the spirit of Hobbes's conception of power as follows:

> (P) The *power* of a person or group is their ability to bring about outcomes, if desired, by employing strategies in their opportunity set.

---

[14] Hobbes (1651, I.16.4, p. 107).

[15] Locke (1690, §3, p. 8).

[16] Hobbes (1651, I.6.7, p. 35).

[17] To be a suicide bomber is surely unreasonable, but it is not necessarily irrational; that depends entirely on what one's goals or aims happen to be.

This neo-Hobbesian view is, roughly speaking, the conception converged on in the recent literature on power. Keith Dowding, for example, defines power in the general sense (which he calls "outcome power" or "power to") as "the ability of an actor to bring about or help bring about outcomes." Similarly, Brian Barry defines power in a "very broad" sense as "the ability to bring about desired states of the world by acting."[18]

3.2.3 The indexical view of power

In situations where outcomes are determined simply by what I decide to do (together, perhaps, with luck), I have the power to bring about (or, at least, to possibly bring about) anything in the relevant outcome space. This outcome space, as we have seen, is defined by the range of strategies I might adopt, which in turn is defined by the physical constraints and the laws of nature, my endowments and capabilities, and other exogenous social facts such as equilibrium prices in a fully competitive market. In other words, my power seems to be a direct function of my means.

Hobbes assumed this was generally the case. Having defined power, he proceeds to offer examples. Thus, to have servants, friends, riches, knowledge of the sciences and arts is power; so is being popular, affable, eloquent, beautiful, and so on.[19] Reflection on his catalog suggests the following line of thought. Since each list item is, let us suppose, a means for obtaining future apparent goods, why not sum all the different means (duly weighting each according to its relative importance in our society) available to different persons or groups, and then assign each an overall score on some uniform index? Of course, since strength, wealth, and so on are positional goods (to be wealthy is to have, relatively speaking, more money than other people), raw scores on this index would not be equivalent to an absolute measure of power. Nevertheless, the relative power of each person or group could be determined from a relative score on the index: thus, we could regard one person or group as more powerful than another whenever the former has a higher indexical score than the latter.

Unfortunately, power cannot be measured on a single scale in this manner, because power is not a direct function of means. One way to see this is by considering the existence of power intransitivities. Suppose that, according to our index, 1 has more power than 2, and that 2 has more power than 3. This would mean, on the indexical view of power, that 1 has greater means than 2,

---

[18] Dowding (1991, p. 48); Barry (2002, p. 160).
[19] Hobbes (1651, I.10.2–15, pp. 58–9).

and similarly 2 has greater means than 3. If power were reducible to its material bases, it would thus necessarily follow that 1 has more power than 3. But this does not necessarily follow. By way of analogy, every sports fan knows that, from the fact that one team can reliably beat a second, and the second a third, it by no means follows that the first can reliably beat the third. This is because the ability of a team to win games is not merely a function of the sum total athletic talent it happens to possess: much depends on how one team's particular talents match up with those of another. Power, similarly, is not always a direct function of means.[20]

Another, and ultimately more significant, reason that power is not a direct function of means is that, as we have observed, outcomes often depend not only on what I decide to do, but also on what others decide to do. This makes things much more complicated. Imagine a schoolyard bully who demands that a wimp hand over his lunch money. The wimp can choose to comply, or not. These are his only strategy options. Depending on what the wimp does, the bully can either beat up the wimp (taking his lunch money in the process), or not. Recalling that strategies are plans for action, the bully thus has four strategy options: always beat up the wimp, never beat up the wimp, beat up the wimp only if he refuses to comply, or beat up the wimp only if he complies. (The bully might also have had the option to not issue a threat in the first place, an option we will ignore so as not to complicate the example unnecessarily.) Both have the *means* to choose any of their available strategies, but this does not in itself indicate their relative power, since the ability of either to bring about any one of the eight possible outcomes (two strategies for the wimp × four strategies for the bully = eight possible outcomes) depends on what the other will do. The power of a person in such cases can be assessed only against their expectations, and as argued earlier, expectations should be based on the assumption of rationality. Let me explain.

Suppose that the wimp prefers to keep his lunch money, but prefers not being subject to a beating even more. Suppose that the bully, for his part, prefers not to go through the effort of beating up the wimp, other things being equal, but prefers getting his lunch money, one way or another, even more. Finally, suppose that all these preferences are common knowledge. Now consider things from the wimp's point of view first. He must suppose that the bully, acting rationally, will beat him up if he refuses to comply with the demand, and not otherwise. Once threatened, therefore, the wimp has the power to bring about either the outcome in which he complies and is left alone, or the outcome in which he refuses and is beaten up; but he does not

---

[20] Here, I abandon the view of power relied on in Lovett (2001, pp. 106–8), and I am grateful to Brian Barry for pointing out some of the difficulties with this view. Cf. Barry (2002, pp. 160–3).

have the power to bring about the outcome in which he keeps his lunch money *and* is left alone. Second, consider things from the bully's point of view. For his part, supposing that he has issued a threat, the bully has the power to either beat up the wimp or not after being given the lunch money. Interestingly, he does *not* have the power to bring about an outcome in which he issues the threat and is refused—this is because he must assume that the wimp, acting rationally, will respond to the threat with compliance. Note that in assessing the bully's power here, it is irrelevant whether he desires this outcome or not: the point is that even if he did (perhaps he relishes a show of force), he could not bring it about. To repeat what was said earlier, power must be understood in desire-independent terms.

Let us now complicate the example by introducing a third character: the watchful principal. Imagine that the principal punishes bullies who beat up other students, and leaves them alone otherwise. This changes things dramatically. Suppose the bully dislikes being punished even more than he dislikes not getting the lunch money; acting rationally, then, he would not beat up the wimp even if he refuses to comply with the bully's threat. If threatened, the wimp now has the power to bring about an outcome in which he keeps his lunch money and is left alone (because the bully, acting rationally, will not carry out his threat: notice our assessment of the wimp's power is again based on the expectation of rationality). The bully may still have the power to not issue a threat, but he now lacks the power to bring about an outcome in which he issues a threat and is complied with (again relying on the expectation of rationality). Instead, he now has the power to bring about an outcome in which he issues a threat, is refused, and does nothing; or an outcome in which he issues a threat, is refused, beats up the wimp, and is punished. The material basis of the bully's power—his physical strength relative to the wimp—has not changed in this second scenario; only the background structure of the relationship has. The bully's power to bring about outcomes relative to the wimp is thus clearly not a direct function of his means relative to the wimp.

The lesson of these examples is that, since power is not reducible to its bare material bases, it cannot be measured on a single index of relative means. Such a measure might be approximately accurate in parametric and other non-strategic situations, but not in strategic ones.

3.2.4 Power and structure

Another lesson to be drawn from the last example concerns the structural character of power. How much power a person or a group has depends, to a large extent, on their structural environment. In Chapter 2, the relevant features of a structural environment were observed to include not only the distribution of natural and social endowments (in this case; the fact that the bully is stronger than the wimp), but also the relevant aspects of the basic structure of society (the fact that the principal will punish bullies who threaten students)—aspects constituted by a particular "alignment" in the behavior of "peripheral social agents," as Thomas Wartenberg puts it.[21] This fact should be obvious, once confusion introduced by the indexical view of power has been cleared away.

It is possible, however, to read too much into this insight, and go so far as to claim that structures themselves, and not social actors, actually have power.[22] This view is commonly attributed to Foucault, and it parallels a confusion, discussed briefly in Chapter 2, that structures themselves can subject persons or groups to domination.[23] What are we to make of the assertion that power resides in structures? There are (at least) three ways we might interpret such a claim, the first two harmless, and consistent with the Hobbesian view developed here, the third misleading and redundant.

First, by asserting that power is a property of structures and not social actors, one might only mean to emphasize the insight explained in Section 3.2.3—namely, that the degree to which a person or a group has power depends, to a large extent, on their structural environment. This is an important insight for at least two reasons. First, it is important because all social actors—both the relatively powerful and the relatively powerless—are to some extent constrained and enabled simultaneously by their structural environments. Second, it is important because these structural environments are to a large extent composed of social, not natural, facts. Both points were noted earlier, in Chapter 2. The system of private property, for example, both constrains me from seizing the property of others, and enables me to reclaim property that others have seized from me; and, of course, that system exists only because people generally act in the various ways that upholding the system requires. Since social facts are in principle amenable to change, the distribution of power clearly might be different than it presently is. On this first interpretation, the assertion that power resides in structures might help remind us of these interconnected observations—though, it is worth noting, the assertion only loosely and metaphorically captures them. (Some forms of

---

[21] Wartenberg (1990, p. 161).

[22] Something like this seems to be the view expressed in Isaac (1987*a*, 1987*b*), Young (1990), and Hayward (2000), for example. Interestingly, Lukes (2005, p. 72) explicitly rejects it.

[23] In my view, this attribution to Foucault is in any case a mistake. If the famous "Two Lectures" on power (Foucault 1980) are read in the context of the complete lecture series (recently published in English as Foucault [2003]), it should be evident that he is discussing authority, not power.

makes it sound
like a possession
you can
carry it
you

power, after all, are not dependent on structures in this way; and in any case, it is always strictly speaking a social actor who *has* the power for which a given structure provides the basis.) So far, we have no reason to question the Hobbesian view of power.

Second, and more interesting, the assertion that power resides in structures might be taken to mean that the structural environments of complex modern societies are often such that persons or groups have power less by virtue of who they are in particular, than by the social roles or offices they happen (for the time being) to fill. For example, a police officer has certain powers that an ordinary citizen does not have. However, she has these extra powers only so long as she continues to hold that position and not longer. Again, this possibility might be highlighted in a loose and metaphorical way by saying that these powers are the property of that structural position itself, not the person who happens to fill it. This second interpretation of the assertion, however, is also perfectly consistent with the Hobbesian view of power as the ability to bring about outcomes. Strictly speaking, it is still the person (who happens to be a police officer) who has the ability in question; if the position went vacant indefinitely, the structure of that position itself would not have the same abilities.

Finally, consider a third interpretation, according to which the assertion should be understood literally, as the claim that structures, not social actors, have power. So interpreted, the assertion should be rejected.[24] Suppose I want to walk to the grocery store, but am prevented by a newly erected fence. The fence clearly constrains me from doing what I would otherwise want to do, but to add that the fence has the *power* to prevent me is redundant. Worse, it is misleading. This is because the fence has no choice in the matter. Taken literally, the structural view (so understood) would apparently not distinguish between my being prevented by a fence, and my being prevented by a dangerous gang leader who likes to terrorize the neighborhood. Surely, there is an important difference here. If we want to use the term power to refer to both sorts of constraint, then we will merely be in the position of having to come up with a new term to cover the latter sorts and not the former. Analogously, it is redundant and misleading to say, not only that the system of private property *constrains* my ability to seize the property of others, but further that it—the system itself, as such—has the *power* to do so. Perhaps whatever constraints are imposed on me by that system are effective only because certain persons and groups (judges, the police, and so on) have the power to enforce the relevant provisions, but this is perfectly

---

[24] The argument here follows Dowding (1991, pp. 8–9).

consistent with the view of power advanced here, and in any case, our recognition of this fact is obscured rather than clarified by the assertion that power resides in structures.

Notice here that we have narrowed our focus somewhat, from a concern with power considered generally, to the sort of power that one person or group might exercise over another specifically. This leads to our next topic.

3.3 SOCIAL POWER

Power comes in many forms: there are myriad ways one might bring about future desired states of the world. Not all these forms are of equal importance in developing a conception of domination, however. Consider two groups who have no social interactions with each other of any kind—perhaps they live on separate continents, and are as yet unaware of each other's existence. One group, by virtue of its having greater natural resources or a different internal social organization, might have more and greater powers (abilities to bring about outcomes) than the other. Presumably, however, we would not want to say, on that account alone, that the second group is subject to domination. This is not what is intended by the imbalance of power conception. The relevant imbalances are rather those of a particular kind, related to what is variously called *social power* or *power-over.* Although the former term is somewhat misleading, in that it falsely implies other forms of power have no social dimension, I will follow the convention in the literature and use these two terms interchangeably. This section outlines a conception of social power that serves as a crucial building block in our overall project of developing a general theory of domination.

3.3.1 Defining social power

Max Weber defined social power as "the probability that one actor within a social relationship will be in a position to carry out his own will despite resistance."[25] To forestall confusion, we must hasten to add that *actual* resistance is not necessary—only that, *if* there were resistance, it *could* be overcome. The state has power over its citizens, even if they happen to prefer doing what the law commands anyway, as many do. The point is simply that, if particular citizens did not want to obey, the state has the power to overcome

---

[25] Weber (1922, p. 53).

their reluctance and compel them. When exercising this power is unnecessary, the state is not less powerful—it is simply lucky.[26]

In the current literature, this Weberian conception is variously described as the ability of one social agent to "strategically constrain" the "action environment" of another; or "the ability of an actor deliberately to change the incentive structure of another actor or actors to bring about, or help bring about outcomes" or "the ability to bring about desired states of the world by acting in such a way as to overcome the resistance of others."[27] The differences between these various formulations are, on the whole, slight. In the language of this study, we might say:

> (SP) One person or group has *power over* another if the former has the ability to change what the latter would otherwise prefer to do—i.e., change the strategy the latter would otherwise select from their opportunity set.

Note that power-over or social power is an instance of power in the general sense: one, but by no means the only, way I might bring about particular outcomes is by getting others to do things they might not otherwise do. Sometimes "power-over" is contrasted with "power-to", where the latter is defined in roughly the Hobbesian sense described earlier. This creates the misleading impression that these terms represent competing conceptions of power, when they do not. More precisely, they represent conceptions directed at two different levels of generality.

Social power, like power generally, comes in many forms. Speaking very broadly, there are two principal methods by which one person or group might change what another would otherwise prefer to do. Either the former can raise or lower the costs and benefits attached by the latter to different options in their opportunity set, or else the former can influence the latter's preferences over those options. This is roughly the difference between reducing the cost of a television set, and making me want one more.[28] The precise line between these methods is not always clear. Indeed, they sometimes bleed into each other: employing the first method, for example, I might elicit preference adaptation as a response; conversely, I might employ the second method precisely in order to enhance responsiveness to the variable costs

---

[26] On this point, see especially Barry (1980).

[27] These definitions are from Wartenberg (1990, p. 85), Dowding (1991, p. 48), and Barry (2002, p. 161), respectively.

[28] We might also consider a third possibility: introducing televisions to a market where there were none before. Is this a sort of power-over? It is not. One person cannot affect the behavior of another by withholding an option the latter does not know she has. Once televisions are introduced, however, the new supplier might be able to take advantage of the fact that people (now) desire televisions in order to induce them to do things they would not otherwise do.

and benefits that happen to be under my control. Nevertheless, the distinction between them provides a reasonably good framework for discussion. It is not important to know whether a particular situation represents an instance of one or the other, provided we keep in mind that either would count as social power.

The method of raising or lowering costs and benefits might be thought of as a *direct* exercise of social power. One can raise the cost of options in another person or group's opportunity set by issuing (credible) threats; one can raise the benefits of options by issuing (credible) offers; or one can do some combinations of these simultaneously. Credibility is, of course, a crucial prerequisite of exercising this sort of power over another, but it is notoriously difficult to define precisely.[29] Roughly speaking, for a threat or offer to be credible, we must suppose that the benefits of carrying it out are greater than the costs. Suppose a thug threatens: "Your money or your life!" Although the thug may prefer not to carry out the threat, all things being equal (otherwise, why bother issuing a threat in the first place?), it may nevertheless be true that he estimates the risk of being caught sufficiently low that he would prefer carrying it out and getting the victim's money to doing nothing at all. Thus, his threat strategy is credible. So too is the bully's threat in the absence of a watchful principal. By contrast, a threat to harm the President by jumping in front of his motorcade is usually not credible, because few people would want to carry out such a threat.

These cases, in which merely short-term costs and benefits establish the credibility of threats and offers, are less typical. More often, threats and offers carry short-term costs and long-term benefits. States punish criminals despite the cost of doing so in the expectation that punishment will deter crime in the long run; crime bosses routinely carry out costly threats for the purpose of establishing a tough reputation; and so on. In such cases, the threat or offer is credible only because we expect the long-term benefits to outweigh the short-term costs.

When one has the ability to raise the cost of an option, we often term this form of social power "coercive" in the narrow sense. But it is not always so clear what amounts to a threat as opposed to an offer, especially in the case of expected benefits. If the government announces that it will no longer contract with discriminatory employers, does it issue a threat or merely rescind an offer? Either description is plausible.

Even if we succeed in restricting the term "coercive power" to threats, many balk at including the ability to make credible offers under the heading of social power generally. Suppose on a very hot day I offer a stranger $10 for the

---

[29] For discussions of credibility, see Schelling (1960, esp. ch. 2) and Elster (1989, pp. 272–87).

soda he is presently enjoying, and he accepts. Would we really want to say that I exercised power over him? In my view, the correct answer is yes. Few would balk, for instance, at saying that Walmart exercises tremendous market power over its product suppliers merely because it issues what are technically offers (not threats) to buy from them only at very low prices. My power over the stranger with the soda is, in this respect, no different, except that it is by comparison very, very small.[30] The only sorts of exchanges we can definitively say involve neither threats nor offers—and thus, no social power—are those made at equilibrium prices in a fully competitive market, for in such cases the exchanging parties, by definition, have no personal influence over those prices. Provided we recognize that threats and offers both count as genuine instruments of exercising power over another, it will usually not be important to determine which has been employed in a particular case.

The other, and often more subtle, way of changing what someone would otherwise do is to influence his or her preferences. This might be called the *indirect* method of exercising social power, and it corresponds roughly to what is called in the literature the "third face of power."[31] Here there is also a range of cases, and the demarcations along this range are quite fuzzy. At one end of the spectrum we have persuasion, either by force of argument or by rhetorical device: Clearly, the persuasive have a sort of power over the easily persuaded. At the other end, we have the more sinister cases of propaganda and preference or belief manipulation. How effective these latter techniques actually are is a matter of some debate, but to the extent that they in fact change what a person or a group would otherwise do, they too count as social power. (The special case of preference and belief manipulation is discussed more fully in Chapter 4.)

The ability to influence preferences is limited as a form of social power in that the manipulator usually cannot benefit from strategic anticipation on the part of the manipulated. The salesman, for instance, must actually succeed in convincing a reluctant customer that he needs a television in order to alter the customer's purchasing behavior. By contrast, merely having the ability to raise and lower costs, provided this is common knowledge, can sometimes effectively induce changes in what other people prefer to do: the beat cop need not

---

[30] For further discussion, see Barry (2002, pp. 163–5).

[31] This expression is due to Lukes (2005) and is now common. This aspect of social power should not be confused with what is often termed "transformative power"—the ability of one social agent to modify (for better or worse) the abilities or capacities of another. There is, however, considerable overlap here: one, but not the only, way a schoolteacher might enhance the capacities of her students is by exercising social power over them; and one, but not the only, reason a schoolteacher might want to enhance the capacities of her students is to change what they would otherwise prefer to do. For further discussion, see Wartenberg (1990, esp. chs. 9–10).

issue any specific threat in order to induce good behavior as he ambles by. The significance of strategic anticipation is highlighted by the paradox of the hated dictator. Consider a universally despised dictator who, with aid of his henchmen, can force anyone in the country to do whatever he wishes. He is, nevertheless, just a man: even the very weakest of his henchmen could kill him easily while he slept. How then is his power maintained? As Machiavelli observed, the difficulty is that no one of his henchmen can be sufficiently confident that a critical mass of the others will support a coup.[32] Thus, the dictator maintains power, despite being hated by all. While it is true that, strictly speaking, his henchmen could ignore the risk calculation and stop following orders at any time, his unfortunate subjects would not do well to conclude thereby that he has no power. Given rational expectations regarding what everyone else is likely to do, each will continue catering to the dictator's wishes, without his having to lift a finger to compel them. Here we again see the importance of rational expectations in discussing power.

3.3.2 Measuring social power

Domination is clearly related to the distribution of social power. Indeed, according to the imbalance of power conception described at the beginning of this chapter, one person or group subjects another to domination if and only if the first has more social power over the second than the second has over the first. Other things being equal, the greater this imbalance of social power, the greater is the degree of domination. In order to make such quantitative judgments, we need some measure of social power, even if it is only a fairly rough one.

To have power over a person or a group is to have the ability to change what they might otherwise prefer to do. Roughly speaking, we can say that the degree of difference one can make corresponds to the degree of social power one has. For example, imagine a simple social relationship with two members: a worker and a manager. Suppose the worker's opportunity set S is a range of levels of effort, and suppose that, other things being equal, the worker would prefer to put forth some moderate level of effort s. Now suppose that by issuing various threats and inducements, the manager can induce the higher level of effort s^* from the worker. We may then say that the degree of power the manager exercises over the worker is roughly given by the equation $SP = s^* - s$. Alternatively, the manager might try to manipulate the preferences of the worker, say, by convincing him of the ethical value of hard work. This too

---

[32] Machiavelli (1532, ch. 19, p. 73).

might induce a higher level of effort, and the extent of this power over the worker again corresponds to the degree of difference she can make. The full measure of the manager's power over the worker might be regarded as the greatest difference she can make in the worker's overall level of effort, using the optimal combination of strategies available to her.

Let us consider another example. Imagine an imperfect market, in which the unilateral decisions of one firm can significantly affect the price of some good. The market power of this firm represents a sort of power over all the potential buyers and sellers of that good. The measure of that power is given by the degree to which the firm can change what the other market participants would otherwise prefer to do, and this of course is a direct function of the unilateral impact the firm can have on prices. If the firm can affect prices only marginally, its power over the market is small, and if it can affect prices dramatically, its power over the market is correspondingly great. In a fully competitive market, by contrast, no buyer or seller can unilaterally affect prices. It follows that (with respect to their market relations, at any rate) the participants in the fully competitive markets do not exercise social power over one another. This confirms what was said earlier.

Given the extensive coercive apparatus available to the state, it can make a great difference in what citizens might otherwise prefer to do; this indicates that the imbalance of power between state and citizen is quite large, which is obvious. But notice that the degree of difference the state can make is at least partly sensitive to, for example, the degree to which a given citizen feels shame at being punished. If one citizen would feel much greater shame at being punished than another, does the state have greater power over the first than the second? The correct answer is yes. How much power does a preacher have over the members of his congregation? That partly depends on the subjective importance those members place on following his guidance. His power over those churchgoers only casually concerned with keeping the faith is relatively small, but his power over those churchgoers who are passionate about their faith might be great indeed. Suppose a suicide bomber is driving toward his target. How much power do security guards have to deter him with the threat of being shot? Given the preferences he happens to have, not much. Clearly, social power is thus to some extent sensitive to the preferences of those over whom it is wielded.[33]

---

[33] Notice that this creates further opportunities for preference and belief manipulation. One way the state can increase its power over citizens is for it to educate them in such a way that they will be very much ashamed of being punished; this might involve employing transformative power as an instrument of social power, though not necessarily.

This does not contradict what was said earlier, that power must be understood in desire-independent terms. This can be seen by considering the citizen again: the fact that I do not want to steal from others does not detract from the state's power to prevent me from doing so, were my preferences different than they are. In my case, the state is merely lucky not to have to coerce me. A refinement on this earlier statement is needed, however. When considering the power one person or group has over another, we must endeavor to hold constant, so to speak, the latter's preferences with respect to outcomes as such, and consider only the differential impact the former can make, *given* those preferences. Although I do not wish to steal, given the fact that I would be very much ashamed to be caught, the state has a great deal of power to prevent me from stealing. Another citizen who would feel less shame might care somewhat less about the prospect of being punished, and the state's power over him is correspondingly diminished (even if it is true that, but for the prospect of that punishment, this citizen might actually prefer to steal). Consider another example. Suppose that two citizens, who both prefer attending Anglican to Presbyterian services, live in a state that commands participation in the Anglican Church. Since this is what both citizens happen to prefer anyway, the state need not actually coerce them, but it nevertheless wields considerable power over them. How much? Suppose the first citizen would be very ashamed of being punished, whereas the second would be less so. In that case, the state has more power over the first. We can see this clearly by reflecting that, if the state were to change course and command Presbyterian participation instead, the former would be more likely to obey than the latter.[34]

The measure of the power one person or group has over another is the difference the former could make in what the latter would otherwise prefer to do, given the preferences the latter happens to have. Even if it will not always be easy to precisely measure the degree of this difference, the rough idea, I hope, should be fairly clear.

3.3.3 Social power and social relationships

To have power over a person or group is to be able to change what they would otherwise prefer to do. As defined in Chapter 2, persons or groups are engaged in a social relationship if they are in some significant respect related to one another strategically, which is to say, if what each wants to do depends on what the others are likely to do, and vice versa. It might appear, then, that

---

[34] I am grateful to Peter Morriss for pressing me to clarify this point.

social power and social relationships are perfectly coextensive: if one person has power over another, then what the latter will want to do must depend on what the former does; and conversely, if what one person wants to do depends on what another does, then the latter must in some sense have power over the former.

Most often, this is indeed the case. But not always. Consider, for example, the game of odds-and-evens. In this game, if the evens player plays one finger, the odds player will want to play two, but if she plays two fingers, the odds player will want to play one. What the odds player wants to do, obviously, depends on what the evens player does. But notice that the evens player is in exactly the same situation: the game is, in other words, perfectly symmetric. This is an example of a situation that is clearly strategic, but in which each player has exactly the same power over the other, which is to say that there is no *imbalance* of power. The same is true of any symmetric strategic situation, whether competitive or not. Pure coordination games, for example, are strategic, though not competitive, and are again not characterized by an imbalance of power. Thus, it is possible for persons or groups to be engaged in a social relationship without there being an imbalance of power between them.

More importantly, it is also possible for one person or group to have power over another but, in a sense, for them to not be related to each other strategically. To see this, we must recall the distinction, discussed earlier, between actions and strategies: a strategy, we said, is a plan for action that might contemplate contingencies. Opportunity sets are composed of strategies, not actions. Now consider the relationship between the schoolyard bully and the watchful principal. Certainly, the principal has power over the bully, insofar as the bully strongly prefers not being punished. But does the bully stand in a strategic relationship with the principal? That depends. Suppose the principal adopts the strategy "only punish bullies when they threaten wimps, and not otherwise." (Notice that this is a strategy contemplating different actions depending on what happens contingently in the schoolyard.) Further suppose that the principal's adherence to this strategy is robust or reliable in some significant respect—say, because it is common knowledge that she will be fired if she ever abandons this strategy. In this case, the principal's strategy—her plan for action—will remain the same, regardless of what the bully happens to do. It does not matter, for example, whether the bully is a brownnose or a churl. (Nor, for that matter, does it matter what the wimp does: whether he is liked by the principal or not, and so on.) From the bully's point of view, he stands in a nonstrategic relationship with the principal. In effect, the principal represents merely another part of the background structure of the social relationship between the bully and the other students, much as the many citizens acting to predictably uphold the law of property constitute a part of the background structure of the social relationship between master and slave. It follows that it is possible for one person or group to have power over another, and yet in a sense not be engaged in a social relationship with them.

These observations, which are useful in clarifying the meaning of social power, will turn out to be significant in other ways as well, as we shall see in Chapter 4.

3.4 POWER AND DOMINATION

Earlier I suggested that it would be counterintuitive to say one person or group dominates another without having any power over them. This intuition is borne out by reflection on our core examples of domination. Slavery provides an easy case: clearly, slave masters have the power to physically abuse and coerce their slaves, so as to induce a greater level of productive effort than the latter would (or should) be willing to provide. Totalitarianism, despotism, and other forms of autocratic government are similarly straightforward cases. The case of feudal domination over the peasantry mentioned at the outset of Chapter 2 is similar, though perhaps the extent of the imbalance of power is somewhat less drastic. And until recently, husbands could exercise a great deal of power over their wives (and children) under the legal and cultural regime in Western countries; their power is certainly more limited today, though perhaps not yet entirely gone. Instances of domination without an imbalance of power are difficult to imagine.

This suggests that an imbalance of social power is indeed a necessary condition of domination, and thus the imbalance of power conception captures some part of the truth about domination. Also, as we have seen, power is what is sometimes called a "dispositional concept": to have power over someone is to have the ability to change what they otherwise prefer to do, whether one happens to make use of this ability or not.[35] The extent to which a person or group has this ability is, to a large extent, determined by the surrounding structural environment. Thus, the imbalance of power conception would count, in the language of Chapter 2, as a structure-based, and not an outcome-based conception of domination. So far, so good.

But is an imbalance of social power *sufficient* to constitute a relationship of domination? At the opening of this chapter, I noted a few social and political theorists who seemed to answer yes. On reflection, however, this cannot be

---

[35] See Morriss (2002, chs. 3–4) and Dowding (1991, pp. 4–5, chs. 2–3).

correct. The owner of a restaurant has the ability to refuse me service if I am rude to the servers: Supposing that I had wanted to dine there, this constitutes having power over me. Similarly, my aerobics instructor (if I had one) has the power to tell me what exercises to perform if I want to avoid being humiliated in front of the class, and this too might constitute having power over me. But we are not inclined to view either of these as genuine instances of domination. Why not? One reason might be that my dependency on either relationship is quite low: I can always find another restaurant or another aerobics class more to my liking, and indeed, I need not dine out or take aerobics classes at all. This only goes to show that, at the very least, we must regard both an imbalance of social power and some degree of dependency as independently necessary conditions of domination.

Conceptions of domination that regard both these two conditions as necessary, and together sufficient, I term *revised imbalance of power* conceptions. This seems to have been the later view of Foucault. Perhaps driven by considerations similar to those discussed, he revised his earlier view and defined domination as what he called "congealed power."[36] Unfortunately, he did not have the opportunity to elaborate much on this definition, but it is plausible to interpret it in this spirit. Something like this view is also sometimes attributed to Max Weber, though (as we shall see in Chapter 4) his view is open to different interpretations.[37] On the revised imbalance of power conception, there would be two strategies by which one might try to reduce domination. First, as we saw in Chapter 2, one might try to lower the dependency of those subject to domination. Second, we can now add, one might try to distribute social power more equally. Consider the potential domination of workers at the hands of their employers. As an example of the first strategy, we can introduce unemployment benefits, so as to make it easier for workers to change jobs; as an example of the second strategy, we can make employer collusion more difficult and union organization easier, so as to reduce the imbalance of bargaining power between them.[38]

The imbalance of power conception is more plausible with this revision. But is it completely satisfactory? In my view, it is not. The complete argument to this effect is made in Chapter 4. But to foreshadow that discussion, consider a college student with library fines. As per its standard policy, the university library has the power to block the conferral of this student's degree until such fines are paid in full. Certainly, this represents a power over the student; indeed, considering the value of the degree, we might say this power

---

[36] Foucault (1988, p. 3ff).
[37] Hayward (2000, pp. 39, 162) seems to attribute this view to Weber.
[38] The formal models in Appendix II further explore these options.

is considerable. Furthermore, having already sunk huge costs in attending this particular university, the student is hardly in a position to walk away and enroll somewhere else; accordingly, we would also want to say that his dependency is quite high. This would seem to satisfy the two requirements of the revised imbalance of power conception. But do we want to say that the student is subject to domination at the hand of his university librarian? Perhaps not. Something is still missing from our conception. In Chapter 4 I argue that what is missing is a third condition—namely, arbitrariness. But we should not get ahead of ourselves.

4

Arbitrariness and Social
Conventions

The imbalance of power conception, discussed in Chapter 3, aims to capture our clear intuition that domination must have something to do with power as directly as possible, by defining domination as a quantitative inequality in the distribution of social power.

At least initially, however, one might have the intuition that not all imbalances of social power should count as genuine instances of domination. Perhaps some other factor, not readily captured in such strictly quantitative terms, distinguishes our core cases of domination—slavery, autocratic government, feudal domination, and so on—from instances like the one involving the university librarian mentioned at the end of Chapter 3. For the moment, this is only an intuition. If no better conception were available, it is perhaps an intuition we should be prepared to drop. In my view, however, there is a better conception. The aim of this chapter is to outline that alternative—what I call the _arbitrary power_ conception of domination—and to argue for its merits as against the imbalance of power conception.

4.1 FORM-RESTRICTED CONCEPTIONS

The imbalance of power conception is sensitive only to quantitative differences in the distribution of social power. That is to say, the degree of domination in any social relationship directly tracks, on this view, the degree of inequality in the distribution of social power among its members (together, on the revised imbalance of power conception, with their relative degrees of dependency). But, surely there are also many qualitative differences in how one person or group might wield power over another. The power of the university librarian over a student is qualitatively (as well as quantitatively) different from the power of a husband over his wife under traditional family law, and both are qualitatively (as well as quantitatively) different from the power of managers over workers. A more refined conception of domination, perhaps, would be sensitive to the qualitative differences ignored by the imbalance of power view.

Recall from Chapter 3 that social power comes in many different forms—coercive power, market power, the power of persuasion, and so on. It follows that we might try to refine our conception of domination by defining it as an imbalance in the distribution of some particular form (or restricted class of forms) of social power and not others. Imbalances of power, on this view, would count as genuine instances of domination only if the power in question assumed the required form or forms. Conceptions limiting the scope of domination in this way will be termed *form-restricted* conceptions.

The following sections discuss and reject form-restricted conceptions, while the remainder of the chapter discusses the arbitrary power conception of domination, which is not form-restricted.

4.1.1 The hegemony conception

Max Weber defined domination as "the probability that a command with a given specific content will be obeyed by a given group of persons."[1] This definition is open to a variety of interpretations. Understood broadly, it might collapse into some version of the imbalance of power conception. Weber is clear, however, that he would regard such a broad understanding as "scientifically useless."[2] Thus, he generally prefers to restrict the term to social relationships in which some persons or groups have the ability to change what others would otherwise do, when the basis for that ability is to some extent specifically due to the fact that the latter believe (rightly or wrongly) that the former hold some form of legitimate authority over them.[3]

This association of the concept of domination with ideologically enabled imbalances of power is common, and it appears in a variety of guises. To give another simplified example, it might be argued that the working classes under the capitalist mode of production are subject to domination by a laissez-faire liberal ideology that makes their subordination seem just and fair, when in fact they are being exploited by the capitalists. Arguments along these

---

[1] Weber (1922, p. 53, cf. pp. 212, 946).

[2] Weber (1922, p. 943).

[3] This is most clear in his discussion at Weber (1922, pp. 942–6), but it is also generally implied by his extended analysis of the various forms the legitimacy beliefs can take—traditional, charismatic, and rational.

lines can be found in the work of Louis Althusser, and also in the critical theory literature, especially as represented by Max Horkheimer and Theodor Adorno, Herbert Marcuse, and Jürgen Habermas. These theories were influenced particularly by the writings of Georg Lukács and Antonio Gramsci.[4]

I would rather avoid getting mired in interpretive debates regarding what any of the above-mentioned theorists did or did not argue; my interest in hegemony is strictly limited to the possibility that it might constitute a viable basis for a conception of domination. Since so many authors seem to employ the terms domination and hegemony more or less interchangeably, it is worth considering whether it would make sense to define domination in this way. In the spirit of Gramsci, I refer to the view that domination should be understood specifically as an ideologically enabled imbalance of power as the *hegemony conception*.[5] The difficulty here, of course, is that hegemony might assume a variety of guises. In what follows, I merely sketch a number of possible accounts of hegemony, without worrying too much about whose views they happen to represent. Some of these accounts, I argue, are not workable as conceptions of domination. Those that are workable will turn out to be form-restricted conceptions. Discussing the hegemony conception will thus provide an entry into our consideration of the merits of form-restricted conceptions in general.

Roughly speaking, we might distinguish two different sorts of hegemony. On the one hand, hegemony might consist in the active manipulation of one person or group's preferences or beliefs by another; this I call *special hegemony*. On the other hand, hegemony might consist in a more sweeping distortion of people's preferences or beliefs for which no particular person or group is directly responsible, but which, as a side effect, at least partially enables the subordination of some persons or groups by others; this I call *general hegemony*. Is either the appropriate basis for a conception of domination? Let us consider the general hegemony first.

---

[4] The relevant works here include: Althusser (1979), Horkheimer and Adorno (1988), Marcuse (1955, 1964), Lukács (1971), Habermas (1971, 1975), and Gramsci (1971). For a review and analysis of critical theory, see either Held (1980) or Geuss (1981). Another variation on this theme discusses the ideological domination of women in patriarchal societies: see Bourdieu (2002), for example.

[5] Note that in other contexts, hegemony has quite different meanings. In international relations theory, for example, hegemony refers to the situation in which one state is sufficiently powerful with respect to its competitors that it need not fear them militarily.

4.1.2 General hegemony

If domination were understood to be general hegemony, then it would be agent-less. In Chapter 2, I argued that there cannot be domination without agents; we must now reexamine that argument.

As always, we should be careful to distinguish shorthand expressions from genuine claims about the meaning of the term domination. Consider, for example, beliefs in the natural inferiority of women commonly held by both men and women in patriarchal societies. Insofar as these beliefs influence the shape of individuals' opportunity sets, they are a part of the basic structure of society, and thus partially constitute the background structural environment of social relationships embedded in those societies. These beliefs might effectively close many career opportunities to women, for instance, and thus increase the dependency of married women on their husbands. This, in turn, might permit husbands to subject their wives to a greater degree of domination.

Now of course beliefs in the natural inferiority of women might have been deliberately encouraged or fostered by men (either directly, or indirectly through women under the influence of men), but in this case we would be talking about special hegemony, which is discussed in Section 4.1.3. However, it is at least possible that, in a given society, no one in particular is responsible for the widespread belief in the natural inferiority of women. This pattern of beliefs might, for example, have arisen through simultaneous preference adaptation: women might have come to hold these beliefs so as to feel less unhappy with their disadvantages, and men so as to feel less guilty about their advantages. If this did indeed happen, we would have a case of general hegemony.

But is it domination? That depends on what one intends to claim. If we say that "patriarchal beliefs dominate women," we might intend this as a sort of shorthand for the complete story—perhaps that men maintain their domination over women partly with the help of the commonly held patriarchal beliefs. There is nothing wrong with saying this, but notice that it does not amount to defining domination as (general) hegemony. On the contrary, the expression assumes that we have some independent grounds for establishing that women are indeed subject to domination (which domination happens to be reinforced through a hegemonic belief system). There must be more to the hegemony view if it is to be a practicable conception in its own right. What might this be? It might be the claim that (to continue with our example) the patriarchal beliefs themselves literally dominate women—and that this is actually what it means to be subject to domination. Such a claim, however, ought to be rejected.

It ought to be rejected, first, because it is unhelpful. Compare the belief in the natural inferiority of women, widespread in many societies, with the belief, once widespread in the West, that combustion was caused by the release of phlogiston. So far as I am aware, no one was systematically advantaged or disadvantaged—and certainly no one was subject to oppression—by the latter belief. How then can it be an instance of domination? It cannot. A commonly held belief, whether true or false, cannot itself dominate anyone, because a belief is not a social agent. To insist on this point is merely to insist on clarity of expression. It does not detract from the observation that the commonly held beliefs—like wealth, guns, and many other things—can, under the right circumstances, be employed by social agents as instruments of domination.

The claim that beliefs themselves can literally dominate persons or groups should also be rejected because it is naive. It tempts us to think that by merely sweeping away some false beliefs or other we can, by that act alone, liberate people from domination. This is rarely, if ever, the case.[6] Even when it is possible to free people from their misconceptions, severe collective-action problems might nevertheless stand in the way of reducing their domination.[7] Liberation is likely to be hard work, and it is best to face up to that fact.

4.1.3 Special hegemony

Let us next consider special hegemony—the active manipulation of preferences or beliefs. The hegemony conception might, correspondingly, be understood as follows: one person or group dominates another to the extent that the former is able, with some degree of success, to manipulate the preferences or beliefs of the latter.

There are at least two sorts of preference and belief manipulation strategies we might consider here. First, if one person or group is in an advantaged position with respect to another, the former might have an interest in raising the latter's dependency on that social relationship. Preference and belief manipulation is one way (among others) to do this. The advantaged person or group might, for example, encourage the belief that the current arrangement is beneficial and natural, that the alternatives are much worse than they might otherwise seem, or that the apparent alternatives do not exist at all. Such strategies were discussed in Chapter 2. The second preference and belief

---

[6] One exception would be cases where the dependency of a person or group rests entirely on false ideas: having cleared such false ideas away, dependency—and in consequence domination—would evaporate. Most often, however, hegemony merely exacerbates material dependency.

[7] See Heath (2000) for a nice discussion of hegemony as it relates to collective-action problems.

manipulation strategy is the sort employed within the context of a social relationship. It consists in one person or group changing what another person or group would otherwise prefer to do by influencing the latter's preferences or beliefs. Managers, for example, might try to encourage efforts from their workers by promoting the idea that hard work is good for the soul (in addition to, or instead of, using direct threats of firing or using offers of higher wages); firms might try to boost their market share by advertising (in addition to, or instead of, lowering prices); and so on.[8] This sort of preference and belief manipulation was discussed in Chapter 3.

If we identify domination with special hegemony, then we have a form-restricted conception: one that qualitatively distinguishes between different forms of social power, and then goes on to restrict the scope of domination to those particular imbalances of power that involve the ability of one person or group to manipulate the preferences or beliefs of another. Unlike the identification of domination with general hegemony, this would constitute a workable conception of domination.

But is it the best conception? It is not. At best, hegemony (so understood) is only one possible instance of domination. This can be shown easily. If any sort of social relationship counts as an instance of domination, slavery should. Surely, however, it would be implausible to argue that many slaves were ever so confused as to believe that their subordinate status was normatively legitimate, and—even supposing this were true—that the existence of such a belief accounts for their general compliance with the system of slavery. Many theories justifying slavery were propagated, of course, but by and large they were not intended for consumption by slaves.[9] What generally ensured compliance, obviously, was the extensive coercive power—thanks especially to the basic structure of the relevant societies—that slave owners had over their slaves, quite apart from whatever the slaves thought about it. Legitimacy beliefs might (controversially), under certain conditions, help establish or sustain domination, but they cannot be said to be necessary for it to exist. Special hegemony represents but one instrument in a wide array of social powers available for this purpose. This shows that the presence of preference or belief manipulation is not a necessary condition of domination.

In rejecting the hegemony conception, we need not reject the possibility that domination *in some cases* might be enabled, in part or in full, by special

---

[8] The discussion here will remain agnostic as to the real-world effectiveness of such strategies, which is subject to extensive debate.

[9] Indeed, the slave owners in the United States seem to have been more confused than their slaves. Upon emancipation after the Civil War, many owners were genuinely shocked and surprised when their former slaves joyfully abandoned them: see Genovese (1974, p. 97ff).

or general hegemony. Rather, we need only acknowledge that, if and when such cases exist, they cannot exhaust the possible instruments of domination. This carries us to a broader point.

4.1.4 Other form-restricted conceptions

The hegemony conception—at least, on its most workable interpretation—restricts the scope of domination to only those imbalances of power that involve the particular ability of one person or group to manipulate the preferences or beliefs of another within the context of a social relationship. It is, in other words, a form-restricted conception. But social power comes in many forms: we can, at times, change what others would otherwise prefer to do not only by manipulating their preferences or beliefs, but also by coercing them, making credible offers, persuading them, excluding them from privileged groups, and so on. It follows that there might be as many form-restricted conceptions of domination as there are different forms of social power. Each such conception would qualitatively distinguish among different sorts of power imbalances by limiting the scope of domination to those instances where the social power in question assumed the required form.

Consider another example. Some define relations of domination as undemocratic social relationships.[10] As in the case of hegemony, this definition is open to different interpretations. If by undemocratic one simply means the "relationships characterized by an unequal distribution of social power," then obviously this is merely a restatement of the imbalance of power conception, and the imbalance of power conception (as noted earlier) seems too crude an instrument for our purposes. Alternatively, however, one might mean something more specific—perhaps that only imbalances of *political* power, in particular, count as instances of domination. Political power might, for example, be understood as the ability of a person or a group to shape the various opportunities and constraints under which people (themselves or others) live out their lives. Understood in this way, the democratic conception would, like the hegemony conception, be a form-restricted conception of domination.

In principle, there are as many form-restricted conceptions as there are distinguishable forms of social power. The forms of social power are simply the various techniques or strategies by which some person or group might attempt to change what another person or group would otherwise prefer to do. On reflection, it should be obvious that not only the hegemony

---

[10] See, for example, Young (1990), Bohman (2004, 2008), and Tully (2005).

conception, but also the democratic conception, and indeed *any* form-restricted conception, is inadequate. To be sure, the agents of domination must
have power of one form or another over their subjects, for it would be strange
to say that one person dominates another but has no power over them. But,
on what possible grounds would we want to insist that some forms of power
should be excluded as possible instruments of domination, at least under the
right conditions? Why should the scope of domination be restricted by
definition to some forms of social power and not others? Any attempt to
develop a form-restricted conception must fail, because it will inevitably be
confined to the historical or cultural circumstances in which those particular
forms of social power happen to be the predominant instruments of domination. The best conception of domination, I argued in Chapter 1, should be
open with respect to the different guises domination might assume, now or in
the future: the best conception, in other words, must be a general one. Form-
restricted conceptions do not meet this requirement.

This returns us to the problem posed at the beginning of this chapter. There
are surely qualitative differences in how persons or groups wield power over
one another, and we would like our conception of domination to be more
sensitive to these differences than it is on the crudely quantitative imbalance of
power view. What then is the best way to capture these qualitative differences?

Rather than restrict the scope of domination to some forms of social
power and not to others, we could instead characterize domination as a
particular *manner or mode* by which one person or group might wield social
power (of any form) over another. To illustrate how this would create a
conception that is nevertheless appropriately general, consider as a parallel
Weber's famous definition of the state. Traditionally, definitions of the state
focused on the particular goals or aims political institutions were supposed to
serve, as for example securing peace, or protecting natural rights. The difficulty with such definitions is that there are no aims a state might not adopt as
its own. Which aims a particular state should or should not adopt is a
separate, though of course important, question for normative political theory.
On the best descriptive conception, a state would not cease to be a state just
because it happens to adopt some aim not on the officially sanctioned list
(even if it thereby becomes an unjust state). The definition Weber offers in
place of the traditional ones is open to new cases in precisely the way we
would want it to be: it does not matter what aims the state adopts, so long as it
pursues them through the characteristic means of successfully asserting a
monopoly over the legitimate use of violence within a defined territory.[11] In

---

[11] Weber (1919, pp. 77–8).

[margin note: historical & therefore not general]

a roughly analogous way, we want a conception of domination that is open with respect to the sorts of instruments that might be employed in subjecting persons or groups to domination, but that nevertheless qualitatively distinguishes among cases according to the manner in which social power is exercised.

Figure 4.1 provides a rough map of the different conceptions I have discussed up to this point. Chapter 2 discussed and rejected outcome-based conceptions in favor of structure-based conceptions. Chapter 3 discussed the imbalance of power conception—a quantitative conception; Section 4.2 expands on the argument against strictly quantitative conceptions. In this section, we have just concluded the argument against form-restricted conceptions, of which the hegemony and democratic conceptions are examples. This leaves unrestricted or open qualitative conceptions of domination, to which I now turn.

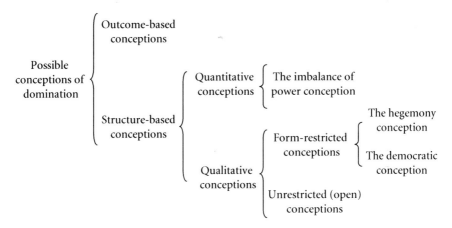

Figure 4.1

4.2 THE ARBITRARY POWER CONCEPTION

Imbalances of social power might assume a wide variety of forms. This is true even when it comes to the core examples of domination we have returned to again and again: feudalism, slavery, domination in the family, autocratic government, the domination of workers, and so forth. In Section 4.1, I argued that there is no good reason to exclude a priori any possible instrument of domination. Any imbalance of social power, regardless of its form, could be a potential basis for domination.

Rather than restrict the scope of domination to some forms of social power and not others, we should instead characterize domination as a particular manner or mode by which social power (of any form) can be exercised over others. The following sections propose an unrestricted qualitative conception of domination along these lines, and argue that it has important advantages over the purely quantitative imbalance of power conception.

4.2.1 Descriptive contouring

Suppose we were to contrast the system of criminal law enforcement in the contemporary United States with that of a totalitarian dictatorship—say, Stalin's Russia or Romania under Ceausescu. Two aspects of this comparison stand out. First, the imbalance of power between the state and its citizens is clearly great in all three cases. (Arguably, in terms of the state's material capacity to coerce its citizens, the United States is more powerful than the others.) Second, the costs of attempting to escape the reach of state power are again, in all cases, quite high. (Perhaps it is somewhat easier exiting the United States than it is a state ruled by a totalitarian regime, but for most ordinary persons the difficulty is still very great—especially once one has come under the suspicion of law enforcement.) According to our definition of dependency as exit costs, citizens in general should be regarded as highly dependent on their respective states. The upshot is that on the imbalance of power conception, even if revised by the addition of a dependency condition, the citizens of Stalin's Russia or Ceaucescu's Romania on the one hand and those of the United States on the other are apparently subject to a comparable degree of domination when it comes to their status under the criminal law.

This cannot be right. Of course I do not mean to suggest that the system of criminal law of the United States is without its problems (far from it). The point is only that, whatever one might think about its failings, surely one would want to say that—with respect to the degree of domination experienced by ordinary citizens at least—it represents something of an improvement over totalitarian dictatorship.

To further press the point, many would argue that the burden of American criminal law does not fall equally on all, but rather falls more heavily on some than others: blacks and other minorities seem to be subject to greater domination than whites, for example.[12] The imbalance of power conception

---

[12] For arguments to this effect, see Cole (1999).

(revised or not) is even less helpful in making this second comparison than the first, since the levels of power imbalance and dependency are here more or less constant.[13]

These are, of course, mere intuitions, whose only point is to illustrate a serious difficulty with the imbalance of power conception when measured against an important desideratum discussed in Chapter 1: practical usefulness. For a conception of domination to be useful, it should be able to do more than say whether some situation or state of affairs counts as an instance of domination or not. Specifically, it should be *descriptively contoured*, in the sense that it should be capable of making clear statements about comparative levels or degrees of domination when one scenario is contrasted with another. *Why* The illustrations I have considered suggest that the imbalance of power conception is not as descriptively contoured as we would like it to be. Can an alternative conception better account for our comparative intuitions here? In my view, the answer is yes.

4.2.2　The arbitrariness condition

With this goal in mind, let us consider the conception of domination proposed by Philip Pettit and others. He argues, roughly, that domination exists whenever one person or group has the "power of interference on an arbitrary basis" over another person or group.[14] *Pett* It is the second part of this definition that is interesting here: namely, the idea of arbitrariness. Now since the expression "arbitrary" can have different meanings in different contexts, it is important to be clear about the meaning intended here.

Sometimes, arbitrary is used to mean "random or unpredictable." In the case of slavery, for example, it is often true that slaves cannot accurately predict when their owners will beat them and when they will leave them alone. This cannot be what makes the imbalance of social power between masters and slaves an instance of domination, however. With long experience, a slave might gradually become better able to predict when his master is likely to abuse him, and thus his master's decisions will appear to him less and less

---

[13] Since minorities are on average less well off than whites, one might argue that this accounts for a somewhat greater imbalance of power and dependency. But even when we compare a middle-class black American with a middle-class white American with an equivalent income, it can still be argued that the former faces greater vulnerabilities vis-à-vis the criminal justice system than the latter.

[14] Pettit (1997, p. 52). Cf. Wartenberg (1990, ch. 6) and Lovett (2001). Something like this view of domination is usually assumed in the civic republican literature defining freedom as non-domination.

random over time. This will be better for the slave, of course. But surely it does not follow that he is subject to less and less domination. Rather, we should say, he is better able to *cope with* the domination to which he is (and remains) subject to. This, then, is not the relevant meaning of arbitrary for our purposes.

"Discretionary" is much closer to the intended meaning, but it is not quite right either. Discretionary power might be delegated to a public agency with a view to advancing certain goals or aims—as, for example, when Congress delegates discretionary authority to the Federal Reserve—and this should not, at least under the right conditions, count as an instance of domination. For example, suppose that a principal delegates discretionary authority to an agent on the condition that the agent remains answerable to a common-knowledge understanding of both the goals and aims it is meant to serve, and the means of achieving those goals and aims it is permitted to employ. Further suppose that the principal can ultimately enforce these understandings against any attempt by the agent to deviate from them. In such cases, we might not regard the discretionary authority as an instance of domination. (This possibility is relevant for discussions of institutional design in Chapter 7.)[15]

What then is the intended meaning of arbitrary here? Traditionally, social power was said to be arbitrary when it could be exercised merely according to the "will or pleasure" of the person or group holding that power.[16] This is the sense of the term relevant for our discussion. More precisely, let us define social power as *arbitrary* to the extent that its potential exercise is not externally constrained by effective rules, procedures, or goals that are common knowledge to all persons or groups concerned. Arbitrariness, so defined, is not merely an excessive sort of discretion. Discretion is an ambiguous umbrella term that covers both unconstrained power as well as power that happens to be constrained in the manner suggested earlier by common-knowledge goals, rather than rules or procedures.[17] In contrast, the degree to which social power is arbitrary is captured by the ratio, so to speak, of its potential uses that are unconstrained to those that are constrained (by rules, procedures, or goals).

Two aspects of this definition of arbitrariness will benefit from further elaboration. The first is that the constraints on social power, whatever they happen to be, must be *effective*—meaning that they must have the actual

---

[15] For a discussion of the conditions under which discretionary authority might not count as arbitrary, see Pettit (1997, chs. 6–7) and Richardson (2002). The need to allow for discretionary authority explains the shift in language from Lovett (2001, pp. 102–3).

[16] O.E.D., 2nd ed., *loc. sit.*

[17] These two senses of discretion roughly correspond to the strong and weak senses, respectively, analyzed in Dworkin (1977, pp. 31–3). I am grateful to José Martí for encouraging me to clarify this point.

capacity to constrain how that social power is exercised. Mere normative standards (e.g., that a power be exercised "fairly" or "with moderation") do not count, unless they are meaningfully backed by some sort of enforcement mechanism. Formal laws—as, for example, the requirement that the police obtain a lawful warrant before searching a private residence—can be effective in this sense, but there is no necessary correspondence between formal laws and effective constraints. This is because, on the one hand, formal laws do not count as effective unless they are actually enforced, while on the other hand, social conventions might sometimes act as effective constraints without their being explicitly codified as formal laws. Both points are clarified in Section 4.3.

The second important aspect of this definition is that effective constraints must be *external* to the power-wielding persons or groups themselves. A husband may choose not to exercise the full measure of power granted to him under traditional family law, perhaps out of a sense of duty and fairness, or perhaps because he happens to be a nice person. These constraints might sometimes count as effective in the sense described earlier, but they are internal in the sense that they depend on the psychology of the power holder himself, and are thus unreliable unless or until they are given some sort of external backing by a third party.[18] The relevant sort of external backing often, though not necessarily, takes the form of a commonly recognized mechanism for appeal. For example, constraints on the police can be given external backing by appeal to the courts, constraints on lower courts by appeal to higher courts, constraints on the Supreme Court by the other branches of government (plus legal and public opinion), and so on.[19] The chain of external constraints need not form a pyramid, of course: 1 might constrain 2, who constrains 3, who constrains 1 in turn. This is possible because, as pointed out in Chapter 3, power is not necessarily transitive.

Hopefully, this clarifies the definition of arbitrariness given earlier. Note that, for the moment, my definition is merely stipulated and not justified. This is significant because, as is evident in later discussion, the relevant sense

[18] Though intuitively sensible, the basis for this requirement runs into deep metaphysical waters, well beyond the scope of this study. Roughly, however, the idea is that important ill effects of domination stem from the peculiar attitude those subject to domination must adopt toward the agents of their domination (more on this in Chapter 5). From the subject's point of view at least, it is impossible to regard the behavior of others as strictly determined by their prior psychological dispositional states (for discussion, see Strawson [1962] and Searle [2001, esp. chs. 1, 3]). Only external constraints can provide the subjective reliability necessary to render social power non-arbitrary.

[19] In discussions of the "unrestrained" authority of the Supreme Court of the United States, it is hardly ever noted that Art. III, §2, para. 2 of the US Constitution grants Congress the authority to define the Supreme Court's jurisdiction virtually at will—a power Congress has been known to exercise.

of arbitrary power to mean "at the will or pleasure of the power holder" admits another, competing interpretation. Relying on the definition as stipulated, however, what I want to do next is to show that it can help explain some of our intuitions in the examples discussed earlier.

What generally reduces the degree of domination suffered by citizens at the hands of the American criminal law system is the presence of a vast web of rules and procedures—established and known to all parties in advance—constraining its operation. As John Locke would say, we enjoy a "standing rule to live by, common to everyone."[20] In theory at least, persons and groups can thus by and large escape the ill effects of their dependency on a criminal justice system wielding tremendous power over them simply by following the rules and planning ahead. In practice, of course, the criminal justice system in the United States suffers from a wide range of well-known problems in this regard, especially with respect to the treatment of minorities. But the comparative point still holds: To the extent that this system of constraints does work, things are at least less arbitrary than they might otherwise be. One can reasonably rely on the fact that, for example, standards of evidence and the definition of crimes will be adhered to. Without even minimal assurances such as these, the defendant in one of Stalin's show trials could only hope to curry favor with the prosecution, perhaps by confessing to crimes he or she did not commit or by accusing other innocent persons.

Thus, we can account for our intuitions with respect to the differences in domination between living under the American criminal justice system on the one hand, and living under that of a totalitarian dictatorship on the other. Likewise, our intuitions regarding the variations within the United States can be accounted for by the fact that the constraints on the criminal justice system are less effective when it comes to protecting minority citizens.[21] The addition of a third, arbitrariness condition to our conception of domination captures both intuitions nicely, and thus supplies the descriptive contouring wanting on the imbalance of power view.

4.2.3 An aside on the rule of law

It is worth mentioning at this juncture the connection—no doubt becoming obvious—between the idea of arbitrariness and the traditional ideal of the

---

[20] Locke (1690, §22, p. 17).

[21] Racial profiling, for instance, effectively grants a wider range of arbitrary powers to police when it comes to deciding whether to stop and search minorities: Cole (1999, esp. ch. 1). For an excellent analysis of discretionary authority in the American legal system generally, see also Davis (1969).

rule of law. Loosely speaking, the power exercised by political and legal authorities over citizens counts as non-arbitrary, in my view, to the extent that those authorities observe the rule of law.

However, the correspondence here is not perfect. For one thing, the concept of non-arbitrariness is much broader in scope, for it applies potentially to all imbalances of power (including those in the so-called private sphere), not merely those between state and citizen. More importantly, however, the correspondence is not perfect because the rule of law ideal—at least as traditionally interpreted—is far more demanding than a non-arbitrariness ideal would be. This can be seen as follows.

On the traditional view, the rule of law requires that no one be punished or "made to suffer in body or goods except for a distinct breach of law established in the ordinary legal manner before the ordinary course of the land."[22] Consider, for a moment, what meeting this standard would require. In the case of criminal law, this is reasonably straightforward: it requires that no one can be punished unless there is some law on the books that the individual can be shown to have violated. But suppose the US Congress were to pass a law modifying the tax code. Clearly, some will do better, and others worse, under these new rules. Indeed, nearly any possible act of government that is not merely symbolic will have some impact on someone, somewhere. On the traditional view, these would count as violations of the rule of law, since their adverse effects cannot be traced to any breach of law on the part of those specific individuals "made to suffer in body or goods." Adhering to the rule of law ideal in its traditional meaning would thus entail, among many other things, all but abandoning social welfare policy.[23]

If non-arbitrariness were defined in terms of the traditional view of the rule of law, it would be far too demanding. A conception of domination including an arbitrariness condition would then fall afoul of the usefulness criterion laid down in Chapter 1, since it would define domination in such a way that domination would be effectively unavoidable. The view adopted here is less demanding. It holds that the exercise of political or legal authority can count as non-arbitrary provided that it is effectively constrained by common-knowledge rules, procedures, or goals. Exactly what this entails with respect to discretionary political authority is discussed further in Chapter 7, but it is certainly not meant to exclude social welfare policy, for example.

---

[22] Dicey (1915, p. 110).

[23] This is precisely why Hayek (1960) wanted to adhere to it, of course. The difficulty of reconciling any sort of regulatory policy with the traditional rule of law ideal is thoroughly analyzed in Rubin (1989); see also Lovett (2002, pp. 64–6).

4.2.4 Further examples of arbitrariness

Adding an arbitrariness condition to the revised imbalance of power conception yields what I call the *arbitrary power* conception of domination. On this view, a person or group experiences domination to the extent that they are dependent on a social relationship in which some other person or group wields arbitrary power over them. Note that this is a structure-based, unrestricted, and qualitative conception of domination.

How does this conception fit with our core cases of domination? Slavery again provides an easy case: in most slave systems, there was little a slave master was not permitted to do to those slaves in his possession. Moreover, what few limitations were imposed by law were frequently ineffective. For example, Frederick Douglass points out that laws protecting slaves in the antebellum American South were almost never enforced for the simple reason that slaves did not have the legal standing to bring cases to court themselves.[24] The other examples we have been using also fit without difficulty. Until comparatively recently in the United States and England, the wielding of arbitrary power within the family was protected by various common-law barriers to action against family members.[25] In the earlier stages of capitalism, employers (especially through their foremen) wielded an arbitrary power to hire and fire employees at will.[26] The situation of the peasantry in early modern Europe is somewhat less clear on this point, but it is interesting to note a general trend, from the early Middle Ages through to the French Revolution, for each group to press against its superiors (the peasants on the nobles, the nobility on the monarchs, etc.) for a more and more explicit specification of rights and duties, so as to reduce the degree of arbitrary rule.

And what of despotic, authoritarian, or totalitarian political regimes? Particularly at the totalitarian extreme, these may seem at first to present a counter-example, insofar as, in the words of Hannah Arendt, such regimes attempt to eliminate "spontaneity itself as an expression of human behavior" by smothering their citizens under a system of rules so dense and comprehensive as to render citizen action entirely predictable.[27] Is this not the very

---

[24] Douglass (1855, pp. 63–4, 127). Indeed, slaves could not even be witnesses in cases brought about by others: Genovese (1974, p. 40). Further discussions of the arbitrary powers of slave masters can be found in Douglass (1855, pp. 121, 262, 429), Genovese (1974, pp. 30, 67), and Patterson (1982, pp. 190–6). When slaves did have greater legal rights, as for example in ancient Rome, we would expect their domination to be marginally lower: see Watson (1989) for an excellent comparative study of slave law.

[25] For an overview of traditional Anglo-American family law, see Holcombe (1983, chs. 2–3) and Mason (1994). See also Mill (1869, esp. parts 1–2).

[26] See Nelson (1995, esp. ch. 3).

[27] Arendt (1968, p. 136).

opposite of arbitrariness? On closer examination, the arbitrary power conception is vindicated once again. It is only the citizens that a totalitarian regime wishes to render predictable, precisely (as Arendt makes very clear) in order to remove any obstacles to the arbitrary power of the rulers. What counts is rather the degree to which the *agents* of domination are constrained, and it is clear that the rulers in despotic, authoritarian, and totalitarian political regimes attempt to free *themselves* from the constraints of law and other social conventions as much as they can.[28]

These core examples are enough, I think, to make at least a prima facie case for connecting domination with arbitrary power. But some other cases are not so easy to reconcile. I am thinking in particular of a rigorously legal system of discrimination. Real-world systems of discrimination—as, for example, Jim Crow laws in the American South, apartheid, or the legal liabilities once imposed on European Jews—are not always characterized by a strict adherence to explicit rules and procedures, of course, but one might imagine a case in which there was genuine procedural non-arbitrariness. Moreover, one might reasonably have the intuition that this should count as another instance of domination. This would seem to count against the arbitrary power conception. I postpone the discussion of this possible counter-example, however, in order to first explain the idea of social conventions. The value of doing so will soon become clear.

4.3 SOCIAL CONVENTIONS

Social power, I have said, is not arbitrary if its potential exercise is externally constrained by effective rules, procedures, or goals that are common knowledge to all persons or groups concerned. But is it even possible to constrain an imbalance of power in this way? Some have argued that it is not. Their view will be discussed shortly.

By way of preparing for that discussion, I first discuss in some detail the idea of *social conventions*. This is a broad term, under which heading I mean to include not only what are often called social norms (e.g., norms against lying), but also simple coordination conventions (e.g., driving on the right) on the one hand, and formal institutions such as laws on the other. The various sorts of social conventions have been analyzed extensively by legal

[28] For further discussion of arbitrariness in totalitarian political systems, see Havel (1992, pp. 181–212) and Podgorecki (1996).

theorists and others; my discussion here is intended to build on their previous work.[29]

4.3.1 Social conventions as Nash equilibria

The general idea of social conventions is most easily conveyed through a set of examples. Let us begin with an everyday one. In many places, there exists what might be called a social rule or norm of standing in line and waiting for service at banks, at checkout counters, at post offices, and so forth. This norm is quite robust, despite the facts that it is rarely enforced officially and that there is no law or statute on the books anywhere requiring it. Why, then, is it so commonly observed?

To some extent, the answer might be unreflective habit. From a young age, most of us are used to waiting in lines and so, in many situations, we do so automatically. This cannot, however, be a complete answer. Imagine someone in a bit of a hurry, who arrives at her bank to find a long line. This personal inconvenience should be sufficient to disrupt her unthinking habit, and prompt reflection: Should I wait in line today, she might think to herself, given that I am in such a hurry? If she decides to observe the rule regardless (as many would), we cannot plausibly attribute this outcome to habit. Two factors, probably in some combination, would no doubt account for her decision. The first is that, on reflection, she might conclude the rule "wait in line for service" is after all reasonable and fair, and thus that she *ought* to observe it, even at some personal inconvenience to herself in this particular instance. The second is that, were she to violate the rule, she might expect others at the bank to express some, more or less subtle, disapprobation. Descriptively speaking, we can think of the former as a sort of internal sanction (she will feel worse for having violated the rule) and the second as an external sanction (others will make her feel worse for having violated the rule).

Which of these two factors is more significant? It is impossible to say for all cases, as the relative contribution of each will vary depending on the person and the situation in question. Fortunately, the answer matters less than one might think. Far more significant is the following observation: Suppose our bank customer arrives to find there is no line, but rather an unruly crowd jostling for service. Will she follow the rule "wait in line for service" in this case? Probably not. She will jostle for service like everyone else. Notice that

---

[29] See especially the signal contributions by Kelsen (1967), Hart (1994), Lewis (1969), Raz (1999), Postema (1982), Elster (1989), and Schauer (1991). The surrounding literature is far too extensive to cite comprehensively.

this remains true, even if we suppose she believes the rule "wait in line for service" is reasonable and fair, and that she (and the others) ought to be following it. The chaos might be, to her mind, regrettable, but this judgment in itself is not likely to prompt her observance of the rule if no one else is observing it. This suggests that social norms derive their robustness largely from expectations: they are observed in large part because people expect them to be observed.

Now let me try to define the idea of a social convention somewhat more precisely. First, we must note that "wait in line for service" is not a complete statement of the rule expressed in the social norm of our example. The complete rule is rather something like this: "wait in line for service, approve of others who wait in line, and disapprove of others who do not wait in line."[30] Recall from Chapter 3 the relationship between actions and strategies. A strategy is a plan that might comprehend multiple actions, some of which respond to future contingencies: in other words, to follow a rule is to adopt a strategy from your opportunity set (and not merely to perform an action). Now consider a group of bank customers N and some arbitrary member of this group i. Suppose that every person other than i in N, by convention designated $-i$, has adopted the waiting-in-line strategy described earlier, which we can designate s_{-i}^*. Given this fact, it will probably be the case that i will also want to adopt the waiting-in-line strategy herself. It does not matter particularly what i's reasons for arriving at this decision happen to be. Perhaps she believes it is the right thing to do; perhaps, given the likelihood of public disapprobation, she believes it is prudent; perhaps this particular bank has a security guard who will enforce the rule; and so on. Most likely, it is some overlapping combination of reasons like these. The important point is that, whatever her reasons happen to be, she prefers the waiting-in-line strategy to anything else in her opportunity set, given what everyone else is doing. When this is true of all i in N, we have what is called a Nash equilibrium, which can be designated $s^* = (s_1^*, s_2^*, \ldots, s_n^*)$.

Roughly speaking, a social convention is a Nash equilibrium writ large.[31] The advantage of thinking about social conventions in this way is that it

---

[30] Postema (1982, pp. 176–7) correctly notes this point. The failure to take it into account has caused some mischief in the literature on social conventions. It is sometimes complained that a descriptive account of social norms cannot capture their "normative character"—that is, the sense in which people usually take the rule expressed in the norm to be itself a reason for doing something. (See Dworkin [1977, pp. 50–1, 53–8, 1986, p. 135–9] and Raz [1999, pp. 56–8]. Hart [1994, pp. 256–9] replies to this complaint.) Below I argue that this feature of social norms can be attributed to their incorporation of external sanctions.

[31] For the association of Nash equilibria and social conventions, I am indebted to Calvert (1995).

reveals the essentially similar nature underlying their apparently diverse types. This point can be illustrated with the help of another example, this time of a different type of social convention commonly called a coordination convention or convention equilibrium. In a well-known scenario anachronistically called a "battle of the sexes" game, a husband and wife must decide whether to go to the opera or to a boxing match after work (see Table 4.1). The husband prefers the opera to the boxing matches, whereas the wife favors boxing matches to the opera, but both prefer spending the evening together, at either event, rather than apart. Now suppose they have regularly been going to the boxing match. In this case, neither will want to deviate from this custom by going to the opera one evening, because (provided they have not had a chance to discuss their plans during the day) each expects that the other will go to the boxing match as usual. Since neither wants to change his or her strategy unilaterally, we have a Nash equilibrium. Fundamentally, this situation is no different than the one described previously: in both cases, it is our expectations regarding the behavior of others that sustains a rule effectively constraining our own behavior. This is what makes both scenarios instances of a social convention. The difference between them consists only in their relying on a somewhat different mix of internal and external sanctions.

Table 4.1

Husband	Wife	
	Opera	Boxing
Opera	2, 1	0, 0
Boxing	0, 0	1, 2

Every existing social convention must constitute a Nash equilibrium (otherwise, it would not be effective). It does not follow, however, that all possible Nash equilibria correspond to existing social conventions.[32] In the "battle of the sexes" game, always going to the boxing match is only one of the several possible equilibria: always going to the opera is another, as is a so-called

---

[32] Further, every Nash equilibrium is a combination of possible strategies, but not all possible strategy combinations are Nash equilibria. For example, each player in the famous prisoners' dilemma game has the strategy "cooperate" in her opportunity set, but the strategy combination in which every player cooperates is not a Nash equilibrium in that game. Most Nash equilibria are, in principle, possible social conventions (an exception will be noted later), but in practice those that require particularly complex strategies are unlikely to arise. As discussed in Chapter 3, people can only select strategies from their subjective, not their objective, opportunity sets.

mixed-strategy equilibrium in which the husband goes to the opera with a probability of two-thirds and the boxing match with a probability of one-third, while the wife does the opposite (the technical game theory details here are not important for the main argument). Further equilibria are possible if we introduce publicly observed events. For example, going to the opera on even-numbered calendar dates and the boxing match on odd-numbered calendar dates could be a Nash equilibrium. The actual social convention is the equilibrium the husband and wife have, in fact, coordinated on, out of the set of possible equilibria.

It is also helpful to note that people may observe social conventions they strongly dislike or of which they disapprove. In the "battle of the sexes" game, it is not a matter of indifference to either the husband or the wife what the custom is. Although the husband has a good reason to go to the boxing match, it is probably not that he believes their observed custom is fair in any normative sense. Indeed, he might well observe the custom of regularly going to the boxing match while vocally criticizing it as unfair. The existence of a social convention is thus consistent with widespread—and even universal—public criticism.[33] It is important, given our commitment to developing a strictly descriptive conception of domination, that we define social conventions independently of any normative judgments we might have of them.

Finally, notice that in the two examples given, the social convention is symmetrical, in the sense that all parties employ the same strategy. Though common, this is not a necessary feature of social conventions. In more complex situations, different strategies might be allotted to different persons or groups. Consider, for example, the social convention of wearing a headscarf if you are a Muslim woman. Muslim men participate in this practice by virtue of their role in disapproving of women who do not wear headscarves, and of other men who fail to show the appropriate degree of disapproval when required. Provided no one wants to change his or her respective strategy unilaterally, given the strategies adopted by all the others, this constitutes a Nash equilibrium of nonsymmetric strategies. Formal institutions such as laws are also like this: they are sustained, in part, by judges, police, and so on, who in equilibrium can be expected to follow specialized enforcement strategies.

---

[33] A social convention might be universally criticized if it is a Pareto suboptimal Nash equilibrium. In this situation, there are several possible equilibria, and the relevant persons happen to be coordinated on one of the inferior ones, worse for everyone than some alternative. They are stuck, however, because no one party can switch strategies unilaterally without making herself even worse off. All the parties have to switch together, and the coordination problem involved in switching together may hinder reform.

4.3.2 The varieties of social conventions

Social convention is, as I have said, a broad term, but it does not cover all possible patterns of social behavior. It is important, in order to avoid confusion, to clarify both what counts, and what does not count, as a social convention. First, what sorts of behavior patterns would not count?

Sometimes people have stable preferences—as, for example, a durable preference for chicken over beef—which will cause them to act in observably predictable ways across a range of circumstances. These might be called *habits*. When a large number of people happen to have the same habits, we will observe a pattern of behavior that might seem to resemble a social convention. Nevertheless, shared habits and social conventions are not the same thing.[34] Shared habits arise accidentally, and they are sustained only so long as the underlying pattern of preferences happens to remain the same. If some particular person in the group changed her mind and decided that she preferred beef after all, she would probably feel no particular reason to adhere to the previous pattern.

Note, however, that shared habits are easily converted into social conventions, the moment some public approbation or disapprobation is attached to observance or non-observance of the general pattern. This might happen with rules of etiquette and customs of dress, for example: what originally arises as a shared habit of acting in particular ways or wearing particular sorts of clothing evolves into a norm backed by public opinion regarding what is appropriate (and what is not appropriate) to do and to wear. In other words, social conventions are distinguished from shared habits by the fact that participants in the former but not the latter have to some extent an external, desire-independent reason for observing the accepted practice.[35] Something like this distinction is often expressed in ordinary conversation. When it comes to habits, people often explain their actions simply with reference to their preferences. If asked why they had chicken, for example, people will usually just reply that they prefer it to beef. When it comes to social conventions, however, people often explain their actions with reference to a rule (which their actions, by assumption, observe). If asked why they removed their hat, people might reply that it is impolite to wear hats indoors. By

---

[34] Hart (1994, pp. 51–61), Raz (1999, pp. 55–6), and Elster (1989, pp. 104–5) each discuss the distinction between shared habits and social conventions. Cf. Schauer (1991, p. 1–3): shared habits are an example of what he terms "descriptive," as opposed to "prescriptive", rules.

[35] Sanctions are external and desire-independent only in the first instance, of course. In a broader sense, sanctions are effective only to the extent that people desire avoiding them. This does not affect the argument here, however.

implication, whether they happen to prefer wearing their hat indoors or not is irrelevant.

Suppose that a person decides to adopt as a rule for herself, "always go running on Tuesdays." This rule provides an additional internal sanction, over and above her mere preference for running on any given day. On some Tuesday in particular, for example, she might, other things being equal, prefer not to go running, and yet do so anyway because she feels committed to the rule. This is sometimes called a personal rule or private norm. What if a large group of people independently happened to adopt the same rule for themselves—would this count as a social convention? It would not. Again, we would observe a pattern of behavior across a group of people that looks in many ways like a social convention, without being one. This is because the sanction in question is not external in the right way. If one of the participants in this practice decided to drop the rule, that would be the end of it from her point of view: there is no external reason for her to retain the rule if she does not so desire.

While not every pattern of behavior counts as a social convention, social conventions are nevertheless quite diverse. Two different sorts of social conventions have already been discussed: social norms and coordination conventions. Roughly speaking, the distinction between these lies in the nature of the desire-independent reason for adhering to the practice in question. Sometimes, the mere fact that others are observing a practice by itself provides a sufficient reason for observing it oneself. While it is true, for example, that people who drive on the wrong side of the road can be punished, both formally (if they are arrested for reckless driving) and informally (if they are criticized for doing so), these punishments are in a sense superfluous: the mere fact that everyone else is driving on one side is enough of a reason for driving on the same side oneself. The sanction, we might say, is "built in" to the coordination convention.[36] By contrast, social norms like the rule "wait in line for service" and the rules of etiquette are generally supported by additional sanctions, and not by the benefits of coordination alone.

Sometimes, there is no substantial reason to prefer one possible coordination convention over another. This is the case, perhaps, with respect to which side of the road people should drive on: what matters is only that everyone drives on the same side, not which side this happens to be. These might be called "pure" coordination conventions. Strictly speaking, pure coordination

---

[36] Of course, we might say that our reason for driving on the correct side of the road is our desire to avoid collisions. Again, what matters is that our reasons be independent of our desires of the first instance—in this case, which side of the road we would prefer to drive on if there were no convention, say. I am grateful to Jack Knight for helping me clarify this point.

conventions are probably rare. Most coordination conventions will be like the "battle of the sexes" game: while everyone prefers coordination to non-coordination, different coordination points will be favored by different people. Many rules of private property might be like this, for example.

In addition to coordination conventions and social norms, social conventions also include formal institutions such as laws. The difference, again, lies in the nature of the external, desire-independent reason for observing the practice. Roughly speaking, we might think of a law as a social convention supported directly or indirectly by the coercive powers of the state (in addition to, perhaps, the informal sanctions of social approbation and disapprobation).[37] Obviously, the exact demarcations between laws, social norms, and coordination conventions will often be unclear. This is not at all important for the argument here. What is important is simply that all social conventions are supported in part by external, desire-independent sanctions. In other words, without knowing much about a person—and, in particular, without having to interpret his or her internal psychological dispositions—we can reliably assume they will have strong reasons for observing the relevant rules, procedures, or goals.

Social conventions are diverse in a second way as well. In many of the examples we have discussed, the social conventions take the form of rules, narrowly understood as straightforward requirements to perform or not perform certain actions under specified conditions. But social conventions might also take the form of procedures or goals. For example, a group might observe a social convention stating that "disputes shall be resolved by majority vote"; or that "the treasurer shall keep accurate records of our finances"; and so on. If these social conventions are supported in part by the approbation and disapprobation of the group's members, they are social norms; if they are supported in part by the coercive power of the state, they are laws. What matters here is only that the rule, procedure, or goal is supported by external, desire-independent sanctions, and thus might operate as an effective constraint on social power.

4.3.3 The reality of social conventions

In Chapter 1, I argued that a conception of domination ought to be useful. From this point of view, it would be a problem for the arbitrary power conception of domination if arbitrariness were impossible to avoid or, at any rate, reduce. Thus, I must consider the possibility that it is impossible to

---

[37] This conception of law is developed with a bit more detail in Lovett (2002, esp. pp. 43–58).

constrain the power one person or group has over another with social conventions. This claim is sometimes referred to as *rule skepticism*, and in legal theory it is commonly associated with legal realists such as Karl Llewellyn and Jerome Frank, or more recently with the Critical Legal Studies movement.[38] Their arguments are addressed to the question of legal systems specifically, of course, but they might apply equally well to social conventions in general.

Broadly speaking, there are two reasons one might doubt the efficacy of social conventions. The first can be called the *realist objection*. Crudely stated, the thought is that one power can be constrained only by another, greater power. In a society like the United States with an independent judiciary, for example, judges often enjoy an area of discretion within which, realistically speaking, no other greater power can override their decisions. It is naive, on the realist view, to think of judges as following rules of law in such cases: rather, a judicial decision is simply an exercise of power, and the rules of laws are at best merely predictions regarding what judges will do, and at worst meaningless ex post justifications of whatever they have already done.

The realist objection is, I think, easily answered. To begin with, it relies on a simplistic notion of power—specifically, on the indexical view discussed and rejected in Chapter 3. Simply because a judge, say, has more power than the litigants, it does not follow that her power is unconstrained. On the contrary, her power is constrained by the appeals system, and the highest court of the appeals system, in turn, by the other branches of government and by legal and public opinion.[39] Since power is not necessarily transitive, it does not follow that there must be a most powerful—and thus unconstrained—person or a group in a complex political system. Even if there were, many social conventions can be maintained even across significant imbalances of power. In the "battle of the sexes" game described earlier, it might be the case that the husband is generally more powerful than his wife, but it does not follow that he has no desire-independent reasons for observing the custom of going to the boxing match. Given that this is the mutual expectation, the fact that he would prefer going to the opera can be more or less ignored, and (even if she is the less powerful party in general) the wife can reliably assume that her husband will continue to observe the convention.

[38] For a discussion of rule skepticism, see Hart (1994, ch. 7). For an overview of the critical legal studies literature, see Kelman (1987), Altman (1990), or Coleman and Leiter (1993). Among political scientists, a version of rule skepticism surfaces in the so-called "attitudinal model" of judicial decision making: see especially Segal and Spaeth (2002).

[39] This point, with respect to the structural constraints on the US Supreme Court, is argued in Epstein and Knight (1997).

The realist objection is effective only against a straw man—someone who sincerely believes that judges, say, are mere "mouthpieces of the law," and not political actors constrained in multiple directions by a complex web of social conventions.[40] The stronger variety of rule skepticism is the second one, based on what can be called the *indeterminacy objection.* All social conventions require that people generally be able to tell what counts as observing a rule, following a procedure, or attempting to achieve a goal, for if we do not know whether some particular behavior counts, we would not know whether it warrants sanctioning or not. But this is not always easy to do. One reason is that it might be impossible to determine by simple observation which rule (procedure, or goal) is being followed. This point is often associated with Wittgenstein.[41] The difficulty he noticed is that any observed pattern of behavior sustained up through time *t* might always be explained with reference to many different rules. For example, suppose the husband in the "battle of the sexes" game is following the rule "always go to the boxing match," whereas the wife is following the rule "go to the boxing match a hundred times, then go to the opera a hundred times, and so on." Unless we have observed a hundred or more cases, we cannot tell which rule the two are following; indeed, they might themselves believe they are following the same rule when in fact they are not.

To some extent, this difficulty can be solved as a practical matter through simple discussion. When there is a genuine social convention, everyone observing it should offer more or less the same rule statement as the reason for his or her actions. But this is not a perfect solution, for the various parties might have different interpretations of what the rule statement means without knowing it. Suppose the boxing arena is closed for repairs one night: in this situation, the husband might believe the rule implies going to the opera instead, whereas the wife might believe the rule implies staying at home. So long as this particular question of interpretation does not arise, the fact that they interpret the same rule statement differently might escape notice.[42]

Although the indeterminacy objection presents some challenging philosophical problems, these cannot be very serious in practice. This must be so because people seem to observe many social conventions in their daily lives without much difficulty or fanfare, and this would not be possible unless problems of this sort were relatively minor. Perhaps cultural similarities

---

[40] This much-maligned expression is due to Montesquieu (1748, XI.6.48: p. 159).

[41] Wittgenstein (1958, esp. pp. 56–88). See also Postema (1982, pp. 188–9), Radin (1989, p. 797–810), and Schauer (1991, pp. 64–8), for discussion.

[42] When it comes to the legal systems specifically, this is the problem of "gaps" in the law—a problem famously debated in Dworkin (1977, esp. chs. 2–4, 1986, esp. chs. 1–2) and Hart (1994, esp. ch. 7 and the postscript).

ensure that even when facing novel situations, most people in a given society will agree that the rule should be extended in one way rather than another.[43] To appreciate the efficacy of social conventions, one need only visit a bank and witness the ease with which people observe them.

We need not imagine that a complete absence of arbitrariness can ever be achieved. It cannot. The arbitrary power conception will be useful provided it is possible to *reduce* arbitrariness. Since reduction is clearly possible, the arbitrary power conception will have the sort of descriptive contouring we are looking for.

4.4 ARBITRARINESS: PROCEDURAL OR SUBSTANTIVE?

This completes my discussion of social conventions. If all has gone well, the reader should now agree, first, that the idea of social conventions is reasonably clear and precise; and second, that social conventions can effectively constrain the opportunity sets available to persons and groups within social relationships. We may now return to the main argument of the chapter.

To the extent that social power is not externally constrained by effective rules, procedures, or goals that are common knowledge to all persons or groups concerned, I have said that we can define it as *arbitrary*. Arbitrariness, so defined, arises when there are gaps in the network of effective social conventions (social norms, coordination conventions, laws, etc.) governing the possible exercise of social power. Sometimes these gaps are accidental or unintended, and sometimes they exist merely because appropriate social conventions have not yet been introduced. Other times, however, these gaps are explicitly created and sheltered by the surrounding configuration of social conventions. An example of the latter is traditional family law, which was specifically designed to prevent external interference with the authority of husbands and parents. This created a zone within which husbands and parents could exercise power over their wives and children according to their unchecked arbitrary will or pleasure. By contrast, university policy presumably leaves no such gaps to the librarian, who is constrained merely to enforce the officially stated policy on late fees. If the librarian were to attempt exercising her power arbitrarily, students could simply appeal to her supervisor.

[43] Something like this is suggested in Taylor (1992).

Combining the idea of arbitrariness with the conditions of dependency and an imbalance of power yields what I have called the *arbitrary power* conception of domination. This conception has the important advantage of supplying the descriptive contouring wanting in the imbalance of power conception (revised or unrevised).

Next we must return to a puzzle left unresolved in earlier discussion—namely, how we should respond to the plausible intuition that a rigorously legal system of discrimination must surely count as an instance of domination, since it would seem to be excluded by the arbitrary power conception.

4.4.1 Procedural versus substantive arbitrariness

Arbitrary power, in the relevant sense, is social power wielded according to the will or pleasure of the power holder. But this somewhat elliptical expression is open to two possible interpretations. On the one hand, we might say that the potential exercise of social power is left to the will or pleasure of a person or group just in case it is not somehow externally and effectively constrained. On the other hand, we might say that the potential exercise of social power is left to the will or pleasure of a person or group when it can be used by them without regard to the relevant interests of the affected parties.

The definition stipulated earlier, according to which social power is arbitrary to the extent that it is not externally constrained by effective rules, procedures, or goals that are common knowledge to all persons or groups concerned, obviously represents an example of the first sort of interpretation. This has the effect, very roughly, of equating non-arbitrariness with the traditional ideal of the rule of law, provided of course that we are willing to loosen and extend this idea considerably. Often, however, and especially in some legal contexts, the term arbitrary is used rather differently. It is commonly said, for example, that it is arbitrary to base hiring decisions on irrelevant criteria such as race or gender; or (more generally) that it is arbitrary for one person to be made worse off than another through no fault of her own. These uses of the term arbitrary represent an example of the second sort of interpretation, which emphasizes the specific thought that decisions made according to the will or pleasure of a power holder often do not reflect the relevant interests of the affected parties. (Everyone presumably has a justifiable interest in being assessed and rewarded according to morally relevant criteria such as merit and effort, and not morally irrelevant criteria such as race, gender, or brute luck.) Let us refer to these as the *procedural* and the *substantive* conceptions of arbitrariness, respectively. On the substantive view it is not enough that power holders be constrained in their exercise of social power, unless they are constrained specifically in a way that compels them to track "the welfare and worldview" of the persons affected.[44]

Which conception is better? Obviously, from a normative point of view, we would want power to be non-arbitrary in both the substantive and the procedural sense. A rigorously legal system of discrimination might be non-arbitrary in the procedural sense, but it cannot, presumably, be non-arbitrary in the substantive sense, since it does not compel power holders to track the welfare and worldview (however defined) of the persons discriminated against. But this is not our present concern. Our concern is rather the narrower one of determining which interpretation of arbitrariness is more suitable in the context of developing a conception of domination.

The principal consideration in favor of the substantive view is our strong intuition that systems of institutionalized discrimination, no matter how carefully framed in scrupulously observed public rules and regulations, must count as instances of domination—along with slavery, autocratic government, and our other core cases. This is indeed a significant consideration. But intuitions are not, in themselves, decisive. In developing a successful conception of domination, other considerations must also be taken into account, and if the latter are found sufficiently weighty on the other side, this is perhaps an intuition we should be prepared, on reflection, to drop. In the next sections, I try first to argue that this is precisely the conclusion we ought to draw in the case at hand, and second to explain what accounts for our contrary intuitions.

4.4.2 Procedural interpretation defended

In order to fairly assess the substantive interpretation of arbitrariness, we need first to say what the welfare and worldview (or relevant interests, etc.) of the affected parties amounts to. Absent such an account, of course, the substantive view would add nothing to the procedural view. In this connection, three alternatives have been suggested. On the first, we should understand the welfare and worldview of persons or groups to mean their objectively defined, normatively justifiable interests; on the second, their subjectively expressed preferences or desires; and on the third, their ideas about their interests as expressed through suitably designed deliberative procedures. These can be

[44] Pettit (1997, pp. 55–6). Note that, as defined, substantive non-arbitrariness necessarily incorporates procedural non-arbitrariness, insofar as being constrained to track the welfare and worldview of the affected parties is to be externally and effectively constrained. This necessity can be avoided only at the cost of abandoning structural conceptions of domination altogether, and reconsidering outcome conceptions (which were rejected in Chapter 2).

called the common good, welfarist, and democratic accounts, respectively.[45]
Let us consider each alternative in turn.

The principal consideration arguing in favor of the substantive view of
arbitrariness, as I have said, is our strong intuition that a rigorously legal
system of discrimination ought to count as an instance of domination. Since
institutionalized discrimination manifestly works against the objectively defined, normatively justifiable interests of the persons discriminated against,
the common good account would characterize such a system as substantively
arbitrary, and thus capture our intuition with ease.

But degree of fit with our prior intuitions is only one of the criteria laid
down in Chapter 1 for a successful conception of domination. Among other
things, it is also important that a conception of domination be useful, and
I have argued that a conception will not be useful unless it observes the
separation thesis: in other words, with the best conception of domination,
it must be possible for us to determine whether or not given persons or
groups are subject to domination strictly on the basis of certain purely
descriptive facts about their situation. The common good account of substantive arbitrariness obviously does not meet this condition. We would not
be able to determine whether one person or group subjects another to
domination until we first established whether the social power of the former
is constrained to track the objectively defined, normatively justifiable interests
of the latter. It follows that an attempt to argue that we should alleviate
domination, so defined, will degenerate into the unhelpful truism that we
should promote people's objectively defined, normatively justifiable interests,
whatever these turn out to be.[46] Given the choice, then, between a procedural
understanding of arbitrariness that is useful and captures most of our prior
intuitions on the one hand, and a common good substantive understanding
that, while capturing nearly all our prior institutions, is useless on the other
hand, surely we must opt for the former. This is especially so when, as I try to
show in Section 4.4.3, we can provide a plausible explanation for the recalci-
trant intuitions in question.

Perhaps one of the other two accounts of substantive arbitrariness will do
better, however. On the welfarist account, we should understand the welfare and
worldview of persons or groups to mean their subjectively expressed preferences
or desires. Since the subjective preferences or desires that people have are, in
principle, descriptive facts, the welfarist account would not fall afoul the separation thesis. Unfortunately, the welfarist account is completely unworkable for

---

[45] Cf. Richardson (2002, ch. 3).
[46] This difficulty is pointed out by Larmore (2004) and Carter (2008), with respect to a
conception of freedom of domination built on a "moralized" account of arbitrary power.

other reasons. To begin with, there will be the well-known problems of interpersonal measurement and preference aggregation, which need not be rehearsed here. Let us imagine these could be overcome. The main point of the substantive view of arbitrariness is to capture our intuition that a rigorously legal system of discrimination ought to count as an instance of domination. The welfarist account of substantive arbitrariness would accomplish this, presumably, on the assumption that most people prefer not to be discriminated against—this would show that institutionalized discrimination was substantively arbitrary, and thus an instance of domination.

But people cannot always be relied on to have the expected preferences. When they do not, our intuitions cannot so easily be captured. Thus it would seem that, on the welfarist view, a person or a group is not subject to domination whenever they happen to believe—rightly or wrongly—that their relevant interests are being taken into account by those wielding power over them. (This was precisely the situation, no doubt, with respect to a great many married women under the traditional system of family law and custom.) When the members of a group disagree on this score, the welfarist account apparently commits us to the view that, though identically situated in all other relevant respects, some of those members are subject to domination and others are not. Indeed, we would apparently be able to render a person subject to domination simply by convincing him that his relevant interests were not being respected, even if this were not true. None of this makes any sense.[47]

In short, the welfarist account of substantive arbitrariness might, unlike the common good account, satisfy the separation thesis, but it is no better than the procedural understanding—and, indeed, probably much worse—at capturing our prior intuitions about domination. What we need, apparently, is an account that is strictly descriptive, but free of the difficulties facing the welfarist account, of what it means for social power to be constrained to track the welfare and worldview of a person or a group.

The democratic account of substantive arbitrariness is supposed to fit the bill: on this view, social power is arbitrary unless it is compelled to track the affected persons' or groups' ideas about their interests as expressed through suitably designed deliberative procedures. Once filtered through such procedures, it is extremely unlikely that people would endorse their own systematic discrimination.[48] No doubt moved by considerations similar to those discussed earlier, and

---

[47] Cf. Ferejohn (2001), who elaborates on some of these difficulties. Chapter 5 will further discuss the various problems with welfarism.

[48] Though not impossible, however—nor can we characterize the relevant deliberative procedures so as to make such an endorsement impossible without transforming the democratic account into what is really a common good account in disguise.

hoping thus to reliably capture the intuition that institutionalized discrimination counts as an instance of domination, Pettit and others take precisely this line on substantive arbitrariness.[49] The issue is whether the democratic account can indeed square the circle. In my view, it cannot.

The central issue is as follows. Rather than contrast a rigorously legal system of discrimination with the absence of such discrimination, we must contrast a rigorously legal system of discrimination with alternative methods for securing similar levels of material advantage and disadvantage. Suppose that for various historical, economic, and cultural reasons, one group in some society manages to acquire a preponderance of social power, which it wields over the other groups in that society directly and without constraint, much to its own benefit (naturally). Since the disadvantaged groups are in no position to directly challenge the social position of the powerful group, they instead demand only that the various rights and privileges of the latter be written down, codified, and impartially enforced by independent judges. Let us suppose that, in time, the powerful group accedes to this demand, on the view that since the rules will, after all, be designed to benefit itself, there will be no significant cost in doing so. Now according to the democratic account of substantive arbitrariness, it would seem that this change does nothing to affect the levels of domination present in the society. This is because the powerful group is in no way compelled by the newly introduced rules to wield social power specifically so as to track the interests disadvantaged groups would express through suitably designed deliberative procedures. But in my view, the situation has indeed changed, and in an important way. Members of the disadvantaged groups now at least know exactly where they stand: they can develop plans of life based on reliable expectations; provided they follow the rules, they need not go out of their way to curry favor with members of the powerful group; and so on.[50] (More on this is explained in Chapter 5.) These are important experiential differences, best captured by saying that the introduction of externally effective constraints on the holders of power constitutes in and of itself a reduction of domination. This is not to say, of course, that the advantages of the powerful group are now perfectly fair. Far from it. Rather, it is only to say that not everything that is unfair must also constitute domination.[51]

---

[49] See Skinner (1998, pp. 26–7), Pettit (1999, pp. 172–3, 2001, pp. 138–9, 156–8), Richardson (2002, pp. 47–52), Maynor (2003, pp. 37–9), and Bohman (2008, pp. 207–8). Note that the language in Pettit (1997) was somewhat ambiguous, leading to some confusion in interpreting his understanding of arbitrariness; it is clear from the later work cited in this footnote, however, that he holds the democratic substantive interpretation.

[50] Cf. Thompson (1975, esp. pp. 258–69).

[51] In this sense, Markell (2008) is surely correct that non-domination alone does not get us everything we want. More on this point in Chapter 5.

Other considerations weigh against the substantive democratic account of arbitrariness as well. Among these is the fact that, without exactly defining domination and democracy as opposites (as Young and some others do), it nevertheless renders the connection between them more or less analytic. In my view, we should resist doing this. This is partly for pragmatic reasons. On the substantive democratic account, it will not be possible to say whether persons or groups are subject to domination until we first determine which interests they would express through suitably designed deliberative procedures. This may not be easy to do. But there are also normative reasons to resist this move. As discussed further in Chapter 7, one of the strongest arguments for democracy is that it tends to reduce domination. This argument is trivialized, however, if we define domination such that it becomes analytically true: the argument would then be analogous to saying that the reason to earn lots of money is because doing so will enable you to buy lots of things. Democracy is one thing, in my view, and non-domination is simply best understood as another.

4.4.3 Accounting for our contrary intuitions

The balance of considerations, it seems to me, favors the procedural interpretation of arbitrariness. But this has the consequence that a rigorously legal system of institutionalized discrimination might not, under certain conditions, count as an instance of domination. This grates against a strong prior intuition. Even if we are prepared, after consideration, to drop this intuition, we may wonder what accounts for it in the first place.

Let us, therefore, consider systems of institutionalized discrimination in somewhat more detail. How do such systems operate? Presumably, they employ an array of public laws and policies that impose special burdens on a group of persons defined racially, ethnically, or in some other way. Examples might be: denying persons in this group the vote, segregating educational facilities, disallowing the members of this group to take up certain professions, prohibiting certain legal actions to the members of this group, and so forth. To be sure, no reasonable person would deny that laws and policies of this sort are bad for those persons unfortunate enough to be members of the group in question, but we must admit that they need not be arbitrary in the procedural sense. Any given member of the group could know in advance that they are not allowed to ø, and the law prohibiting their ø-ing could be enforced with absolute impartiality and procedural fairness (in the sense that only members of the specified group are punished for ø-ing, they are punished if and only if they have in fact ø-ed, and the punishment imposed is no more or less than the rules require in that event).

Of course, as argued in the previous chapters, institutions are not themselves social actors, and thus cannot be said themselves to dominate anyone. Rather, institutions (and social conventions more broadly) constitute the structural environments of social relationships. For there to be domination, strictly speaking, there must be a social relationship in which one person or group wields arbitrary power over some other person or group. Now in many instances, discriminatory laws and policies create precisely this situation. One example would be a law that effectively blocked legal actions in defense of the members of some defined group: this would allow other people to arbitrarily harm the members of that group with impunity. Under Jim Crow laws, for example, this result was more or less effectively obtained by excluding blacks from the jury pool. Arbitrariness in the procedural sense is thus involved here after all, and so we may correctly speak of there being domination.[52]

But in other instances, discriminatory laws or policies do not create situations of this sort. An example of this might be the laws that once prohibited European Jews from entering into certain professions. Generally speaking, laws and policies of this sort do not themselves create problems of procedural arbitrariness.[53] Again, this is not to say that such laws are not bad for other reasons: for example, they certainly result in an unequal distribution of opportunity, and on many accounts of moral and political philosophy this should be regarded as a bad thing. (Indeed, in Chapter 7 I argue that, under certain conditions, social inequalities are bad because they can indirectly lead to domination.) Real-world systems of discrimination tend to combine laws and policies of both sorts into a single, complex mass. Not unreasonably, we view the mass as a single problem because it stems from a single source: the desire—born of self-interest, of hatred, of misunderstanding, etc.—of some persons in one group to systematically disadvantage the members of another group. Some of the laws and policies in this mass create relations of domination, while others do not. It is natural, in the absence of a precise conception of domination, to come to regard the whole mass as implicated in the domination of one group by another. This accounts, I think, for our strong prior intuition with respect to such cases.

---

[52] A number of commentators have remarked on how systems of discrimination create "free-fire zones" (Adam 1978, p. 28) for those who would harm the members of the discriminated-against class. Cf. Pettit (1997, pp. 120–5).

[53] Under certain conditions they might, however. Suppose the members of some class are disallowed from being lawyers. This might result in a legal incapacity similar to the one described earlier—but then, of course, we bring arbitrariness back into the picture, and the procedural view is unharmed.

Our question is purely the conceptual one of whether or not the particular laws and policies that do not themselves create opportunities for the exercise of procedurally arbitrary power should be regarded as constituting domination. In my view, for the reasons stated earlier, they should not. Political and social institutions and practices are implicated in domination only when they specifically enable one person or group to wield (procedurally) arbitrary power over another.

This conclusion is less worrisome than it might appear. In Chapter 5, I argue that domination is a very bad thing. But it is by no means the only bad thing. It is bad to starve, for example, but it does not follow that to be starving is to be subject to domination. It is also bad to treat others unfairly in the distribution of goods and opportunities, but it does not follow that this is, as such, to subject them to domination. Domination is one thing, and unfairness is another (much as democracy is one thing, and non-domination another). To collapse these terms is only to make both less clear and precise than they might otherwise be.

4.5 THE FINAL DEFINITION OF DOMINATION

In this section, I bring together the various strands of Part I into a final statement of my preferred conception of domination—what I have referred to as the *arbitrary power* conception. In plain English, we can say that persons or groups are subject to domination to the extent that they are dependent on a social relationship in which some other person or group wields arbitrary power over them.

Notice that domination, so defined, may come in degrees. Specifically, dependency is a matter of degree, the imbalances of power are a matter of degree, and the scope of arbitrariness left to the agent of domination by existing social norms, laws, and so forth is a matter of degree. It follows that the domination suffered by a person or group is, one might say, continuously variable in three dimensions. Formally, we might imagine a continuous function $f: d \times p \times a \to D$ that maps levels of dependency, power, and arbitrariness into levels of domination as follows:

$$D = f(d, p, a) \tag{4.1}$$

Since, other things being equal, greater degrees of dependency, power, or arbitrariness each yield higher levels of domination, we would expect all the first-order partial derivatives of equation (4.1) to be positive: $f_d > 0$, $f_p > 0$, and $f_a > 0$. Obviously, precisely specifying a function of this sort would be no easy task; these comments are only meant to illustrate the general idea.[54]

Alternatively, we might express the arbitrary power conception as a set of conditions. To correctly describe person or group 1 as dominating person or group 2, the following individually necessary and jointly sufficient conditions must obtain:

1. 1 and 2 must both be social actors.
2. 1 and 2 must be engaged in a social relationship with each other.
3. 2 must be dependent on the social relationship to some degree (the *dependency* condition).
4. 1 must have more power over 2 than 2 has over 1 (the *imbalance of power* condition).
5. The structure of the social relationship must be such as to permit 1 to employ power over 2 arbitrarily (the *arbitrariness* condition).

The first condition rules out agent-less domination. The second excludes from the set of dominating agents those who only indirectly enable domination, e.g., through their participation in the basic structure of society. The third entails that there would be no domination at equilibrium in a perfectly free market. The fourth rules out mutual domination. (Suppose that 2 has some power over 1, but 1 has even greater power over 2: since power is effective only to the extent that its exercise is credible, 2's power is useless in the face of a greater counterthreat from 1. The power that counts is 1's, so 2 cannot dominate 1.[55]) Finally, the fifth condition restricts domination to cases where social power can be wielded in an arbitrary manner.

Since the arbitrary power conception is agnostic with respect to the bases of dependency and the forms of social power, it is in principle a perfectly general conception, applicable to a wide range of historical and cultural circumstances. Since domination, so defined, comes in degrees, the conception is capable of discriminating among cases according to their level or degree of domination; and since each of its various working parts—social relationships, dependency, power, arbitrariness, and so on—are carefully defined in descriptive terms, the

---

[54] Appendix II aims to further develop some formal models of domination, however. Note that I have not commented on the possible interdependence of the variables in equation (4.1)— for example, whether increasing dependency, other things being equal, tends to increase the imbalance of power, and so on. These are interesting questions, but their resolution will not affect the main argument.

[55] But suppose 1's power is neutralized in some way: now 2's power, previously ineffective, comes into play, and 2 can dominate 1. In this way, a person or group subject to domination may have the latent ability to dominate their dominators when conditions change. I am grateful to Jeremy Waldron for raising these issues.

conception also satisfies the separation thesis. Thus, it is both descriptively and normatively useful. Finally, the arbitrary power conception captures most of our stronger intuitions regarding such core cases as slavery, feudalism, autocratic government, and domination in the family.

This is not to say our conclusions are entirely unsurprising, however. Some common pre-existing intuitions have required revision. By way of concluding Part I, it might be worthwhile to review some of the more significant points of controversy, and reiterate the considerations guiding us toward the arbitrary power conception as it finally stands here. The most prominent point of controversy, no doubt, is the one discussed previously in this chapter—namely, the rejection of rigorously legal systems of discrimination (and like cases) as genuine instances of domination, which does not correspond with many people's prior intuitions. I argued, however, that the cost of covering these particular prior intuitions would be too high, insofar as doing so would undermine the conception's usefulness, and in any case, that a plausible alternative account of the same intuitions can easily be supplied.

Not all the possible surprises concern what the arbitrary power conception excludes, however: at least some might concern what it includes. For example, it might have been our prior intuition that domination must always involve some sort of material disadvantage on the part of those subject to it. But, it turns out, this is not necessarily the case: a given slave under a particularly benevolent master might do very well for himself indeed, and nevertheless be subject to domination. This follows from our commitment to having a structure-based conception of domination. The alternative (an outcome-based conception) would lead us to believe that a slave becomes less and less subject to domination as he becomes better and better able to assess his master's psychological dispositions. This cannot be right. To have a master—good, bad, or indifferent—is to be subject to domination.

Having committed ourselves to a structure-based conception, however, it was perhaps surprising that we limited the set of dominating agents to the set of persons or groups directly holding arbitrary power over others. Why not also include those who have an indirect causal role in enabling domination, for example, through their participation in the maintenance of the basic structure of society? Expanding the conception to include such external enablers, I argued, would undermine the coherence of our conception, by including fundamentally distinct experiences under a single head. Apart from any descriptive fuzziness that might result (how significant an indirect causal contribution would a person or a group have to make to qualify as an agent of domination?), this would render our normative commitments toward domination harder to discern with precision. Since the moral position of external enablers is likely to be different from that of the actual agents of domination, it is far better to keep the two distinct.

As has been emphasized, this is not to suggest that external enablers bear no moral responsibility for the domination they indirectly support, any more than excluding rigorously legal systems of discrimination from our list of genuine instances of domination is meant to suggest that discrimination as such is not a bad thing. Since there are many bad things worthy of consideration, perhaps it would be helpful to mention what I see as the connection, if any, between some of them and the particular phenomenon of domination.

Apart from hegemony, discussed at length in this chapter, the term domination is most often associated with coercion, exploitation, and oppression. To coerce someone, I noted in Chapter 2, is to change what he or she would otherwise prefer to do by raising the costs associated with one or more of his or her options. For one person or group to have the ability to coerce another, in other words, is for the former to have a form of power over the latter. Coercion might thus constitute a basis for domination—indeed, it might be the most common such basis. Since social power comes in many forms, however, it is not the only possible basis. Exploitation (in the relevant sense) might be described loosely as the extraction of valued goods and services from a person or a group beyond what, in some sense, might reasonably be due. As will be discussed in Chapter 5, exploitation is a possible—and indeed likely—outcome in relations of domination. (It might also be the likely outcome of other, nondominating relations.)

Coercion and exploitation are thus, in some ways, narrower concepts than domination. Oppression, by contrast, is much broader. We might describe persons or groups as oppressed whenever their opportunities are reduced or restricted in some significant respect, especially by systematic institutional forces.[56] Domination would nearly always constitute oppression, so defined, as would nearly any system of discrimination. Insofar as people subject to domination find their opportunities restricted by external enablers who maintain the basic structure of society, we might plausibly say the former are oppressed by the latter (though they are *dominated* only by their particular masters). Even more broadly, we might describe people as being oppressed by abject circumstances, or by a heavy tax burden, and so on. In my view, the concept of oppression is probably too broad to be of much practical use in theories of moral or political philosophy: it covers problems having widely diverse origins, best addressed by distinct and sometimes competing strategies.[57] Others will naturally disagree, but defending my view on this score would take us

---

[56] Cf. the roughly similar definitions in Frye (1983, p. 4) and Young (1990, p. 38).

[57] This is evident from the discussion in Young (1990), for example. "Oppression" in her work seems to operate merely as an umbrella term for diverse sorts of systematic social harms: in her detailed analysis of those harms, the concept of oppression itself performs no real work.

far afield our main subject. The claim important to me, and defended in Part II, is that the concept of domination, at least, is very useful.

Not everyone, perhaps, will concede that the arbitrary power conception, as I have developed it here in Part I, is the best available conception of domination. Nevertheless, I take its meaning as settled in Part II. Once it is put to work in the context of a broader normative theory, I hope it is even more clear why this particular conception is so compelling.

Part II

Normative Analysis

5

Domination and Human Flourishing

Domination is a bad thing. It is terribly unjust if persons or groups are subject to avoidable domination, which is to say that anyone able to reduce such domination lies under a prima facie moral obligation to do so. These are strong claims that require explanation and justification. In this study, I have insisted on maintaining a strict separation between the descriptive and the normative aspects of a complete theory of domination. It follows that all the work of showing why we should regard non-domination as an important human good remains to be done. This chapter aims to undertake that task.

5.1 THE GOOD OF NON-DOMINATION

Why might there be a general obligation to reduce avoidable domination? Before attempting to answer this question, let me make a few stipulations. First, I regard the expressions "domination is bad" and "non-domination is good" as equivalent, and use them interchangeably. Second, I regard the expression "domination is bad" itself as a sort of shorthand, meaning roughly that all people lie under a prima facie moral obligation to reduce domination (their own, or anyone else's) whenever and wherever they can. Since, as we have seen, domination comes in degrees, we might add that this obligation is stronger when the domination in question is more severe. It follows from these stipulations that to show why we have compelling reasons to reduce domination is simply to show why non-domination should be regarded as an important human good, and vice versa.

The first stipulation probably requires no explanation, but the second might. Unfortunately, a complete discussion would take us too far afield, so I comment only briefly. In my view, the atomic units, so to speak, of moral and political philosophy are reasons for action. Moral facts, in other words, are facts about the valid reasons we have for doing or not doing certain things (and the conditions under which those reasons apply). Human beings are capable of doing things not only because they happen to *want* to do them, but also (at least sometimes) because they believe they have good or valid *reasons* for doing them. What we want to do and what we have good reasons to do will not always conflict. Even when they do, however, we often do things we do not want to do because we have (or believe we have) good reasons for doing them: we ingest medicine that tastes bad, for example, because it will make us better; we refrain from punching a jerk because it is wrong to resort to violence unnecessarily; and so on. The terms good and bad operate as shorthand for large bundles of reasons related to one another in some way. Rather than listing in detail the many reasons we have for acting in various ways under a variety of circumstances so as to promote health, for example, we simply say that "health is a good." Similarly, to say that non-domination is an important human good is just to say that there are many interrelated reasons for acting in diverse circumstances so as to reduce domination.

This does not, of course, constitute a defense of my assumptions.[1] I state them here only to reduce confusion in what follows.

5.1.1 The preference-based account

Most people, most of the time, strongly prefer not to be subject to domination; indeed, many people have accepted considerable costs so as to escape it—risking death, for example, to topple an autocratic government. This much is fairly obvious. Of course, not *all* people have this preference, and among those who do, not all have it to the same degree. Even supposing a person does have a strong preference for non-domination, it is nevertheless possible that he or she might (reluctantly) *choose* domination if the price of securing non-domination instead were simply too high. Still, it is safe to assume that a reasonably strong preference for non-domination is widespread.

If we are inclined to accept this empirical generalization, it might seem to follow that the reason we lie under an obligation to reduce avoidable domination is precisely the fact that so many people would prefer not to

---

[1] It is also, however, a view that others share, and (directly or indirectly) they have discussed it in much greater detail. See, among others, Kelsen (1967, chs. 1–3), Ross (1968), von Wright (1968), Raz (1999, chs. 1–4), Parfit (1984, 2002), and Schauer (1991).

experience it. All we would then need to prove our case once and for all, it might seem, is an empirical study definitively validating our assumed empirical generalization.

This is not my view. Of course, the fact that most people prefer non-domination might be taken as *evidence* that non-domination is a good, but it is not, in my view, what *makes* it a good. In order to explain why, we must first distinguish two different things one might mean in advancing the suggested argument.

On the one hand, one might believe there are no such things as moral facts (i.e., facts about the sorts of reasons we have for doing things), and that, in the absence of moral facts, the only thing we have to go on are the preferences that people actually happen to have. We need not spend much time dismissing this view. Suffice it to say that one cannot consistently believe that the fact that a person has a preference gives us a reason to satisfy that preference, if one does not believe there are such things as reasons to begin with. If there are no reasons, it does not matter what the facts are.

On the other hand, one might believe there are moral facts. In particular, one might believe that the empirical fact that a person has a preference *does* give us a valid reason, other things being equal, to satisfy that preference. Thus, on this view, we lie under some obligation to reduce domination because people generally prefer non-domination. Unlike the former sort of argument, this one is perfectly coherent; indeed, it amounts to a version of welfarism.[2] Nonetheless, it is not my view.

The main difficulty with welfarism is that people's preferences are adaptive and (at least sometimes) susceptible to manipulation.[3] People living under hardships—as, for example, under severe domination—may adapt their preferences to suit their limited circumstances. If the only reason we have for reducing domination is the fact that people would prefer not to experience it, then it follows that as this preference weakens or disappears, our obligation diminishes correspondingly. What is worse, it also follows that we should be indifferent (at least as a matter of principle) between reducing some group's

---

[2] The two arguments sketched here are often confused. This confusion is analogous to the even more common confusion of skepticism with egoism: skepticism is often thought to entail some sort of egoism, and egoism, in turn, is often though to rest on some sort of skepticism. In fact, egoism and skepticism are mutually exclusive: both cannot be true, although both can be (and, in my view, are) false.

[3] This is not, of course, the only problem with welfarism, but for our purposes it is decisive. The problem of preference adaptation has been discussed widely, but in this context, see especially Elster (1983b, ch. 4) and Millgram (2000).

domination, and brainwashing its members so they dislike their domination less. Either consequence is unacceptable.

The usual strategy for extricating welfarism from this objection is to insist that we rely only on what might be called *authentic preferences*—that is to say, not the preferences people actually happen to have, but rather the preferences they would have, if their preferences had developed under normal circumstances. Unfortunately, in order to recover these authentic preferences, we need a prior account of the ideal circumstances for preference development, and this inevitably turns out to be a non-welfarist account of the good. It is precisely *because* we support gender equality that we should discount the expressed preferences to the contrary of women in severely patriarchal societies; likewise it is *because* domination is bad that we should discount the expressed preferences to the contrary of people who are subject to severe domination.[4] Since working out a non-welfarist account of the good is a precondition of developing an acceptable welfarist account anyway, we might as well get on with it.

My argument for regarding non-domination as an important human good is not preference-based. This, of course, is consistent with believing that people generally prefer not to experience domination. Indeed, I do believe this, and I rely in various ways throughout this study on the assumption that it is generally true (the significance of possible exceptions is discussed later in this chapter). The point here is only that non-domination should not be regarded as a good *because* most people prefer it; on the contrary, most people prefer non-domination because it is, in fact, good.

5.1.2 Domination and human flourishing

Domination is bad because, given the sorts of creatures we are, it presents a serious obstacle to human flourishing. Put another way, enjoying some significant degree of non-domination is a crucial condition of human flourishing (along with health, education and care, sufficient material goods, cultural membership, and so on). For the moment, I only offer a list of reasons for believing this to be the case; by no means should this list be

---

[4] The most ambitious attempt to carry out this sort of welfarist program has been undertaken by Roemer (1993, 1996, 1998): he has developed a sophisticated model that controls for involuntary circumstances, so as to determine the degree to which a society has achieved equality of opportunity for welfare. But Roemer (1996, p. 279) has no method for determining what should count as an involuntary circumstance, except to say that it is "envisioned to be, for each society, a subject of political debate."

viewed as comprehensive.[5] Supposing my arguments are generally sound, and provided that we do indeed have reasons to promote human flourishing, it follows that we should aim to reduce domination when we can. This is what it means, on my view, to say that domination is bad. Note that, for the purposes of the argument here, I merely stipulate without further elaboration that human flourishing can roughly be understood as success in achieving autonomously formulated, reasonable life plans, through fellowship or community with others, over a complete life.[6]

[margin note: human flourishing pithy]

In what ways does domination present an obstacle to human flourishing? The direct material harms of domination are perhaps the most obvious: these are the actual injuries that result when one person or group wields arbitrary power over another. Typically, the agents of domination take advantage of their situation to coercively extract valued social goods from those subject to them: for example, slave masters extract productive labor from their slaves, members of the class of nobles extract feudal dues from members of the peasant class, husbands extract household and/or sexual services from their wives, and so on.[7] In a manner reminiscent of Marx, we might refer to this common feature of domination as *exploitation*. Insofar as they suffer exploitation, those subject to domination will find their success in carrying out their own life plans diminished. *[margin note: not a necessary condition]*

[margin note: also a facet of Young's oppression]

This, however, is only typically the case. Though the temptation to exploit others may often be difficult to resist, there will of course be some benevolent agents of domination who decline such opportunities. But it is important not to restrict the scope of exploitation to the valued social goods actively coerced from those suffering under domination. This is because, as we have seen, those subject to domination might frequently engage in strategic anticipation—surrendering valued social goods on their own initiative in the hopes of forestalling the unpleasant experience of active coercion. This might be termed *indirect*, as opposed to direct, exploitation. Indirect exploitation is possible because it is common knowledge that the agent of domination could choose to exercise her arbitrary power, even if, in fact,

---

[5] The discussion in this section follows in some respect that found in Pettit (1997, pp. 85–9). His first and third items correspond more or less to my second and third, respectively. His second (strategic deference) is incorporated by my first (exploitation). Comparison might also be made with Young (1990, pp. 48–63), whose first, fifth, and fourth "faces of oppression" correspond roughly with my first, second, and third items, respectively.

[6] This idea of human flourishing derives ultimately from Aristotle, but there are also many contemporary accounts: see, for example, Rasmussen (1999), Nussbaum (2000, ch. 1), and Pogge (2002, ch. 1).

[7] Patterson (1982, ch. 12), goes so far as to define slavery as in essence a form of "human parasitism."

she does not.[8] Relationships of domination are thus "infused by an element of personal terror," as James Scott writes, such that, even when the agent's powers are not exercised, "the ever-present knowledge that they might [be] seems to color the relationship as a whole."[9] (The tendency of those subject to domination to apparently conspire, as it were, in their own exploitation has often been observed.[10]) If this is correct, then it will turn out that the subjects even of benevolent masters will, to some extent, lead less flourishing lives than they might have otherwise.

In addition to the harms of exploitation, the subjects of domination are likely to suffer the additional harms of insecurity. So long as the agents of domination possess arbitrary social powers over their subjects, the latter will be severely restricted in their ability to autonomously formulate their own life plans. This is because it is obviously difficult, and at the extreme impossible, to plan in the face of uncertainty.[11] An ongoing sense of insecurity has both material and psychological consequences. On the one hand, insecurity necessitates precautionary measures. Ever concerned that they might face coercion, the subjects of domination must adopt a defensive posture—overcompensating and taking evasive measures against these dangers, hoarding goods as insurance, and lowering life expectations as required (this overcompensation effect is further analyzed in Appendix II). On the other hand, those subject to domination additionally suffer from psychological anxiety and a sort of paralytic sense of helplessness. At the extreme, this may result in complete resignation and social withdrawal: recognizing the improbability that even modest life plans will come to fruition, the victims of domination may give up the idea of formulating goals or aims for themselves at all.[12]

Finally, consider the impact of domination on self-respect. Relationships characterized by domination develop a distinctive symbolic or ritual structure in addition to their more "objective" structure of exploitation and uncertainty. The symbolic face of domination—which Scott refers to as the "public transcript"—involves rituals of respect, deference, and debasement on the part of the subject, and rituals of disrespect, dishonoring, and contempt on

---

[8] Of course, I assume here that relevant facts regarding arbitrary power and dependency are indeed common knowledge; in my view, these facts are bound to be revealed, intentionally or unintentionally, in any ongoing social relationship through the actions of its members.

[9] Scott (1990, p. 21). Pettit (1997, pp. 58–61, 70–2) emphasizes the common-knowledge aspect of domination.

[10] See, for example, Sidanius and Pratto (1999, ch. 9).

[11] Cf. Nozick (1974, pp. 65–71).

[12] For further discussion, see Adam (1978, pp. 54–7, 93–9). On insecurity and slavery in particular, see Douglass (1855, pp. 173–8) and Genovese (1974, pp. 637–48). On insecurity and totalitarianism, see Podgorecki (1996, esp. pp. 25–7).

the part of the agent.[13] The reason for this particular pattern may be obvious: on the one hand, the subjects of domination hope to secure lighter treatment through flattery; on the other hand, the agents of domination seek to rationalize their advantageous position (to themselves, at the very least). Whatever the causes, however, both aspects to the symbolic structure of domination tend to undermine the subjects' self-respect or sense of personal worth.[14]

At the milder end of the spectrum, we might consider the effects of the "courtier spirit" encouraged by absolutism: whereas "a king must be ador'd like a Demigod," according to John Milton, the citizens of a free commonwealth "are not elevated above thir brethren" and "may be spoken to freely, familiarly, friendly, without adoration."[15] Alexis de Tocqueville was concerned lest an unrestricted power of the majority might introduce something like the courtier spirit even in democratic republics.[16] This symbolic structure of deference on the one side and disrespect on the other suppresses free expression on the part of those subject to domination: consider, in this light, how Victorian society regarded quiet deference a virtue of women and of members of the lower classes. As domination becomes more severe, some subjects' habitual self-debasement may lead them to inflict psychological violence on themselves—to believe in their own lack of worth, if only in order to come to terms with their unhappy condition.[17] In relatively severe cases such as slavery, the fear of speaking incorrectly can produce stammering in those who suffer no true speech impediment.[18] And at the limit, we may find what is called the Stockholm syndrome, a phenomenon named after a group of hostages in Sweden who developed unexpected positive feelings for their captors.[19] This sort of personal debasement not only hampers a person's success in achieving his or her goals or aims, it also stands in the way of genuine fellowship or community with others, which at some level is predicated on a mutual recognition of personal worth.[20]

[13] Scott (1990, p. 2, *passim*).

[14] Contrary to Hegel (though he might be read less literally), the condition of slavery does not seem to have been very good for the self-respect of slaves, even if we as observers come to respect those who suffered under slavery: see Patterson (1982, pp. 10–13, ch. 3). More on this is explained in Section 5.2.

[15] Milton (1660, p. 120).

[16] Tocqueville (1835, I.15, pp. 266–8).

[17] Adam (1978, pp. 69–77, 83–9, 99–101), explores such self-destructive effects of domination. Cf. Memmi (1971, pp. 5, 10, 86) and Sidanius and Pratto (1999, ch. 4).

[18] Genovese (1974, pp. 646–7); Scott (1990, p. 30).

[19] For discussion, see Flynn (1989, pp. 100–7).

[20] Here we might recall Plato's adage, *Rep.*, 575e–576a, that friendship with tyrants is impossible. For further discussion of how persons or groups subject to domination are "discursively disenfranchised," see Pettit (2004, esp. pp. 89–93).

For these reasons, non-domination must be regarded as an important condition of human flourishing. To repeat what was said above, this list is not meant to be comprehensive; there may be further features of domination relevant to a more complete evaluation that could easily be added. (Possible additions might include the tendency of domination to atomize the members of subject groups and to encourage in-group hostility.[21]) The argument here is the empirical one that—given the sorts of creatures we are—the exploitation, insecurity, and undermined self-respect necessarily attending the experience of domination present serious obstacles to human flourishing. In generating these effects, notice that it is the subjective dependence of a person or a group that matters. Suppose that, from an external observer's point of view, no basic interest of mine depends on my remaining in a particular social relationship of domination; nevertheless, if I perceive exiting as costly for some reason, I will find myself beset by insecurity, compelled to engage in strategic anticipation, and unable to engage with the agent of my domination as an equal in moral worth. This reinforces a point made in Chapter 2. Similarly, in Chapter 4, we observed that social power is arbitrary unless it is externally constrained. Suppose that the agent of my domination happens to be a nice person and thus self-restrained in the exercise of his power over me; nevertheless, without the assurance of some external constraint, I will find myself bound to strive after his uncertain continued good favor, since we cannot help but regard others as free agents, always capable of acting against their usual dispositions.[22]

Although, as I have been arguing, the experience of domination always produces these deleterious effects, they are not themselves a part of the strictly descriptive definition of domination developed in Part I. We could, perhaps, imagine a possible world in which, the human condition being very different than it is, domination would not have these effects. In such a world, human beings could flourish even if subject to domination. That is not our world, however. Since, in our world, domination always inhibits human flourishing, we have strong reasons for reducing it whenever we can.

5.1.3 Intrinsic and instrumental goods

I have argued that enjoying some degree of non-domination is a condition of human flourishing, and therefore it ought to be regarded as an important

---

[21] See Adam (1978, pp. 55–6, 106–14) and Memmi (1971, p. 11). On American slavery in particular, see Genovese (1974, pp. 5–6), though he later presents some evidence to the contrary (Genovese, 1974, pp. 622–37).

[22] Strawson (1962).

good. My account is not, of course, complete. For one thing, non-domination is clearly not the *only* condition of human flourishing, and I make no effort here to spell out all the others (health, education and care, sufficient material goods, cultural membership, and so on). More importantly, while I have presented an argument to the effect that we should reduce domination because it is an obstacle to human flourishing, I have presented no argument to the effect that human flourishing itself is something we should aim to promote.

Is this a problem? In my view, it is not. In the empirical (natural or social) sciences, no one—no matter how comprehensive his or her project—aims to explain everything. Rather, one always attempts to explain the less familiar with reference to the more familiar. For example, social scientists might explain poorly understood events like social revolutions or economic growth by showing how they arise out of (purportedly) better-understood events like failed expectations or capital investment. Moral and political philosophers, analogously, attempt to show how less obvious reasons for action can be deduced from more obvious ones we are already inclined to accept.

Many people already have the strong intuition that domination is bad, and the remainder of this study is dedicated to showing what taking this intuition seriously would entail. To be sure, not everyone has this intuition, but then neither does everyone agree that capital investment is a less puzzling social phenomenon than economic growth. This does not undermine the value of either enterprise. I will have done enough if I can suggest how our reasons for reducing avoidable domination might in turn be derived from other, more primitive (and presumably less controversial) normative commitments most of us already share. Nearly everyone, I hope, is committed to the view that we have reasons to promote human flourishing, other things being equal.

One might ask where the chain of moral reasons ends. Must there be a "first reason" analogous to Aristotle's prime mover unmoved for the argument to get off the ground? Not necessarily. Just as progress in the social and natural sciences does not require agreement on what the first cause was, progress in moral and political philosophy does not depend on our establishing what the first reason is. The contrary view involves a misunderstanding of either enterprise.

Having clarified these points, I would like to address the question of whether we should regard non-domination as an intrinsic good or an instrumental good. Usually, what is meant by an *intrinsic good* is that its value is not based on or derived from the value of some other good. Now on my view, the term good is always shorthand for a bundle of reasons, and thus "intrinsic good" must mean a reason or set of reasons whose validity does not depend on the validity of some other reason or set of reasons. Since I have just dismissed the quest for a first reason as chimerical, obviously I do not regard non-domination as an intrinsic good in this sense.

But at the same time, to call non-domination an instrumental good might be misleading. There are at least two ways in which one might regard a good as instrumental. First, there is a weak sense in which a good might be called instrumental, insofar as its value is based on or derived from some other good. Non-domination is an instrumental good in this sense, because all goods are. But there is a second sense in which a good might be called instrumental, insofar as its value is limited or contingent on particular conditions being satisfied. Acetaminophen is instrumentally valuable as a means of reducing headaches and fevers, for example, but its value is limited and contingent. For one thing, when a person does not have a headache or a fever, acetaminophen loses its value for that person; for another, it is obviously not always better to have more acetaminophen rather than less: only the right amount of it is a good thing.

Non-domination is not an instrumental good in this second sense. Domination as such is always an obstacle to human flourishing, and it is always better to have more non-domination rather than less, other things being equal. It is, in other words, an example of what John Rawls calls a "primary good."[23] This is equivalent, on my view, to saying that we always have a prima facie reason for reducing domination when we can, and moreover that the more severe the domination in question, the greater is our obligation to reduce it. This claim might still seem too strong to be correct; later (in Sections 5.3 and 5.4), I defend it against the usual sorts of objections.

5.2 IS DOMINATION SELF-DEFEATING?

So far I have argued that we have strong reasons to reduce avoidable domination because it presents serious obstacles to human flourishing. In presenting this argument, I assumed it was the flourishing of those *subject* to domination that we should be concerned about. But some have argued that, in addition to its being bad for those subject to it, domination might also be bad for those wielding it. In a sense, then, domination might turn out to be self-defeating.

Perhaps the most famous argument along these lines can be found in the "lordship and bondage" sections of Hegel's *Phenomenology*.[24] He begins by

[23] Rawls (1971, pp. 62, 92). Pettit (1997, pp. 90–2), similarly argues that non-domination should be regarded as a primary good in Rawls's sense.

[24] Hegel (1807, §178–96, pp. 111–19). See also the useful discussions in Taylor (1975, pp. 152–7), Norman (1976, ch. 3), and Wartenberg (1990, pp. 121–6).

arguing that a person can attain complete self-consciousness of herself as an independent and autonomous being only through the recognition of others. This leads to a struggle for recognition—which struggle eventually resolves itself, upon the victory of one party or the other, into a lordship–bondage relationship. Self-recognition, on this view, is one of the important goods people hope to obtain by subjecting others to domination.[25] If this is correct, however, then domination may turn out to be self-defeating. This is because, by denying the subject of domination complete recognition as a human being, the agent thereby renders whatever recognition he receives in turn completely worthless; and at the same time, by putting the subject of domination to work in satisfying the desires of the agent, the latter thereby hands the former the very means of realizing her own self-consciousness as an independent and autonomous being, able to transform nature according to her own ends. Far from securing the desired good of recognition for the agent, domination in the end may supply this good to the subject instead.[26]

Other examples of the self-defeating argument can be found in the various antislavery writings of early American political thought. Thomas Jefferson's discussion more or less served as the model for later writers. His argument runs as follows: the institution of slavery, by its nature, demands "a perpetual exercise of the most boisterous passions, the most unremitting despotism on the one part, and degrading submissions on the other." Now imagine a (freeborn) child raised in an environment where the institution of slavery is widespread: clearly, we would expect the brutality of the master–slave relationship to leave a powerful impression. "The man must be a prodigy," writes Jefferson, "who can retain his manners and morals undepraved by such circumstances."[27] In the long run, then, domination inevitably inflicts severe moral harms on its agents, in addition to whatever harms it inflicts on its subjects. Exactly the same argument appears later, in Frederick Douglass: "The slaveholder, as well as the slave, is the victim of the slave system." This is because "man's character greatly takes its hue and shape from the form and color of things about him," and "there is no relation more unfavorable to the development of an honorable character than that sustained by the slaveholder

---

[25] This claim is given some support by Patterson, who argues that since slavery was often an economic burden on societies practicing it, it must be explained in part through the desire for goods like recognition: see Patterson (1982, esp. ch. 3).

[26] Patterson (1982, p. 99), points out what seems to me a potentially fatal mistake in this line of argument: if 1 enslaves 2, she may indeed receive no worthwhile recognition from 2, but what about from 3, a non-slave third party? Indeed, it may be precisely the point of primitive slavery, Patterson argues, for masters to secure honor in the eyes of one another (and *not* in the eyes of their slaves).

[27] Jefferson (1788, p. 214).

to the slave."[28] Analogous arguments along these lines can easily be found in other contexts. J. S. Mill, for example, points out much the same with respect to the domination suffered by women under traditional family law—that for the children of families characterized by inequality, "the family is a school of despotism," whereas it ought to be "the real school of the virtues of freedom."[29]

A third example of the self-defeating argument, again relating to the particular case of American slavery, receives extensive treatment in Tocqueville. Here the claim is that—apart from whatever moral harms accrue to the slaveholders—slavery as an institution, in the long run at least, is destructive to the economic well-being of those who practice it. The reasons for this are diverse and complicated, and Tocqueville runs through a number of them in the course of his discussion. The main support for his claim, however, comes from the indisputable empirical fact that after the Northern states abolished slavery, their economic growth outstripped that of the Southern states, which retained the institution.[30]

I sympathize with arguments of this sort. The possibility that domination turns out to be self-defeating on any of the above grounds is intriguing and counter-intuitive, and insofar as such arguments turn out to be useful in reducing domination, I would support them. Nevertheless, there are important grounds for caution.

To begin with, one might wonder whether the added value of such observations is worth the possible risks. Once we have shown that domination is bad for those subject to it, we have strong reasons for reducing it when we can, other things being equal. Perhaps the fact that domination is also sometimes bad for its agents gives us an additional (comparatively weaker) reason for reducing it, but of course if domination turns out to be on the whole good for its agents, surely this is no reason for changing our minds. It is unclear, therefore, what significant normative contribution the former observation would offer, even if correct. Domination is clearly bad for those who suffer under it, and establishing this fact should be enough.

Now one could always reply, as suggested above, that whereas it is not directly relevant whether domination is beneficial or harmful to its agents, nevertheless its effects on those agents might be instrumentally relevant in the

---

[28] Douglass (1855, p. 80).

[29] Mill (1869, p. 518).

[30] Tocqueville (1835, I.18, pp. 361–8). A nascent version of the same argument is made by Jefferson (1788, p. 215), who notes the deleterious impact of slavery on the work ethic of slave masters. It is, of course, disputable whether the abolition of slavery causally contributed to the North's economic growth; indeed, the North may have economically benefited from the retention of slavery in the South. We may leave such questions aside here, however.

struggle against it. If the self-defeating argument were correct, this might weaken possible countervailing reasons against reducing domination, and thus better motivate people in the effort to do so. There is a stronger and a weaker version of this view. On the stronger version, one might regard it as impossible to get people to do anything that cannot be shown to be in their self-interest overall.[31] In this case, it might prove essential for combating domination that we convince at least a few of its agents that they would be better off surrendering their arbitrary social powers. On the weaker version, one might regard the self-defeating argument as merely good rhetoric for softening the opposition.

Consider the stronger version of the instrumental claim first. Obviously, wielding arbitrary social power over others carries some costs and some benefits. Now either these overall costs outweigh the overall benefits, or else they do not. If they do not, then no agent would ever surrender his or her arbitrary social powers, because *ex hypothesi* no one would ever act against his or her own self-interest; but if the costs do outweigh the benefits, then it is a mystery why the agents ever assumed their arbitrary powers in the first place, for exactly the same reason. Only on the dubious assumption that the agents of domination are seriously confused about the costs and benefits of their situation would this argument seem to have utility.[32]

This leaves the weaker version of the instrumental claim, in which the self-defeating argument is employed simply as a rhetorical tactic for softening opposition to the struggle against domination. The problem here, of course, is that the tactic might backfire. Suppose we are debating whether or not some particular instance of domination should be reduced or eliminated. Raising the issue of whether domination is harmful or beneficial to those holding arbitrary power shifts the location of debate to inherently less favorable grounds. Moreover, it suggests if one *could* show domination was good for its agent, this would be a reason for *not* reducing or eliminating it. This is not the sort of argument we want to get into.

Part of the appeal of the self-defeating argument, I suspect, is the hope that one need only expose the internal contradictions of some unjust social institution for it to be overcome. This hope is dangerously naive. Social

[31] Tocqueville (1840, II.8, pp. 121–4) comments on the peculiar American habit of always trying to show that it is in a person's interests to do the right thing.

[32] Let me note two possible counter-arguments I would have to consider in a fuller discussion of this topic: first, that domination is on the whole beneficial to the agent at an earlier date, but then later becomes on the whole costly; second, that there might be a sort of prisoners' dilemma situation, in which it is individually advantageous but collectively disadvantageous for the members of a group (e.g., slave holders) to establish domination. Tocqueville, in my view, was making some version of the second of these points in discussing American slavery.

institutions rarely, if ever, collapse under the weight of their own logical contradictions.[33] (American slavery, certainly, did not.) One reason for this is that reforming unjust social institutions often requires overcoming substantial collective-action problems. It will often be hard work, and we should not be under any illusions as to this fact.

5.3 DOMINATION AND MORAL PLURALISM

Earlier I claimed we *always* have a prima facie reason for reducing domination when we can. This claim might seem too strong. In this section and in Section 5.4, I consider a number of examples that seem to contradict it. Some of these contradictions will turn out to be only apparent, resting on confusions that are easily dispensed with. Even genuinely contradictory examples, however, will be shown not to detract from the claim that non-domination should be regarded as a primary good—as something it is always better to have more of rather than less, other things being equal.

To organize the discussion, I loosely distinguish between two different sorts of possibly contradictory examples. The first involve cases where, so it is claimed, the value of non-domination is defeated by the value of some other good with which it comes into competition. The second involves cases where people apparently consent to their own domination, and it is wondered whether we should aim to reduce their domination regardless. This section considers the former and Section 5.4 the latter.

5.3.1 Moral monism and moral pluralism

It is always better to have more non-domination rather than less, other things being equal. But other things are not always equal. While non-domination is an important good, it is not the only good. This claim is an example of what is sometimes called *moral pluralism*. Before discussing the implications of moral pluralism for my argument, I would first like to make some general comments by way of clarification.

It is obvious that people value lots of different things to differing degrees. Historically, however, many philosophers and others have believed this diversity to be illusory. Why might they have thought so? Some have thought there is, in fact, only one truly valuable thing—salvation, say—and that other

---

[33] I am grateful to Patchen Markell for suggesting this turn of phrase.

things only falsely appear valuable. Others have thought that all the many different things people seem to value are, in fact, only valuable insofar as they instrumentally contribute to some single overarching good—happiness, say. Those holding a unified theory of the good of either sort are *moral monists*. While this was not always the case, moral monism is today the minority view. Most people now believe that there are many different valuable things, whose respective independent values cannot be reduced to a single overarching good. Moral pluralism is, in other words, now the majority view.

Moral pluralism comes in different varieties, however. For example, one might believe that, although there are many different valuable things, their value can be ranked and that this ranking is absolute. Thus, when one thing is more valuable (say, respecting individual rights), no amount of some other, less valuable thing (say, securing greater equality of opportunity), is worth even a slight loss in the first. When a set of options are equivalent with respect to the more valuable thing, however, the less valuable thing can act as a tie-breaker. This is called a lexical ranking or ordering of human goods. Moral pluralism combined with a strict lexical ordering of goods is really a sort of weak monism in disguise. If the lexical ordering is complete, then there will be one most valuable thing at the top that trumps all the others, and admitting other lesser goods in by way of breaking ties amounts to a minor concession. The early Stoics were strong monists, believing that the only valuable thing was virtue, and that all other things (wealth, health, family, etc.) were, strictly speaking, indifferent. Later Stoics realized that they could admit other goods as having secondary value in the lexical sense without having to greatly modify their overall system.

Two other forms of moral pluralism are not versions of monism in disguise. According to the first, there are many different and independently valuable things, and their relative value is simply incommensurable. This view might be called *strong moral pluralism,* and it can be contrasted with the view that, although there are many different and independently valuable things, these values can in principle be compared and reasonable trade-offs can be made among them. This latter view might be called *weak moral pluralism.* Note that weak moral pluralism is consistent with believing that some goods are more valuable than others: this only means that the more important goods should be given greater weight when it comes to making trade-offs. In other words, even if one good is (let us say) twice as important as another, it is still reasonable to trade 100 units of the first for 250 of the second.

Strong moral pluralism is implausible as a moral or political philosophy. It would commit us to some incredible and unacceptable beliefs. Suppose, for example, we thought liberty and equality to be incommensurable goods. That is to say, we might believe that there is no answer as to whether a substantial improvement in equality is worth a significant loss of liberty or vice versa. Given the complexity of many social and political problems, the appeal of this belief is understandable. But notice that, if taken literally, it commits us also to the view that there is no answer as to whether a substantial improvement in equality is worth a trivial—even imperceptible—loss of liberty (or vice versa). This cannot be right. Unfortunately, there is no way to avoid making choices that entail trade-offs among different values, and it would be irresponsible not to at least try to make those choices as reasonably as we can. To accept this responsibility is to concede that different goods *must* be compared with one another, and ergo that they are, at least in principle, comparable. The attractiveness of incommensurability stems, no doubt, from the fact that making these comparisons—which is to say, assigning relative weights to the many different and independently valuable things—can be very difficult, and sometimes can entail having to make agonizingly tragic choices. But denying that such choices can be made as a matter of principle is just burying one's head in the sand. It is the coward's way out.

This leaves us with weak moral pluralism. There are many different and independently valuable things, but their value can in principle be compared, and thus better and worse trade-offs can be made among them. Of course, reasonable people disagree as to how these trade-offs should be made, which is to say, as to what relative weights should be assigned to each of the many human goods. This is pluralism of a different sort—what, following Rawls, is generally called "reasonable pluralism." Reasonable pluralism arises from the fact that people hold differing conceptions of the good.[34] This is not unlike the sort of reasonable pluralism that exists among scientists who disagree as to the age of the universe, or the validity of string theory. Reasonable disagreement as such does not entail that there are not better and worse answers, only that we must learn to be content, for now, with different answers. Fortunately, reasonable disagreement of this sort is not all that difficult to live with, and indeed (as I will attempt to show in the following section and in Chapter 6), we can make do remarkably well without having to resolve that disagreement.

5.3.2 Trade-offs in non-domination

Non-domination is one good among others. It is, however, an especially important good, in the sense that it should be given considerable weight

---

[34] Rawls (1993, pp. 3–4, *passim*). Note that moral pluralism need not be a prerequisite of reasonable pluralism: two reasonable monists might hold differing unified conceptions of the good. Nor does moral pluralism entail reasonable pluralism: even if there are many different goods, reasonable pluralists might agree on their relative ranks or weights.

relative to many other goods. Even so, its value is not absolute. This means that, at a certain point, it will sometimes be reasonable to live with a certain amount of domination in order to obtain a lot more of some other valuable good. It is also the case, in my view, that the value of all goods, including non-domination, is generally subject to diminishing marginal returns. In other words, the first unit of non-domination is comparatively much more important or valuable than the last unit, much as $100 is more valuable to a starving man than it is to a millionaire. These observations can be summarized as in Figure 5.1.

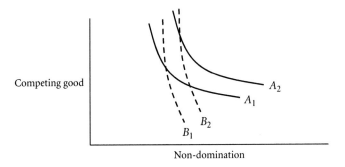

Figure 5.1

Here A_1 and A_2 represent indifference curves in the trade-off between non-domination and some other competing good. That is to say, we are indifferent between combinations or bundles of non-domination and the competing good when they fall on the same curve, but any combination on the curve A_2 is better than any combination on the curve A_1. The curves B_1 and B_2 capture the idea that non-domination should be given greater weight than the competing good—notice that large gains in the competing good are required to compensate for even small losses in non-domination.

Now, at last, let us consider some examples that apparently contradict my claim that we always have a prima facie reason for reducing domination when we can. Suppose there is a trade-off between non-domination and national security, and suppose that two societies have made different choices with respect to this trade-off: society *A* has opted for relatively more non-domination at the price of somewhat less national security, while society *B* has opted for relatively more national security at the price of somewhat less non-domination. First, observe that the fact that society *B* has opted for more national security does not demonstrate that it does not regard non-domination as a good. If it could enjoy greater non-domination for free (i.e., without any loss in national security), presumably it would. This is just what it means to say that we always have a reason to reduce domination, other things being equal. The difficulty is that other things are not equal: further reductions in domination would come at a price, and society *B* has opted not to pay that price. Second, observe that it does not even follow in this example that societies *A* and *B* disagree with respect to the relative value of non-domination; indeed, it might be that they place exactly the same weights on the two values. The difference in their choice might instead be due to differing circumstances: society *B* might face a more dangerous security environment than society *A*, from which it follows that the cost of reducing national security is greater for *B*. Faced with similar circumstances, society *A* might make an identical trade-off.

Analogously, women in the nineteenth century often accepted marriage, together with the domination it entailed, rather than face the severely limited prospects of "spinsterhood," given that these were the only two choices available to them. It does not follow that they necessarily valued their non-domination less than do women today, who benefit from broader opportunities. Or again, Andrea might choose to accept some domination at the hands of a harsh employer rather than refuse the job and starve, if these are the only choices she has; it does not follow from this that she values non-domination less than Bob, who, being well off, has a wider range of choices open to him. Many apparent differences of opinion regarding the value of non-domination can be explained simply with reference to differences in circumstances like these. And, naturally, these do not detract from the claim that it is always better to have more non-domination rather than less, other things being equal.

A slightly more complex case arises from the fact, mentioned earlier, of reasonable pluralism. So far I have assumed that people agree on the relative weights of different goods, but this is not always the case. Some people or groups will value non-domination relatively more or less than others. It follows from this that in at least some cases of identical circumstances, people or groups will make different choices. Given identical security environments, if society *A* happens to weight non-domination somewhat more heavily than society *B*, it will opt for a somewhat different balance between non-domination and national security. Nevertheless, this does not detract from the general claim. Even if society *B* values non-domination somewhat less than *A* does, it does not follow that it does not value it at all, or that it would not want to enjoy more non-domination rather than less, other things being equal. The only serious challenge to my claim is a person or group that genuinely does not value non-domination *at all*, or gives it such a small weight as to be inconsequential. Such cases are considered in Section 5.4.

5.3.3 Benevolent domination and similar cases

Are there situations in which domination might actually be a good thing? My claim is that there are not, but some have argued otherwise. This argument is most commonly presented through the example of a benevolent caregiving relationship. Parents clearly possess some degree of arbitrary power over their dependent children, and so it would seem that children suffer under some degree of domination as I have defined it. But surely, one might suppose, the parent–child relationship is (at least in most cases) an extremely valuable one. Isn't this sort of domination a good thing? More generally, one might argue that certain sorts of goods can be obtained only through the experience of suffering under domination: for example, the nearly absolute respect for authority required of a good soldier might be impossible to obtain except through the humiliating experience of basic training under the arbitrary power of a commanding officer. If these or other similar examples are sound, then it would seem that non-domination is not something a reasonable person would always want more of rather than less.

There are three possible responses to this observation. The first is to redefine domination so as to exclude such cases. Our revised conception might look something like this: persons or groups suffer under domination if and only if they are dependent on a social relationship in which some other person or group wields arbitrary power over them *contrary to the former's overall interests.* Since loving parents presumably wield arbitrary power over their children in their children's interests, this and similar cases would be handily excluded by definition, and the claim that we always have a reason to reduce domination so defined could be retained.[35] The second possible response is to retain the conception of domination roughly as developed in Part I, and instead weaken the claim that non-domination is something we would always want more of rather than less, other things being equal. We might then think of non-domination as an instrumental good in the stronger sense described in Section 5.1.3—as something that is good only under the right circumstances. Given the benefits of being raised under loving parental authority, such caregiving relationships are one of those circumstances in which we would not want more non-domination rather than less.[36]

Both of these first two responses should be emphatically rejected, on grounds that I will explain momentarily. Fortunately, however, neither is required. The alleged problem arises only due to an elementary

---

[35] This is more or less Wartenberg's strategy (1990, pp. 119–21), and also Friedman's (2008, pp. 253–6).

[36] Ferejohn (2001, p. 86), endorses this strategy.

conceptual error—what philosophers call confusing the part for the whole. It is undeniable, at least in the ordinary course of things, that parent–child relationships are extremely valuable on the whole. But it does not follow from this that they are valuable in each and every part. Their benefits stem from the value of intimacy, love and respect, personal warmth, particularized familiarity, etc., on the one hand, and from the disadvantages of raising children in any other fashion on the other. These benefits outweigh the costs in terms of the child's being subject to some degree of domination. It does not follow, however, that this domination is, as such, a good thing. On the contrary, if the benefits of parental care could be obtained without subjecting children to any domination at all, that would be better still. In other words, the case of benevolent domination is simply another instance of the need to make trade-offs among competing goods. The only real difference from the examples discussed in Section 5.3.2 is that, in this case, the competing goods are so closely entwined that it is easy to miss the fact that they are indeed distinct.

It should be clear now what the third and correct response is—namely, to reject the intuition that the domination of children under parental authority is a good thing, as such. The importance of adopting this position can be seen if we consider the general history of Western family law. Under the traditional view, children were regarded as the property of their parents, more or less to be dispensed with according to the wishes of the latter. The legal consequences of this view varied, of course. Under Roman law, a father theoretically held the power of life and death over his children. In Anglo-American common law, children were effectively regarded as family assets, to be exploited as their parents saw fit. And so on.[37] Gradually, however, this older view gave way to the modern idea that parents are merely the temporary trustees of their children's welfare during the period in which children cannot effectively care for themselves. In family law, this led to the gradual recognition of various rights on the part of children, and obligations on the part of parents, which are both common knowledge and (at least to some extent) publicly enforced both in law and convention.[38] According to the arbitrary power conception, this represents a reduction in parental domination.[39] Further-

---

[37] See Nicholas (1962, pp. 65–8) and Freeman (1983, pp. 14–15).

[38] See Mason (1994), for example, which describes this shift with respect to American culture and law.

[39] This view accords with Pettit (1997, pp. 61, 119–20), who suggests that in the absence of legally backed children's rights, even benevolent parental authority should count as dominating. This leads Ferejohn (2001, p. 82), to wonder whether moral education—of parents, of slave masters, etc.—might not reduce domination. In my view, it might. But this is simply because social norms, to the extent that they provide external, desire-independent reasons for observing a given rule, may count as social conventions (see Chapter 4), and thus reduce arbitrary power.

more, we would surely want to say that this change was a good thing, even if ✓
eliminating parental domination altogether is impossible. It might be impossible either because other goods like privacy or efficiency begin to take
priority at the margin; or because further reductions in the domination of
children cannot be had without introducing greater domination at the hands
of state agencies; or because of some combination of these, and other, considerations.

[margin note: sometimes the trade off for reducing dom. is not worth it]

   The belief that the introduction of children's rights was a good thing is best
captured by the claim that we always have a prima facie reason to reduce
domination if we can, which is to say that non-domination is always something we should want to have more of rather than less, other things being
equal. That we cannot have more non-domination in this instance without
accepting costs we are unwilling (for now) to accept is neither here nor there.
The first two responses would obscure this conclusion, and potentially blind
us to opportunities for reducing domination in the future.

[margin note: nondomination i'm though not necessarily 100%]

5.4 CONSENSUAL DOMINATION

Sometimes, people agree to suffer under domination. For example, migrant
laborers, who will inevitably find themselves exposed to the arbitrary power of
their employers in the United States and elsewhere, nevertheless volunteer to
work under such conditions. Traditional Anglo-American family law granted
husbands extensive arbitrary power over their wives, and yet millions of
women agreed to marriage. Whole societies have apparently embraced autocratic governments whose establishment might have been avoided (e.g., in
Weimar Germany, or perhaps in Russia today). And many cultures seem to
endorse the view that women should be strictly subordinate to men, children
to their parents, etc.—so much so that they would not want to abolish these
forms of domination, even if they had the opportunity. In this section,
I consider what we are to make of this fact. In particular, do we lie under an
obligation to try to reduce the domination of those who accept or endorse it?

[margin note: false choices?]

   Of course, people are often deliberately confused, misled, or intimidated
into accepting the condition of domination. According to one common view,
these cases should not count as genuine consent, and so they would not pose a
serious challenge to the claim that we should always aim to reduce domination when we can; the real issue arises only in cases of *genuinely consensual*
domination. If one held this view, it would be important to determine
the requirements and conditions of genuine consent, and this is something
that has proved notoriously difficult to do. As it happens, I believe we

should *always* aim, other things being equal, to reduce avoidable domination, whether it is consensual or not. It is thus not important for me to determine the conditions of genuine consent.[40] For the sake of argument, however, I assume that we have defined genuine consent, that there are at least some instances of domination answering to that definition (if not the examples suggested earlier, then others like them), and that we are discussing only such cases here. It would be unfair to defend my position with the assertion that domination cannot be consensual by definition, and I will not do so.

Should we, then, aim to reduce the domination even of those persons or groups who have, by assumption, genuinely consented to live under that domination? Broadly speaking, there are two quite different reasons a person or group might consent to domination. The first and more obvious reason is that they happen to have unusual preferences—that is to say, either they do not particularly dislike being subject to domination, or else they perhaps even enjoy it. Persons or groups with such preferences would happily agree to suffer under domination so as to obtain other goods, or perhaps even for its own sake. Such preferences are "unusual" in the sense of being strange, of course, only from the point of view of those (like myself) who have a strong preference for non-domination. As it happens, I believe they are also unusual in the sense of being statistically rare, but of course this is irrelevant from a philosophical point of view.

Not all cases of genuinely consensual domination, however, can be explained with reference to unusual preferences. This brings us to the second reason a person or group might consent to domination, namely, that they happen to face a dismal choice scenario in which they must choose between domination and other alternatives they consider even worse. As important as avoiding domination is to many people, it is not the only important thing. Even perfectly reasonable people with the usual sorts of strong preferences for non-domination will choose to suffer domination rather than starve, for instance. Given the limited options open to women before the twentieth century, it is perfectly understandable that nearly all chose marriage—even though this entailed accepting some degree of domination. In exceptional circumstances, societies as a whole might also face dismal choice scenarios. Faced with the prospect of defeat and conquest by a brutal enemy, societies might accept nearly any burden—including subjecting themselves to extensive government or military domination. A lack of acceptable alternatives is, I think, the most common explanation of consensual domination.[41]

---

[40] Except, perhaps, as a matter of law or policy. But that is a different story, beyond the scope of this discussion.

[41] People can be misled into believing their choice scenarios are worse than, objectively speaking, they really are. Given what they believe their options are, such people might then reasonably choose domination. It is sometimes erroneously inferred from this choice, however, that they have unusual preferences. This does not follow; to choose domination because I (mistakenly) believe the alternatives are even worse is not to desire domination for its own sake.

In a few cases, these two explanations might overlap. Persons or groups facing (what are commonly thought to be) dismal choice scenarios might happen to have unusual preferences, in which case they would not regard those choice scenarios as particularly dismal. This means that there will be a third possibility to consider.

Let us first consider the case of persons or groups with usual preferences, who face dismal choice scenarios. Should we aim to reduce their domination? Obviously, we should. That this does not always seem obvious is only due to the (unwarranted) assumption that aiming to reduce their domination must mean interfering with their choices—in particular, prohibiting those choices that would entail their subjecting themselves to domination. It is natural to want to respect the choices that people make. It would seem unfair and disrespectful to interfere with the choices of people who, after all, are only trying to do the best they can for themselves under difficult circumstances. Indeed, not permitting people to do the best they can for themselves under difficult circumstances adds insult to injury. I agree with this sentiment. We should not restrict the choices of persons or groups who face dismal choice scenarios (except perhaps in a few cases, as a matter of policy, if necessary to prevent fraud and intimidation). But aiming to reduce their domination does not require that we do this. On the contrary, it is far more likely that we will succeed in reducing their domination if we improve the choice scenarios they face. Given better options, people with usual sorts of preferences will likely not opt for domination, and the overall domination suffered will thereby be reduced. We should try to do this. The reason we should is because non-domination is an important human good that it is always better to have more of rather than less. To argue that we have no good reason to provide a person with the new options *C*, *D*, and *E* simply because among options *A* and *B* she happened to choose *B* is perfectly *non sequitur*.

In subsequent chapters, I discuss some ways in which we might try to improve people's choice scenarios so as to reduce their domination. The important point here is that my main claim stands—that we always have a reason to reduce domination if we can, other things being equal.

But what if the persons or groups facing these dismal choice scenarios happen to have unusual preferences, such that they endorse their own domination? This is the third possibility mentioned earlier. Should we aim to reduce their domination? Again, at least provided that our strategy is to expand their options rather than restrict them, the answer is clearly yes. If they genuinely prefer domination, providing additional options will not at any rate do them any harm. But there are also several strong positive considerations in favor of improving their options, regardless of their expressed preferences.

The first is that the preferences of others can be difficult to interpret. This is particularly so across cultures: what appears to be consensual domination from the point of view of our culture might turn out not to be on closer inspection or from a different perspective. While it is my view that there is always a fact of the matter with respect to domination, it is also my view that cross-cultural observation can be a tricky business. It would be a dangerous mistake to decline to improve the opportunities of women in severely patriarchal societies, for example, merely because that society's culture appears (to us) to endorse patriarchal domination. This leads to a second consideration, which again arises in the case of cultures that apparently endorse domination. It is all too easy in such cases to commit a fallacy of composition—in other words, to take the preferences of a society as a whole to stand for the preferences of each and every one of its members. Consent to domination cannot be given by proxy. It is only persons' or groups' preference for being subject to domination *themselves* that is relevant (if anything is). That some people (men, say) historically or today might prefer that some other group (women, say) be subject to domination is irrelevant. Of course, it is always possible that with sufficient care we might avoid such dangers in interpreting consent. This brings us to a third and final consideration, which applies equally well to individuals and groups, and is by itself decisive, even when we are confident we have the facts about expressed preferences right. This is the problem discussed in Section 5.1.1 that persons and groups often adapt their preferences to suit their circumstances. Imagine that one group successfully subjects another to domination, and that the latter subsequently adapts its preferences to match its new situation. Those adapted preferences cannot now be taken as justification for perpetuating that domination. At most, they can provide pragmatic reasons for not forcing people into non-domination before they are psychologically ready. But of course I do not propose that we do this. Rather, I only suggest that our obligation to reduce avoidable domination entails that we try to improve their opportunities so that they might (gradually, perhaps) begin to choose non-domination for themselves. That they do not presently desire non-domination is not, it seems to me, a reason for refusing to give them the choice.

One case remains. Suppose we have improved opportunities such that a person or group no longer faces a dismal choice scenario. If the relevant persons have, or will eventually develop, the usual sort of strong preferences for non-domination, they will then by assumption choose to avoid domination, and our job will be done. What remains, then, are those cases of bona fide dissent—cases in which persons or groups remain committed to their unusual preferences, despite having a full range of opportunities not involving domination. Once we have screened out confusions due to the difficulties of cultural interpretation, situations where the preferences of one group are being taken as proxy for the consent of another (men for women, parents for children, etc.); and of course fraud or intimidation; the number of genuine examples remaining will be, I believe, quite small. I do not mean, of course, to deny their existence altogether, only to point out there are many fewer instances than might initially be thought.[42] But this does not answer the question: Should we continue to aim to reduce domination even in such cases? Other things being equal, we should. When subject to domination, human lives are less flourishing than they might otherwise be, whether a particular person recognizes this fact or not.

Of course, we must always consider what, pragmatically speaking, would be the best method for reducing domination. Direct coercion is hardly ever the most effective method: education is, usually, a far more desirable strategy, and Chapters 6 and 7 consider other strategies as well. And, of course, we must also consider the costs. Domination is not the only thing that detracts from human flourishing, and it might well be that we cannot eliminate the last degree of domination except at a cost (in terms of personal autonomy, perhaps) we are not prepared to accept. But these are pragmatic considerations. They do not detract from the main claim, which is that we should always aim to reduce domination if we can, other things being equal.[43]

5.5 ADDENDUM: NON-DOMINATION AND POLITICAL LIBERTY

Non-domination and political liberty seem related to one another. Contemporary civic republicans, in particular, have argued that political liberty should simply be defined as non-domination. Without reviewing the extensive literature on political liberty in detail, this section considers a few reasons for regarding this identification as both plausible and potentially appealing.

---

[42] As it happens, I cannot think of any clear examples. S/M practices do not constitute domination because they do not involve dependency (using "safe words" one can always exit, and so on). I recognize, however, that this does not mean bona fide dissent could not exist.

[43] I do not mean to reject toleration as a (non-instrumental) value altogether. But no plausible theory of moral or political philosophy can tolerate *everything*, and my only claim is that domination is one of the (perhaps few) things we should not tolerate. Toleration and cultural accommodation are discussed further in Chapter 7.

5.5.1 Positive and negative liberty

It is notorious that there are several competing conceptions of political liberty. The now standard account was laid down most influentially by Isaiah Berlin in his famous lecture, "Two Concepts of Liberty."[44] According to the first, *negative* conception, people are free simply to the extent that their choices are not interfered with. There are many variations on this conception, depending on how exactly one wants to define the term "interference," but they all have in common the basic intuition that to be free is, more or less, to be left alone to do whatever one chooses. This idea of negative liberty Berlin associates especially with the classic English political philosophers Hobbes, Bentham, and J. S. Mill, and today it is probably the dominant conception of liberty, particularly among contemporary Anglo-American philosophers. In Mill's well-known words, "the only freedom which deserves the name, is that of pursuing our own good in our own way, so long as we do not attempt to deprive others of theirs."[45]

The second, *positive* conception of liberty, is not quite so easy to define. Roughly speaking, persons or groups are free in the positive sense to the extent that they exercise self-control or self-mastery. It is not agreed, however, what exactly constitutes self-mastery in the relevant sense. According to one particularly influential account, to be free in the positive sense is to be able to act on one's second-order desires.[46] For example, the addicted gambler may be free in the negative sense not to gamble—since no one actually forces him to do so—but he is not free in the positive sense unless he can actually succeed in acting on his (presumed) second-order desire not to desire gambling. To be "driven by appetite alone is slavery," one might say, whereas "obedience to the law one has prescribed for oneself is liberty."[47] Berlin associates this second conception especially with such continental philosophers as Spinoza, Rousseau, and Hegel; although it also found some support among English Hegelians like T. H. Green, those who advocate the positive conception of liberty have generally been in the minority among contemporary Anglo-American philosophers.

The troubling implications of the positive conception of liberty are well known, and need not be rehearsed here. For the most part, they stem from the problem that freedom in the positive sense would seem to sanction fairly extensive coercion on behalf of individuals' allegedly "real interests"—for

---

[44] Berlin (1969).
[45] Mill (1859, p. 17).
[46] Frankfurt (1971).
[47] This famous expression is from Rousseau (1672, I.8.3, p. 151).

example, coercively forcing the gambler to quit on the presumption that this *that's not* is what he *really* wants to do (even if he does not say so). Regarding this *self-deter-* danger, Berlin writes: *mination*

> It is one thing to say that I may be coerced for my own good which I am too blind to see: this may, on occasion, be for my benefit.... [But] it is another to say that if it is my good, then I am not being coerced, for I have willed it, whether I know this or not, and am free (or "truly" free) even when my poor earthly body and foolish mind bitterly reject it, and struggle against those who seek however benevolently to impose it.[48]

Liberals like Berlin have thus understandably rejected the positive—and emphatically embraced the negative—conception of liberty. The question remains whether the received view of negative liberty as non-interference adequately captures the political ideal we should be most committed to. Contemporary civic republicans argue that it does not.

Consider the following scenarios; both are standard examples in the republican literature. In the first, imagine a group of slaves with a generally well-meaning master. While the latter has an institutionally protected right to treat his slaves more or less as he pleases (he might start whipping them just for the heck of it, say), let us suppose that this master in particular leaves his slaves for the most part alone. Now to the extent that he does not in fact interfere with his slaves on a day-to-day basis, we are committed to saying—on the non-interference view of liberty—that they enjoy some measure of freedom. Some find this conclusion deeply counter-intuitive: if there is anything to the idea of political liberty, one might think, surely it cannot be found in the condition of slavery!

Even if we are willing to accept this conclusion, the non-interference view of liberty commits us to others that are perhaps even more paradoxical. For one thing, notice that we are committed to saying that the slaves of our well-meaning master enjoy *greater* freedom than the slaves of an abusive master down the road. Of course, the former slaves are better off in some respect than the latter, but do we really want to say that they are *more free*? In the words of a seventeenth-century English republican:

> The weight of chains, number of stripes, hardness of labour, and other effects of a master's cruelty, may make one servitude more miserable than another: but he is a slave who serves the best and gentlest man in the world, as well as he who serves the worst.... For this reason the poet ingeniously flattering a good emperor, said, that liberty was not more

---

[48] Berlin (1969, p. 134).

desirable, than to serve a gentle master; but still acknowledged that it was a service, distinct from, and contrary to liberty.[49]

Or consider the slave who, over time, comes to understand his master's psychological dispositions better and better. Taking advantage of this improved insight, he manages to keep on his master's good side and is, consequently, interfered with less and less: thus, on the non-interference view of liberty, we are committed to say that his freedom is increasing over time. Again, while it is clear that the slave's greater psychological insight improves his own well-being in some respect, do we really want to say that it increases his *freedom* specifically?

Now consider a second scenario. Imagine the colony of a great imperial power. Suppose that the colonial subjects have no political rights, and thus that the imperial power governs them unilaterally. But further suppose that the imperial power, for one reason or another, chooses not to exercise the full measure of its authority—that its policy toward the colony is one of more or less benign neglect. From the point of view of liberty as non-interference, we must conclude that the colonial subjects enjoy considerable freedom with respect to their government for, on a day-to-day basis, their government hardly ever interferes with them. Next suppose that the colonial subjects revolt successfully, and achieve political independence. The former colony is now self-governing. We may imagine, however, that the new government is somewhat more active than its imperial predecessor, passing laws and instituting policies that interfere with people's lives to a greater extent than formerly was the case. On the view of liberty as non-interference, we must say that there has been a *decline* in freedom with independence.[50] As in the first scenario, many find this counter-intuitive. Surely, a nation that has gained independence must have *increased* its political liberty.

5.5.2 Republican liberty

What these examples are driving at is that political liberty might better be understood as a sort of structural relationship that exists between persons or groups, rather than as a contingent outcome of that relationship. Whether a

[49] Sidney (1698, III.21, p. 441). Algernon Sidney (a favorite of Thomas Jefferson and others) was once widely known as a republican martyr, having been executed for treason by King Charles II of England in 1683; he fell into obscurity in the nineteenth century.

[50] Berlin (1969, pp. 129–30), is quite explicit on this point: negative liberty "is not incompatible with some kinds of autocracy, or at any rate with the absence of self-government" and "is not, at any rate logically, connected with democracy."

master chooses to whip his slave on any given day, we might say, is a contingent outcome; what is not contingent (or at least not in the same way) is the broader configuration of laws, institutions, and norms that effectively allows him to do so or not as he pleases. Contemporary civic republicans aim to capture this insight as directly as possible by defining liberty as the absence of domination.[51] Note that this is, at least in the broad sense, a negative conception of political liberty. One need not do or become anything in particular to enjoy political liberty in the republican sense: one need not exercise self-mastery, on any view of what that entails, nor succeed in acting on one's second-order desires. Republican freedom merely requires the absence of something—namely, dependence on arbitrary power or domination. It is a less demanding ideal than full-fledged autonomy, for example, which requires not only an absence of domination, but also sufficiently developed capacities for critical reflection and perhaps other things as well.[52]

Despite some broad similarities, however, republican freedom is not equivalent to the received view of negative liberty as non-interference. In contrast to the non-interference view, republican freedom easily accounts for our intuitions in the two scenarios described earlier. The slave lacks freedom because he is vulnerable to the arbitrary power of his master, whether his master happens to exercise that power or not. Likewise, what matters with respect to political freedom on the republican view is not *how much* an imperial power chooses to govern its colony, but the fact that the former may choose to govern the latter as much and however it likes.

Moreover, the republican conception captures in a more intuitively satisfying way what would improve either situation with respect to political liberty. Most people are not inclined to say that slaves enjoy increasing freedom just because, with experience, they improve their insight into their masters' psychological dispositions. But many *would* be inclined to say that their freedom is enhanced, other things being equal, if some effective reform in the laws, institutions, or norms sharply regulates their masters' authority over them. This is not necessarily to say that the slaves enjoy greater well-being, all things considered—only that, because their domination is lessened, they enjoy greater freedom to that extent. And of course, no matter how benevolent their particular masters happen to be, slaves cannot be completely free until

---

[51] See especially Skinner (1984, 1991, 1998), Pettit (1989, 1996, 1997, 2001, esp. chs. 6–7, 2004), Spitz (1995), Viroli (2002), Maynor (2003), and Lovett (2005). Note that a large part of the contemporary civic republican scholarly agenda has been to show that the classical republicans (Machiavelli, Harrington, Milton, Sidney, etc.) held something like this conception of political liberty as non-domination. See also Appendix I.

[52] In my expression, the goods of non-domination, health, education, and so forth are *conditions* of human flourishing, whereas autonomy is a *component* of human flourishing.

the institution of slavery itself is abolished. Political freedom, in other words, is the upshot of rightly ordered laws, institutions, and norms, and thus only changes in how those laws, institutions, and norms effectively structure the relationships existing among the various persons and groups in a community can affect the level or degree of freedom they enjoy.

One final advantage of the republican view should be mentioned here. On the view of negative liberty as non-interference, any sort of public law or policy intervention counts by definition as an interference and, ergo, a reduction in freedom. Being committed to the received view of negative liberty, liberals thus tend to be overly hostile to government action. On the republican view of political liberty, by contrast, public laws or policy interventions need not necessarily count as reductions in freedom. Provided that a law or policy is adopted and implemented in an appropriately non-arbitrary manner, the freedom of the citizens can remain relatively untouched. Indeed, if the law or policy ameliorates dependency or curtails the arbitrary powers some exercise over others in a given community, the freedom of citizens may be enhanced. In the classical tradition, this idea was often expressed as Blackstone, for example, puts it: "laws, when prudently framed, are by no means subversive but rather introductive of liberty" and thus "where there is no law, there is no freedom."[53]

Obviously, I am sympathetic with the republican conception of freedom. In Chapter 6, I argue that we should understand social justice as minimizing domination, and if we accept the republican conception of freedom, we can describe justice as the advancement of freedom—an idea that is both conceptually elegant and rhetorically compelling. However, the arguments in this study do not, for the most part, hinge on our accepting this view, which in any case I have not fully defended here. So long as one accepts the claims that non-domination is an important condition of human flourishing, and that we always lie under a prima facie obligation to reduce domination when we can, the aims of this chapter will have been met.

---

[53] Blackstone (1765, I.1.12, p. 122).

6

Domination and Justice

Chapter 5 made the case for regarding non-domination as an important human good—which is to say, for believing that we all lie under a prima facie obligation to reduce domination whenever we can, other things being equal. This chapter has two aims: the first is to sketch a conception of social justice that builds on the claims of Chapter 5; the second is to contrast this theory with several leading competitors, and argue for its comparative merits.

6.1 THE SCOPE OF SOCIAL JUSTICE

Justice is a broad idea. In different contexts, the expressions "just" or "unjust" can describe individual actions or lines of conduct, the character or disposition of a person, a distribution of goods, the operation of a law or policy, a scheme of government, the behavior of different governments toward one another, and more.

It is natural, perhaps, to believe this is not merely an accident—that the best account of justice would be one directly applicable in all these diverse uses of the term. Plato, for example, held something like this view: it is important, on his account, that we find a person just on the same grounds that we find political institutions just. But why must this be? Perhaps the word "justice" is simply a homonym. Or more likely, even if there is some connection between the various uses of the word, perhaps the role of the concept of justice nevertheless varies according to the context. In my view, there are no good a priori grounds for rejecting an otherwise apparently sound account of social justice, say, merely because that account cannot serve equally well in all other contexts. (To the extent that it can, of course, so much the better.) With this caveat in mind, the discussion in this chapter focuses on the question of social justice specifically.

The subject of a conception of social justice is the basic structure of an independent and ongoing society. This idea obviously derives from John Rawls.[1] Let us say that the basic structure of a society (as discussed in Chapter 2) consists of the complete set of political and social institutions and practices that constitute the relatively stable background conditions or expectations against which the members of that society live out their lives. This includes, but is not limited to, what people ordinarily think of as political institutions in the narrow sense (the form of government and the system of laws); it also includes, for example, the mode of economic production, the configuration of many public policies, significant social norms and conventions, and so on. Since the basic structure of a society will often have a substantial impact on how well or badly the lives of its members tend to go in the long run, its organization will obviously be a matter of great importance. A conception of social justice, then, is simply an account of what sort of basic structure would be best, from the point of view of justice. To say that a basic structure is best from the point of view of justice is to say, very roughly, that in respecting and upholding its institutions and practices in the process of living out their lives, people would, in the traditional expression, be giving each their due.[2]

Put another (and perhaps more useful) way, a conception of social justice provides, for some independent and ongoing society, a principle or set of principles for rank ordering feasible basic structures, from the most to the least just. Must this ordering be the same for all societies, regardless of their background cultures and historical circumstances? This is a complicated question, and different theories of social justice give different answers. It is important, however, not to confuse this question with another only apparently similar one: namely, whether the set of *feasible* basic structures is the same for all societies, regardless of circumstances. Since the answer to the second question is almost certainly *no*, it follows that the most just feasible basic structure will not necessarily be the same for all societies. But since a rank ordering over both feasible and infeasible basic structures might nevertheless be universal, this helps little with respect to answering the first question. In this study, I ignore this problem by assuming (unless otherwise noted) that we are talking about societies roughly like our own—that is, societies that are large; reasonably well developed and prosperous; and

---

[1] Rawls (1971, esp. pp. 3–11, 54–8, 84, 1993, pp. 257–88). See also Pogge (1989, ch. 1) and Scheffler (2006).

[2] We may take "giving each their due" to represent the *concept* of justice, whereas a *conception* of social justice is a construction or interpretation of that concept specifically as it applies to the basic structure of an independent and ongoing society. For the distinction between concepts and conceptions, see Chapter 2.

racially, ethnically, and culturally diverse. We can always return to the question of universality down the road, once our conception is better developed.

Social justice is a broad topic, but a theory of social justice is neither a complete moral philosophy, nor even a complete theory of justice if the latter is taken to include all the contexts in which our use of that concept might be considered appropriate. The assumption that we are discussing more or less independent and ongoing societies, for example, excludes the topics of global and transitional justice; and the focus on the basic structure of society excludes the topic of direct interpersonal justice. The conception of social justice sketched in this chapter may or may not be directly applicable to these broader topics. While some issues related to the topics of interpersonal, transitional, and global justice are discussed briefly at the end of Chapter 7, the argument for my preferred conception of social justice should not be seen as hinging on how such extensions turn out.

Social justice is, perhaps, the most distinctive virtue of basic structures, but it is worth emphasizing that it is not the only such virtue. Justice is not the only thing that matters. Basic structures might be more or less efficient in terms of their productivity and rates of economic growth, for example. Since, other things being equal, a more efficient basic structure is presumably better than a less efficient one, efficiency might also be considered a virtue of (though not distinctive to) basic structures. Unfortunately, justice, efficiency, and other applicable virtues do not necessarily run together, and thus we will have to make difficult trade-offs when they conflict. I return to this important point at the end of this chapter.

6.2 JUSTICE AS MINIMIZING DOMINATION

Suppose, following the argument in Chapter 5, that we regard freedom from domination as a particularly important human good. What might this entail with respect to the justice or injustice of the basic structure of a society? One especially direct way to answer this question is simply to define social justice as the minimization of domination. Stated more formally:

> (JMD) Societies are just to the extent that their basic structure is organized so as to minimize the expected sum total domination experienced by their members, counting the domination of each member equally.[3]

---

[3] Note the use of the term "expected" here: it is assumed that in cases of uncertainty, we are to employ the standard tools of probability calculus in deciding among the various options.

This is not, as we shall see, the only way one might build a conception of social justice on the value of non-domination for human flourishing. But, from a certain point of view, it is the simplest and the most obvious: if domination is bad, it seems only natural that we should want there to be as little of it as possible. From the point of view of social justice, this seems to entail designing the basic structure of a society in such a way as to minimize domination. As it turns out, things are not so simple, and much of this chapter will be devoted to ironing out the various complications. But in terms of capturing the basic idea, the principle as stated earlier is not far off, and indeed, in many cases, it will suffice as an adequate account of social justice.

Before considering arguments for and against justice as minimizing domination (JMD), it is worth first clarifying what sort of conception of social justice it is. Obviously, it is similar in structure to utilitarianism, with the important difference that non-domination has taken the place of happiness as the object of maximization. It follows from this substitution that JMD is not a welfarist theory: whereas utilitarianism directs us to maximize the sum total happiness (generally understood as the satisfaction of preferences), JMD directs us to minimize domination as such, whether people happen to prefer this or not. On the assumption that most people strongly prefer not being subject to domination, lowering the sum total domination will often incidentally raise the sum total happiness, but this is neither the aim nor the justification of the theory. Aside from this, however, the parallel with utilitarianism is fairly strong, and perhaps instructive to examine in further detail.

6.2.1 The comparison with utilitarianism

In practical or ethical philosophy, it is common to distinguish conceptions of the good from conceptions of the right. A conception of the good is, roughly speaking, an account of what makes a human life go better or worse; a complete theory of the good would thus be a complete account of human flourishing. By contrast, a conception of the right is roughly an account of morality—that is, an account of right and wrong, or of what human beings owe to one another in their capacity as morally responsible agents.[4] Theories

---

[4] Note that this does not conflict with what I asserted in Chapter 5, that the term "good" is a shorthand for a bundle of interrelated reasons for doing certain things. To say that health is good, for example, is to say that we have a bundle of interrelated reasons to promote health, other things being equal; this would be one part of a complete account of human flourishing. But this does not tell us, for example, whether we should promote aggregate health or equal health, to what extent individuals should be held responsible for their own health, and so on; all this belongs to a conception of the right.

of social justice are, strictly speaking, a part of the latter. Nevertheless, the good and the right are connected ideas, and thus it is common to characterize theories of social justice according to the various assumptions about this connection they build on.

Some theories of social justice start from the assumption that the right derives its justification independent of any particular conception of the good, and thus that the former has a certain sort of priority over the latter—that the right limits or constrains the acceptable conceptions of the good, perhaps. These sorts of theories are generally called *deontological* theories. Rawls's theory of justice as fairness is a clear example. By contrast, other theories of social justice start from the contrary assumption that the right derives its justification from some independently established conception of the good, and thus that the latter has a certain sort of priority over the former. These are generally called *teleological* theories. Among the latter, some theories specifically define social justice as the maximization of some independently established good (or, equivalently, as the minimization of some independently established bad), and so they might be called *strictly teleological*. Other teleological theories might define the right as the honoring of an independently established good in some way other than by maximizing it.[5] Both JMD and utilitarianism are strictly teleological theories of social justice: both start with an independently established good (non-domination and welfare, respectively), and define social justice as its maximization.

Theories of social justice also make assumptions about how a complete conception of the good itself ought to be specified. One might, for example, assume that there is a single sort of human life that is best or most excellent for everyone: theories based on this assumption are generally called *perfectionist* theories. Two examples frequently discussed in the contemporary literature are civic humanism and liberal perfectionism. According to civic humanism, the best human life is one of active citizenship and civic virtue in a broadly democratic community; according to liberal perfectionism, the best human life is one based on autonomous self-reflection.[6] Traditional Stoic and Christian theories are also perfectionist, insofar as they are based on a conception of human excellence as a moral or religious virtue. Indeed, historically speaking, perfectionism has more or less been the norm. Many

---

[5] The "ethical liberalism" developed in Dworkin (1990, 2000) might be an example. Note that the converse hybrid is also possible: Nozick (1974, pp. 28–35) contemplates (but rejects) a right-maximizing theory according to which we ought to minimize the sum total rights violations.

[6] The former is commonly associated with Arendt (1958, 1990, 1993), Rahe (1992), and Pocock (1975), among others; the latter with Raz (1986, 1994) and others. Recall from Chapter 5 that the ideal of autonomy is considerably more demanding than the ideal of freedom from domination.

contemporary theories, however, are not perfectionist: that is, they are to some extent agnostic toward differing conceptions of the good, at least as a matter of principle.[7] Such theories are variously described as neutral, impartial, or anti-perfectionist, though each of these terms can be seriously misleading. This is because perfect neutrality or impartiality toward all possible conceptions of the good is impossible to achieve, and in any case, it is not always (or even often) the direct aim of such theories. A more appropriate, if less elegant, term might simply be *non-perfectionist*.

These two issues are sometimes confused with each other. For example, it is frequently assumed that perfectionist theories are necessarily teleological (indeed, Rawls himself apparently assumed this).[8] This is an easy mistake to make, for it is natural to assume that if a theory holds one sort of human life to be the most excellent for all, then it must also define the right as the promoting or the honoring of this particular excellence. But the traditional Stoic and Christian theories provide clear counter-instances: both start with an independently derived conception of the right as moral or religious virtue, and then go on to define a good human life as one lived in accord with those particular virtues. In other words, they are deontological, but nevertheless perfectionist, theories. Conversely, it is possible for a teleological theory to be non-perfectionist. Indeed, both utilitarianism and JMD are examples of this, albeit for somewhat different reasons. Utilitarianism is not a perfectionist theory because it defines the good in a way that is (within limits) agnostic toward what gives people happiness: it directs us to maximize the degree to which individuals' preferences are satisfied, regardless of what those preferences happen to be.[9] JMD is not a perfectionist theory because it makes only the limited assumption that an acceptable conception of the good must include freedom from domination as an important condition of human flourishing. Among the many possible conceptions of the good meeting this requirement, JMD is generally agnostic.

In these two respects, then, JMD and utilitarianism have a similar structure. In some other respects, however, their similarity depends on how one interprets the latter. Consider, for instance, the somewhat technical (but, as we shall see later, significant) issue of whether we should interpret utilitarianism

[7] I say "as a matter of principle" here, because any theory of social justice might, in its operation, encourage or discourage particular conceptions of the good as an unintended side effect. While sometimes (perhaps) lamentable, this is unavoidable. See Barry (1995, p. 11, *passim*) for a discussion of this point.

[8] Rawls (1971, p. 25).

[9] I say "within limits" here, because there may be circularities in the theory unless we exclude some other-regarding preferences, especially those having to do with the degree to which other people's preferences are satisfied. See Rakowski (1991, esp. pp. 25–9).

as what is called a *personalist* conception of social justice or not.[10] This issue is most easily explained by way of illustration. Suppose we face a choice between two different population policies: under the first, ten people will be born, who will each enjoy ten units of preference satisfaction over the course of their lives; under the second, a completely different set of twenty people will be born, who will each enjoy six units of preference satisfaction over the course of their lives. Utilitarianism directs us to maximize the sum total preference satisfaction. The difficulty is that, although the second policy seems better from a sum total utility point of view, there is no one it is better for, so to speak, since the different sets of people do not overlap. So interpreted, utilitarianism would violate an extremely compelling basic proposition in moral philosophy—often called the "person-affecting principle"—according to which something cannot be good (or bad) unless there is someone it is good (or bad) for.

In my view, the person-affecting principle must be true, and so a more compelling interpretation of utilitarianism would be a personalist one—meaning that it directs us to maximize the sum total preference satisfaction of whatever people there are, rather than the sum total preference satisfaction as such.[11] (Others, however, disagree.[12]) It is important to stress that JMD should also be interpreted as a personalist conception of social justice. The detail of what exactly this entails is discussed later, in Section 6.4.3, but notice that if we were to interpret JMD in non-personalist terms, we would apparently be able to make a society more just by simply reducing the number of people who would otherwise have lived (on the assumption that each would have experienced at least some degree of domination at some point in their lives). JMD should not be understood in this way.

6.2.2 Initial appeal of the conception

The detailed defense of JMD begins in Section 6.3. Here, I want to mention only a few reasons for initially finding it appealing, based on what has been said so far.

[10] I borrow this term from Pettit (1993, pp. 23–6).

[11] Rawls (1971, pp. 161–6) and others have thought that this must entail some versions of average utilitarianism, but this is not the case. Average utilitarianism might violate the person-affecting principle for exactly the same reason classical utilitarianism might: considering again the two possible population policies discussed, average utilitarianism tells us that the second is worse, but who is it worse for? It cannot be worse for the persons born under the second policy, for they would not have lived under the first.

[12] Sidgwick (1907), for example, and Parfit (1984).

First, it sits nicely with some strong intuitions many people have concerning social justice. For example, we now generally regard slavery and tyranny as obviously unjust, and the emancipation from either as a gain in human freedom. By conceptualizing domination and freedom as opposites (see Chapter 5), and social justice as the minimization of domination, JMD handily accounts for both beliefs and moreover connects them as directly as possible. It captures, in other words, our deep sense that freedom and justice must run together. Other theories of social justice might capture these intuitions as well, of course, but not in so elegant and straightforward a manner. Another intuition nicely captured by JMD is the sense that social justice is a "negative" ideal, meaning that it is primarily about removing the barriers or obstacles to human flourishing, rather than a "positive" or utopian expression of what sort of a people we want to be. As suggested in Chapter 1, it is better to construct a theory of social justice from the ground up, so to speak, on the basis of a concrete and specific *summum malum*, rather than to start from a vague and ephemeral *summum bonum*.

A second appealing feature of JMD is its impartiality, understood in the following sense: namely, that it regards no one person's freedom from domination as more or less important than anyone else's. Much as Jeremy Bentham was alleged to have said regarding utilitarianism, each counts for one, and no one for more than one.[13] This expresses an intuition that no contemporary moral or political philosopher would deny: namely, the fundamentally equal moral worth of all human beings.

Third and finally, JMD has the advantage of being theoretically thin and empirically thick. In other words, as compared with the elaborate conceptual apparatus required by some alternatives (though not utilitarianism in this case), our theory quickly hands things over from the political philosopher to the social scientist. This should be regarded as a virtue, because it means that JMD will remain robust and dynamic in the face of changing empirical conditions. Put another way, JMD instructs us to keep ever in view as our goal minimizing domination, and to not substitute for this a commitment to some specific set of political or social institutions or practices presumed at one time most likely to serve this goal. On the contrary, the basic structure of society should be regarded as permanently revisable in the light of historical experience.[14]

For these reasons, JMD might seem, initially at least, an appealing conception of social justice. To reiterate what was said earlier, my discussion for the

---

[13] The expression is attributed to Bentham by Mill. Sen (1992, ch. 1) argues persuasively that any plausible theory of justice must be impartial in at least this basic sense.

[14] Pettit (1997, pp. 146–7) makes a roughly similar point.

most part is limited to this topic. Utilitarianism, in contrast, is sometimes interpreted as a complete account of moral philosophy. It is disputed whether this is a good interpretation of utilitarianism, but regardless of how this dispute turns out, JMD need not be so understood. The conception I have proposed is only a conception of social justice. Even if (as I happen to believe) it could be extended reasonably well, so as to describe a complete theory of justice, it would never constitute a complete moral philosophy.

Put another way, it is not my view that justice is the only thing that matters—certainly not from the point of view of practical philosophy in general, and not even from the point of view of moral philosophy, narrowly speaking. I return to this point later on, and I mention it here only for emphasis. JMD is appealing as a conception of social justice (and, possibly, as a conception of justice more broadly), but not as a general moral philosophy.

6.3 THE ARGUMENT FOR THE CONCEPTION

Theories of social justice have both what might be called a horizontal and a vertical architecture. The horizontal architecture consists in the various working parts or modules, so to speak, that fit together in a distinctive principle or set of principles of social justice. In Rawls's conception of justice as fairness, for example, these parts or modules include the account of primary goods, the difference principle, the just savings principle, the various priority rules, and so on. By contrast, the vertical architecture of a theory of social justice consists in the relationship between the conception of justice itself—its distinctive principle or principles—and its proposed justificatory apparatus on the one hand, as well as its proposed applications in the design of political and social institutions and practices on the other. These three— the justificatory apparatus, the conception itself, and the applications of the conception—constitute three distinct levels of analysis in a complete theory.

Chapter 7 considers the various possible applications of JMD. In this chapter, I am concerned with the two other aspects of the theory, starting with its justificatory apparatus, but focusing mainly on the arguments for its various parts or modules.

6.3.1 Methods of justification

There are many competing conceptions of social justice. On what grounds are we supposed to choose among them? Unfortunately, nearly as many choice procedures have been proposed as there are conceptions of social justice to choose.

For all intents and purposes, however, only three have a serious following among contemporary political philosophers and theorists.[15] The first choice procedure proposes that the best conception of social justice is the one that would most advance the prudential self-interest of the persons who would live under its guidance. On this view, we can think of a conception of social justice as representing terms of mutual cooperation that a group of self-interested and prudential bargainers would agree to, those terms then presumably deriving their normative justification from some version of ethical egoism. Theories of social justice relying on this sort of justificatory apparatus are often described as *mutual advantage* theories. Justice as mutual advantage has a distinguished pedigree: versions of the argument are first discussed in Plato's *Republic*, later defended by Epicurus, and finally given a sophisticated exposition in Thomas Hobbes. More recently, mutual advantage arguments have been made for both utilitarianism and liberal contractualism, but they are employed most often on behalf of libertarianism.[16]

Mutual advantage theories suffer from a number of serious defects; since these have been thoroughly vetted in the literature, I will only mention what I see as the three chief difficulties.[17] The first is that they would, in their operation, merely replicate whatever imbalances of power exist prior to the terms of agreement: this is because the prudential self-interest of all the parties dictates that they each make the best use of their respective bargaining power in securing terms favorable to themselves. The second (related) difficulty is that mutual advantage can give no account of our obligations to persons from whom we have no reason to expect benefits—for example, the members of future generations. These are, of course, external complaints. The third difficulty is internal to the mutual advantage theory itself. Suppose that a group of self-interested and prudential bargainers agree on terms of social justice that would be mutually beneficial if generally complied with. Still, the question remains, what reason does any given member of that group have to comply with those terms on the occasions when unilateral defection would

---

[15] Others that are now generally dismissed (in my view, with good reason) are choice procedures based on authority (e.g., the authority of God), nature, or convention. This is not to say, of course, that these do not each still have their adherents.

[16] Edgeworth (1881, pp. 52–6) sketches a mutual advantage argument for utilitarianism (which Rawls [1971, pp. 169–71] shows to be faulty); Binmore (1998) attempts to derive liberal contractualism from mutual advantage; Gauthier (1986), Narveson (2001), and others employ mutual advantage on behalf of libertarianism.

[17] For further discussion of the difficulties mentioned here, however, see Parfit (1984, ch. 1), Barry (1989, 1995, ch. 2), and Roemer (1996, ch. 2).

happen to promote her self-interest? Within the mutual advantage frame-work, there is no workable answer to this last question.

The second, and perhaps dominant, view is that the best conception of social justice is the one that reasonable people would choose under fair conditions. This choice procedure retains the idea that we should think of social justice as representing terms of mutual cooperation, but it replaces self-interested and prudential bargainers with reasonable persons, and adds that the agreement must be made under the right conditions. In this context, reasonable persons are generally understood to be persons suitably motivated to find fair terms of cooperation acceptable to all; and the right conditions are generally understood to be (at a minimum) conditions of equal bargaining strength. Theories of social justice relying on this sort of justificatory appara-tus might be called *consent-based* theories. Consent-based arguments have been advanced for utilitarianism, but they are employed almost always on behalf of liberal contractualism.[18]

In my view, consent-based choice procedures suffer from a deep and ultimately fatal ambiguity.[19] Briefly, the issue is how we are to interpret the relationship between the consent-based choice procedure on the one hand, and the principles of social justice that would be chosen using that procedure on the other. Should we view the principles as expressing the right account of social justice because they (and not others) would be chosen by reasonable persons under suitable conditions, or would reasonable persons under suit-able conditions choose those principles (and not others) because they express the right account of social justice? On the first, voluntarist, reading, consent-based choice procedures must face the well-known (and, in my view insur-mountable) difficulties posed in the literature on social-choice theory. Unless we assume—and we have no good reason to assume this—that people have beliefs about social justice that conveniently aggregate without inconsis-tency into a collective agreement, we must acknowledge the possibility that the procedure might generate irrational results. Permitting the parties to deliberate beforehand will only help if we have good a priori reasons to expect that such deliberations will generate consensus on a unique solution. But it is unclear what our reasons for expecting this would be, unless we believed that a best account of social justice exists independently of the deliberative

---

[18] Harsanyi (1953, 1955) proposed a consent-based argument for utilitarianism; the best-known consent-based arguments for liberal contractualism include Rawls (1958, 1971, 2001), Scanlon (1982, 1998), Barry (1989, 1995), and Nagel (1991).

[19] In Lovett (2004, 2007), I have made the argument that follows in greater detail. Pettit (1982) and Parfit (2002) address similar issues from different points of view.

procedure (which we would then naturally expect it to converge on, at least given sufficient time). This brings us to the second, rationalist, reading.

On the rationalist reading, the consent-based choice procedure operates as a sort of heuristic device—as an aid for reflecting on what the best account of social justice really is. Once we figure this out, we can be confident that reasonable people will, under suitable consent-giving conditions, choose it for themselves (and if they do not, that it must be either because they are not being sufficiently reasonable, or else because the conditions of their deliberation are not sufficiently fair). So interpreted, however, the consent-giving apparatus is at best an unnecessary diversion, and at worst a positive hindrance.[20] That it might be an unnecessary diversion can be seen when we reflect that asking which arguments a reasonable person would agree to under suitable conditions is merely a roundabout way of asking which are the best arguments—something we can perfectly well do directly. That it might be a positive hindrance can be seen when we observe that in order to ask the roundabout version of the question we must take on board considerable conceptual baggage, some of it highly controversial in its own right, which would otherwise be unnecessary. (Here I am thinking about our accounts of moral personality, motivation, boundary problems, and so on.)

This brings me to the third choice procedure, which of course is the one I prefer, namely, the method of *reflective equilibrium*, according to which the best conception of social justice is the one that sits well with the moral (and other) intuitions we have decided, on reflection, to keep. This is the same procedure introduced in Chapter 2 for Part I, now applied to normative political theory. Since it was discussed there, I need not discuss it further here.

6.3.2 The competing conceptions

Let us turn now from the question of justification to the substantive principles of social justice. With respect to its horizontal architecture, JMD has three main components. The first is the selection of non-domination as the appropriate object of concern from the standpoint of social justice; the second is the weighting of each person's freedom from domination equally; and the third is the *minimization principle*, according to which we should aim to minimize the sum total domination. Of these, the second is clearly the least controversial. It is an expression of our fundamental commitment to the equal moral worth of all human beings, and few moral or political philosophers today would dispute this commitment. My discussion, therefore,

---

[20] McGinn (1999) canvasses similar objections here.

focuses on the other two, each of which requires a separate justification. Before proceeding to that justification, I will say a few words about what I see as the main competing conceptions, emphasizing the ways in which they would dispute the selection of non-domination as the relevant object of concern, the minimization principle, or both.

Our first major competitor is obviously utilitarianism. It is a major competitor for (at least) two reasons. The first is because it has long been regarded as an especially powerful conception of social justice, and rightly so. Everyone must contend with utilitarianism for this reason. The second reason is, somewhat paradoxically, because it is so similar to JMD. It follows from this very similarity that nearly any argument for JMD is an argument for utilitarianism. Indeed, supposing that we adopt the most compelling interpretation of utilitarianism, the two conceptions differ only at a single point: namely, in the substitution of non-domination for preference satisfaction as the relevant object of concern from a social justice point of view. The whole argument for JMD as against utilitarianism will thus hinge on the advantages of the former as against the latter.

Our second major competitor is the group of theories I have referred to in this study as liberal contractualism. By far, the most significant example of liberal contractualism is Rawls's theory of justice as fairness, but there are many others as well, variously referred to as theories of justice as reciprocity, justice as impartiality, liberal egalitarianism, and political liberalism.[21] For the most part, these liberal-contractualist theories share the consent-based justificatory apparatus to which I objected in Section 6.3.1. But it is the substantive principles of social justice we are interested in here, and one might imagine liberal-contractualist principles advanced on other grounds. What then are its characteristic substantive principles? Naturally, there is considerable variation. However, in terms of defending JMD, two points of comparison stand out, and on these two points, all the liberal-contractualist conceptions of social justice more or less agree. The first is that all liberal contractualists would reject the selection of non-domination as the relevant object of concern from a social justice point of view, in favor of a broader view along the lines of Rawls's account of primary goods. The second is that all would reject the minimization principle in favor of something more egalitarian—either an equality principle, the difference principle, or perhaps (as in Rawls's conception) some combination of these. My argument for JMD will thus concentrate on defending these two aspects of its principle of social

---

[21] For examples, see Rawls (1958, 1971, 1993, 1999, 2001), Barry (1995, 2001, 2005), Nagel (1991, 2005), Moon (1993), Scheffler (2001, esp. chs. 8–10), and Kelly (2005).

justice; having done this, I will have demonstrated its advantages over the substantive principles offered by liberal-contractualist theories.

These are, in my view, the two main alternatives I must contend with. However, it might be worth mentioning a few others for the sake of completeness. To begin with, there are welfarist conceptions other than utilitarianism—equality of welfare conceptions, for example.[22] The case for JMD as against equality of welfare will, of course, be sufficiently addressed by the arguments for non-domination as against preference satisfaction, and for the minimization principle as against some more egalitarian alternative. Three other sorts of conceptions will not be sufficiently addressed here, however. The first are the various perfectionist conceptions, civic humanism, and liberal perfectionism among them (see Section 6.2.1). The second are communitarian conceptions, and the third of course is libertarianism. A more complete discussion would have to address these as well; my only excuse for not doing so is that I have little to add to the many able critiques made by others.

6.3.3 The argument for non-domination

In Chapter 5, I argued that we should regard freedom from domination as an important human good, and in this chapter I am taking that issue as settled. Why then does this component of the conception require further defense? Because, as was also pointed out in Chapter 5, non-domination is not the only human good, and even if we suppose it to be an especially important one, the question still remains why it and not the others should be the exclusive concern of a conception of social justice.

Let us consider the alternative of welfarism first. On a welfarist theory like utilitarianism, social justice should be concerned with the degree to which people's preferences are satisfied. This view has a number of difficulties. One difficulty, touched on in Chapter 5, is that subjective preferences are vulnerable to adaptation and manipulation. Put crudely, we can satisfy people's preferences either by giving them what they want, or else by ensuring that they want whatever we choose to give them, and welfarist theories would seem to be indifferent between these strategies as a matter of principle. Consider two societies: in the first, goods (including non-domination) are distributed more or less broadly, while in the second, goods are hoarded by a small elite. In both, it is possible that everyone will, in time, adapt their

---

[22] Equality of welfare theories are advanced by Arneson (1989), G. A. Cohen (1989) and Roemer (1985, 1996, 1998).

preferences to more or less fit with the larger or smaller shares they expect to receive, and so we might easily imagine that the levels of preference satisfaction will end more or less uniformly distributed, both across individuals and across the two societies. Must we then say that these two societies are equally just? On a welfarist theory, apparently yes. This is a good reason for rejecting such theories.

There are other reasons as well. As frequently pointed out, it is not necessarily desirable to count all subjective preferences equally.[23] For example, some people might enjoy subjecting others to domination. Welfarism would seem to require that these preferences be given no less weight than other, more benign, preferences.

Since JMD is not a welfarist theory, it does not face these sorts of familiar objections. In this connection, it might also be worth mentioning another advantage of non-domination as against preference satisfaction. Once a person is perfectly free from domination, there is no further non-domination for her to experience. Of course, for reasons discussed in Part I of this study, it is impossible (practically speaking) to reach this limit; nevertheless, it sets a definite upper bound on the level of non-domination any one person can enjoy. This rules out the non-domination equivalent of what are called "utility monsters"—persons capable of such extreme levels of happiness that the sum total preference satisfaction might be maximized by devoting all of a society's resources to their exclusive consumption.[24]

Next let us consider the other, in my view more difficult, challenge. Suppose we agree that non-domination is an important human good. Nevertheless, there are certainly others. Among these are those bundles of resources that Rawls lists as primary goods: basic rights and liberties, powers and prerogatives of office, income and wealth, and so on.[25] The question is, Why should social justice be concerned with non-domination exclusively, and not with all primary goods? Consider two equally hard-working and otherwise equally deserving persons. Through no fault of their own, it is possible that one might end up with a substantially larger share of wealth than the other—say, because one happens to be born with a greater natural talent for playing baseball, or because the other is the victim of some unforeseeable (and, let us suppose, uninsurable) disaster. This is certainly unfair, and thus it has seemed to many that correcting for this sort of unfairness, at least to some

---

[23] These and other related problems are discussed in Rawls (1971, pp. 30–1), Sen (1979, pp. 471–9), Dworkin (2000, pp. 21–8, 48–62), and Rakowski (1991, pp. 25–9, 45–52, elsewhere).

[24] This term derives from Nozick (1974, p. 41).

[25] Rawls (1971, pp. 90–5, 1982, 1993, pp. 178–90). Other resource-based theories have been developed by Nagel (1977), Dworkin (2000, esp. ch. 2), and Rakowski (1991, esp. chs. 3–7).

degree and under some conditions, must be a matter of social justice. If so, then all primary goods, and not merely the good of non-domination, must be the appropriate concern of a theory of social justice.

In response to this line of reasoning, first let me emphasize that JMD is by no means indifferent to the distribution of other primary goods. This is for the obvious reason that levels of domination will often be affected by the distribution of rights and liberties, income and wealth, etc., and thus, to the extent that this is the case, the aim of minimizing domination will supply instrumental reasons for being concerned with the distribution of these other goods as well. (Indeed, I argue precisely this with respect to income and wealth in Chapter 7.) My claim is merely that the primary goods other than non-domination are not themselves a *direct* concern of social justice.

Second, I should reiterate that justice is not the only virtue of political and social institutions and practices: they can also be more or less efficient with respect to economic productivity, for example. As it happens, it is also my view that they can be designed to correct for more or less unfairness in the distribution of primary goods through risk-pooling social insurance schemes—and, indeed, that they should correct for rather more unfairness than they do at present (at least, say, in the United States). My contention is only that a reasonably wide range of unfairness correction might be consistent with social justice, provided of course that the instrumental concerns suggested above are sufficiently addressed.[26] In other words, if two societies have done an equally good job in reducing domination, one would not be less just merely because it does not correct for as much unfairness as the other, much as one would not be less just merely because it is less efficient than the other. Duties of fairness, unlike duties of justice, specifically arise out of our associative obligations: one part of what it means for us to form a community is to agree to collectively share certain risks and burdens according to our own notions of solidarity. Justice, by contrast, is not particularistic in this way: anyone affected by an institution or practice (regardless of community membership) in principle has a claim at the bar of justice with respect to that institution or practice. This must be so, if justice is not to be blatantly parochial. Merging our duties of justice into our duties of fairness, as Rawls attempted to do, seemed attractive only so long as it was possible to regard the set of persons affected by a community's institutions and practices as effectively coextensive with the members of that community. It has become increasingly obvious, however, that these two groups are not

[26] And, of course, provided that other, more urgent humanitarian obligations are not at issue. The assumption that we are discussing reasonably well-developed and prosperous societies sets aside such concerns for the moment. More on this in Section 6.5, however.

coextensive, and the deeper difficulties with the Rawlsian approach have thereby gradually been revealed, especially when it comes to the problems of intergenerational and global justice (discussed later in this chapter and in Chapter 7, respectively).

With these caveats, then, here are some grounds for identifying freedom from domination as the particular concern of a theory of social justice. If we believe that justice is, in Rawls's words, "the *first* virtue of social institutions," then we must be able to account for that priority in some way.[27] It is not my view that concern for the distribution of primary goods as such, independently of whatever impact that distribution might have on levels of domination experienced, adequately captures the priority of justice. Societies that succeed in minimizing unfairness might still be less than fully just. This is suggested by the fact that many people historically have been willing to struggle for freedom from domination even at great material cost to themselves, and even sometimes when they had few complaints regarding their share of other goods. It is unlikely that those struggling against feudal, colonial, or patriarchal domination, for example, shared any views regarding what a fair distribution of primary goods would be; indeed, they almost certainly disagreed widely. Their willingness to struggle for justice taps into something deeper and more fundamental: specifically, I believe, it taps into our yearning to be free of domination. JMD captures more directly than other theories the intuitions that justice is a negative ideal, and that freedom and justice must run together.

6.3.4 The argument for minimization

Suppose we agree not only that freedom from domination is an important human good, but also that it should be the exclusive concern of social justice. It remains to be shown why the minimization principle best expresses these commitments. There are two separate complaints that might be leveled against the minimization principle.

The first is that, as an outcome-oriented principle, it fails to respect the so-called separateness of persons.[28] Suppose that by increasing somewhat the domination of a few, we could greatly reduce aggregate domination in society overall. On the minimization principle, this would be an improvement, but it seems to entail using some people as a means for improving the situation of

---

[27] Rawls (1971, p. 3), emphasis added.
[28] Versions of this familiar complaint can be found in Rawls (1971, pp. 26–7), Williams (1973, p. 99), Nozick (1974, pp. 30–3), Gauthier (1986, pp. 244–5), and Nagel (1991, p. 66ff).

others. Indeed, one might say it amounts to treating *all* people (whether they fare well individually or not) as a means to the end of minimizing the sum total domination, in the sense that we are apparently indifferent to who actually experiences whatever domination remains. People are, in a sense, merely carriers or vectors of non-domination. This does not, so the argument goes, adequately respect the independent value attached to each separate human life.

Before directly responding to this first complaint, I should point out that it applies equally well to many other sorts of distributive principles. Suppose we were aiming for equality. Consider the distributions of non-domination (4, 2) and (3, 3). An egalitarian distributive principle would endorse a move from the first distribution to the second. But surely, just as much as in the previous instance, this move would amount to treating as a means the person who must sacrifice some of her non-domination in order to bring about an egalitarian result overall; moreover, with just as much plausibility as before, we can say that *both* persons are treated as mere carriers or vectors of non-domination toward the end of achieving an equal distribution. In order to avoid the separateness of persons complaint—at least as it stands—we would need to abandon distributive principles altogether. The alternative would be some sort of side-constraint view, according to which we should never act so as to raise a person's domination.

But should the separateness of persons complaint stand as it is? It should not. The point of aiming for equality is surely to benefit people, and the egalitarian principle of distribution is merely a device for accomplishing this. Likewise, if our grounds for minimizing the total domination were that the achievement of a low total somehow represented an accomplishment of society as such, then indeed we would be treating the members of that society merely as means. But these are not our grounds for minimizing the sum total domination. Rather, we regard domination as bad for the individual members of society themselves. (To reiterate what was noted earlier, this is what it means for JMD to be a personalist theory.) The minimization principle is merely a device for freeing people from avoidable domination.

The real issue is how best to respect the independent value attached to each separate human life. It is by no means clear that we adequately respect the independent value of a person's life when we fail to reduce the (severe) domination to which she is subject to merely because we cannot do so without (slightly, let us say) raising the domination of another. Indeed, quite the opposite seems true to me.[29]

---

[29] This point is nicely made in Scheffler (1982, esp. ch. 4).

Nevertheless, this first complaint is independent of the second: namely, that minimization is the wrong distributive principle. What might we substitute instead? One option is that we aim to achieve the highest degree of non-domination possible for one person or group, regardless of what the sum total domination turns out to be. We might accomplish this, for example, by enslaving the majority of a society's members, thus enabling a free minority to experience an extremely high level of freedom from domination unachievable in any other way. This might be thought a worthy objective if one held an aristocratic view of society, according to which the absolute value or worth of a society is determined by its greatest accomplishments. Let us call this the aristocratic principle of distribution.

Few now would take the aristocratic principle seriously, of course.[30] More likely, the plausible alternatives to the minimization principle are what might be called the equality principle, the difference principle, and the sufficiency principle. The first would direct us to achieve the lowest possible equal distribution of domination; the second to minimize the domination of the most dominated group; and the third to ensure that as many people as possible were subject to no more than some minimally acceptable threshold level of domination.[31] (It is unclear what the grounds for a specific threshold might be: if some non-domination is good, isn't more better? I ignore this problem, however.)

How should we choose among these principles (minimization, or one of the three plausible alternatives)? If one of them generated intuitively appealing results in every possible scenario, the choice would be easy. Unfortunately, this is not the case. Each of the contenders can be shown to generate deeply counter-intuitive results under some imaginable conditions. This shortcoming is widely recognized in the case of the minimization principle. For example, imagine a society in which subjecting a very small minority to abject slavery would permit us to lower somewhat the domination of a much greater majority. Provided that the second group is large enough relative to the first, the minimization principle would seem to endorse this policy, and this

---

[30] Tocqueville at times expresses some nostalgia for this idea, however, and on some (perhaps dubious) interpretations this is roughly the view of Nietzsche.

[31] Note that, as specified, all three principles are incomplete. To fully specify the equality principle, we would have to supply a rank ordering of different possible states of inequality: for example, is the distribution (10, 10, 1, 1) more or less equal than the distribution (11, 5, 5, 1)? To fully specify the difference principle, we would have to add that, having minimized the domination of the most dominated group, we should next minimize the domination of the second most dominated group, and so on. And to fully specify the sufficiency principle, we would have to clarify whether it is better to bring a few people just over the threshold than it is to bring many people close, but just under it.

is (rightly) thought to be problematic. But in other imaginable scenarios, the proposed alternative principles can be shown equally problematic, as we shall see. In the absence of a principle that will work in every *possible* scenario, we are compelled (more modestly) to choose the principle that works best in the most *likely* scenarios. From this point of view, I argue that the minimization principle is at least no worse, and may sometimes be better, than its three serious competitors.

Let us begin by reflecting on what it would mean to put any of the proposed principles into practice. At any given time, there will be many groups subject to varying degrees of domination in a society. Let us suppose:

> (1) The political, social, and economic resources available for reducing domination are relatively scarce. Not all avoidable domination can be reduced at once.

In the short run, at least, this is a very plausible assumption. It follows that we must choose how to best employ our limited resources. On elementary efficiency grounds, it would seem that whatever resources we have should be employed so as to produce the greatest possible benefit (as defined by our preferred distributive principle). Now let us further suppose:

> (2) Other things being equal, it is easier to reduce severe domination than it is to reduce mild domination.

In other words, a given unit of available resources can affect proportionally larger reductions in the domination of a group subject to severe domination than it can in the domination of a group subject to mild domination. Why might this second assumption be plausible? As we have seen, there are three main strategies available for reducing domination: we can reduce dependency, we can reduce imbalances of social power, or we can reduce the arbitrariness with which social power might be wielded. Now it stands to reason that each of these strategies must be subject to diminishing marginal returns. For example, while it may be fairly easy to reduce severe dependencies, it is difficult or impossible to eliminate dependency altogether. If this is generally the case, then it will be easier to reduce the domination of those subject to comparatively severe domination than that of those subject to comparatively mild domination. This assumption is further supported by the thought that severe domination will usually be more obvious, and thus supply a firmer basis for the mobilization of political action against it; whereas milder domination will usually be subtler and harder to see, thus rendering the mobilization of political action against it more difficult.

Given these first two assumptions, what will each of the proposed distributive principles direct us to do in the short run? They will all direct us to employ whatever resources are available in reducing the domination of the most dominated group first. On the minimization principle, this is because doing so will bring about the greatest net reduction in the sum total domination. On the equality principle, this is because doing so will bring about the greatest possible reduction in inequality. And so on. Thus, given our first two assumptions, the minimization principle does no worse than the alternatives, for the trivial reason that all the principles issue the same directives.

Admittedly, this convergence may only hold true in the short run. In the long run, if there are enough improvements, we may eventually reach a time when resources are no longer scarce, in the sense that the available resources will actually be sufficient to achieve equality, or sufficiency, or whatever. As this limit is neared, the proposed principles begin to diverge. But how soon is this divergence likely to occur? Consider next:

(3) In any society, new forms of domination will continually emerge.

Stated at this level of generality, this third empirical assumption is also extremely plausible. Persons or groups experience domination to the extent that they are dependent on other persons or groups wielding arbitrary power over them. But the bases of dependency and social power have continually shifted throughout history. During the Middle Ages, for instance, salvation was a highly valued good; indeed, it was so valuable that people readily exchanged other goods (such as wealth) in order to secure it for themselves and their relatives. Outside the church there was no salvation. Christians were thus highly dependent on the Catholic Church, which in turn wielded considerable arbitrary power over them. In this context, the Protestant Reformation might be seen as a dramatic reduction in one form of domination. But in the long run, many new forms of social power and dependency rose in place of the old, giving rise to new forms of domination.[32]

It is not clear how quickly new forms of domination are likely to emerge, relative to our ability to bring about domination reductions. One hopes that the latter will (eventually) outpace the former. Given the third assumption, however, we should not expect the conditions of divergence to arise any time soon. This makes choosing among the proposed principles much less important, in practice, than it might otherwise appear. We might then select the minimization principle on the grounds of theoretical simplicity and elegance. Nevertheless, for the sake of completeness, I mention some additional problems with the alternatives.

---

[32] Cf. Walzer (1983, ch. 1), who employs a similar argument against simple equality.

Imagine a society with two large groups of citizens, the first subject to severe domination, the second to only mild domination. Suppose a dictator comes to power and promptly increases the domination of the second group so that it more or less matches that of the first. On the equality principle, this development would apparently constitute an improvement, despite the fact that no one is better off, and many are much worse off.[33] This is implausible. The aforementioned person-affecting principle tells us that something cannot be better if there is no one it is better for.

Let us change the example slightly. Suppose that the first group were political allies of the dictator, who facilitated his rise to power. As a reward for their support, the dictator first lowers their domination very slightly, and then substantially increases the domination of the other group to match this new level. On either the equality principle or the difference principle, this also would appear to constitute an improvement, despite the fact that no one is more than very slightly better off, and many are much worse off. Strictly speaking, this is no longer a violation of the person-affecting principle; nevertheless, it is not very appealing. Indeed, it is even less appealing when we reflect that, on either principle, it does not matter how large the second group is relative to the first. The first group might constitute only a tiny minority, and yet both principles would endorse the dictator's moves as bringing about an improvement.

And what about the sufficiency principle? There are two possibilities. Either the first group, before the dictator's coming to power, is above the threshold level of acceptable domination, or it is not. If it is above the threshold, then the dictator's move brings it slightly closer to the acceptable level. Suppose that the dictator then raises the domination of the second group, not to match, but rather just up to the threshold: on the sufficiency principle this constitutes an improvement, despite the fact that no one is more than very slightly better off, and many are much worse off. If the first group is not above the acceptable threshold of domination before the dictator comes to power, then the dictator's policies do not affect who is above or below the threshold. It follows, on the sufficiency principle, that things will not be worse than they were before. Either way, the conclusion is not very appealing.

Each of the alternatives to the minimization principle thus has disadvantages. It is possible, of course, that some combination of principles might perform better than any one of them individually. But we should keep in mind that, as I tried to show, there will be little practical difference between them for the foreseeable future. What then would be the use of

---

[33] This, of course, is merely a redescribed version of the "leveling-down" problem: see Parfit (1995, pp. 16–18, 23–4, 28–34).

such refinements? At least until refinements are needed, it is best to adopt the simplest and most straightforward option, and this is the minimization principle.

6.4 SOME TECHNICAL REFINEMENTS

Having completed the main argument for JMD, I turn next to ironing out some stubborn technical problems. No conception of social justice is free from such difficulties, and none of the particular difficulties addressed here is unique to JMD. Thus their resolution should not, in my view, count either for or against the conception. I address them primarily for the sake of completeness, and to pre-empt unwarranted criticisms.

While the issues discussed in this section are somewhat technical, no theory of social justice that fails to address them can be considered complete.[34] Readers uninterested in such details are free to skip ahead.

6.4.1 The opportunity problem

The first issue concerns whether we should aim to minimize domination as such, or rather to maximize opportunities for avoiding domination.

Often, achieving these aims in practice will amount to the same thing. On the assumption that most people prefer not being subject to domination, providing people with the opportunity to avoid it will generally lead to its reduction. Likewise, the most efficient strategy for reducing domination (if that is our direct aim) may be an indirect one. Political and social institutions and practices have limited capacities for generating specific outcomes in detail. Thus it may well turn out that expanding people's opportunity sets to include domination-avoiding options will bring about the lowest sum total domination we can practically hope to achieve. Here I am interested rather in the theoretical question: Which should be our direct aim, and which should be (in most cases) its indirect by-product? To make things more concrete, let me pose three examples that more or less cover the relevant field.

Consider first the punishment of crimes. Prisons, at least as they are presently administered in the United States, for example, are clearly sites of

---

[34] Intergenerational justice, in particular, is sometimes viewed as an extension of a theory of social justice. This is not correct: without an account of intergenerational justice, a theory of social justice is simply underspecified, and thus incomplete.

domination.[35] However, at least in principle, everyone has the opportunity to avoid prison by obeying the law. If our aim were to maximize the opportunity for avoiding domination, then we would want to focus on ensuring that the laws were clear, that no innocents were punished, and that the opportunity to avoid prison was a real opportunity. The fact that (guilty) prisoners are themselves subject to domination in prison would not be of a direct concern on this view, since they previously had the fair opportunity to avoid that domination.

Consider next the assumption of risk. People are often presented opportunities to take gambles in the hope of some reward. At least in some cases, it would seem, they should be held responsible for the choices they make in such situations. For example, suppose that a well-informed and reasonably well-off individual declines to purchase health insurance. Subsequently, he is inflicted with crippling health expenses, which he can only afford by trading away some of his non-domination (perhaps he volunteers to become the indentured servant of a wealthy patron). If our aim were to maximize the opportunity for avoiding domination, we would in such cases want to focus on ensuring that individuals were well informed and that they had sufficient opportunities to decline risk, should they so choose. It would not, however, be our concern to reduce any domination that results from the genuinely voluntary assumption of risk.

Third, consider cases of what in Chapter 5 I called "unusual" preferences. It is at least imaginable that some people might enjoy being subject to domination, and thus, given the opportunity, would choose it for themselves. Again, at least assuming that such people are fully informed and have had a fair opportunity to avoid domination (otherwise their unusual preferences might be due to adaptation or manipulation), it seems we should not be concerned with reducing the domination they have chosen for themselves.

What connects these examples is the following idea: at least under the right circumstances, we want to respect the choices that people make. Respecting choices means holding people responsible for the (good or bad) outcomes of their choices. It would seem to follow that our prima facie obligation to reduce domination whenever we are able is cancelled, so to speak, when domination in a particular instance results from the genuinely voluntary choices of responsible individuals. Thus, our direct aim should be to maximize opportunities for avoiding domination, trusting that (for the most part) this will lead to less domination overall as an indirect by-product.

---

[35] It does not follow that prisons must be so, of course: Braithwaite and Pettit (1990), for example, aim to work out a system of punishment that would minimize domination.

This is not my view. The fact that, in any given instance, domination directly or indirectly results from the voluntary choices of responsible individuals does not itself cancel our prima facie obligation to reduce that domination if we can. This is because the opportunity-maximizing view is necessarily parasitic on the direct minimization view. It is indeed important to give people the opportunity to avoid domination, if they so choose. But is it equally important to give people the opportunity to taste caviar, if they so choose? It is not. This must be because freedom from domination is inherently a more important good than caviar. But then our reason for wanting to give people the opportunity to avoid domination is precisely that non-domination is intrinsically an important human good. Expanding opportunities is the (often effective) means, not the goal itself. If expanding opportunities as such were the goal, then it would seem we should be indifferent as to the character of the opportunities we give people, provided we give lots of them. But this is implausible. It is no real benefit to be given a large number of trivial options.

What are the consequences of accepting this view in the three examples discussed? First consider the case of criminal punishment. It may not be possible to inflict punishment on criminals without subjecting them to some degree of domination. Nevertheless, it will often be possible to *reduce* this degree of domination—for example by reducing the range of arbitrary discretion granted to prison guards. The direct minimization view gives us a reason to do this, whereas the opportunity-maximizing view does not. This argues in favor of the former.

The case of risk assumption is similar. It is neither possible nor desirable to eliminate all opportunities for the assumption of risk from society, but we should aim to reduce the likelihood that domination will result from such risk taking. There are many ways we can do this. For example, in the United States, involuntary servitude is constitutionally prohibited. This takes one form of domination off the table, so to speak: no series of gambles, no matter how risky, can terminate in slavery as an outcome. In Chapter 7, I discuss other strategies as well.

Finally, we have the case of unusual preferences. This, obviously, is the most difficult case, and we have encountered it before (in Chapter 5). It is particularly difficult because, unlike the previous cases, it involves the deliberate and direct choice of domination, rather than a choice that has domination as its indirect and (perhaps) unintended consequence. It is my view, as expressed in Chapter 5, that our obligations to reduce such domination are not cancelled by the mere fact of voluntary choice, but they might be outweighed by competing considerations, which we can call *reasons of toleration*. I discuss reasons of toleration in Chapter 7.

6.4.2 Future generations

In minimizing domination, we must take into consideration not only the present generation, but also future generations. This is because decisions we make today might obviously affect the well-being of people in the future—in particular, the amount of domination the latter might experience.

The first question we must ask is: Should the domination of future generations count the same as the domination of present generations? Some have thought not. When an individual compares present gains or losses with those in the future, it is natural for her to discount the latter: having a car today, for example, is more valuable than having the same car a year from now. The best explanation for this is that no one can be certain whether she will still be alive at a given future date. The more temporally distant an event, the less likely she will still be around to experience it (for good or for ill), and thus the more she will discount its (positive or negative) value. Discounting expresses, so to speak, an intimation of mortality in the language of economics.

Individual discounting (at least, within moderate bounds) is perfectly sensible. The question is whether the same reasoning should apply to our moral evaluations across generations—i.e., whether there should be what is called *social discounting*. Given the choice between benefiting some people now, and benefiting other people in the future, should we discount the latter benefits, simply on the grounds that they will occur later? We should not. There are several reasons for this. The most important—and decisive—reason is that social discounting fails to respect the equal moral worth of all human beings. The fact that one person happens to live later than another should make no difference from a moral point of view. Imagine we discover (and safely defuse) a bomb that someone has set with the intent of injuring a large number of people. This person has clearly done something morally blameworthy. Now imagine that the same person had set the bomb with a time delay such that, had it not been discovered and defused, it would have detonated fifty years from now. Has he done something less blameworthy, merely because the injuries would have occurred later in time? He has not.[36]

According to JMD, the domination of all persons should count equally, regardless of when they happen to live. This does not, however, resolve the main issue: namely, how should non-domination be distributed across generations? This turns out to be a remarkably complex question. In order to

---

[36] See Barry (1977, pp. 273–5), Parfit (1984, pp. 356–7, 480–6), and Cowen and Parfit (1992). Note that uncertainty regarding the future does not detract from this point. This is because the uncertainty specifically due to temporal distance (as distinct from uncertainty due to the inherent risk of different policies) applies to all our options equally.

render it manageable, let us begin with a few simplifications. First, let us assume that all generations are exactly the same size; and second, that generations are discrete and sequential. Both assumptions are clearly false, and both will be dropped in Section 6.4.3. Let us also assume that we do not know how many generations there will be. This third assumption is clearly true, and it is likely to remain so for a long time.

Given these assumptions, it may at first seem that we should aim to reduce the sum total domination experienced in all generations, counting the domination experienced in each generation equally. Unfortunately, this will not work. The difficulty is that by accepting a higher level of domination now, the present generation might enable a later generation to achieve a much lower level of domination in the future. It might be able to do this, for example, by starving itself of non-renewable resources that could otherwise have been used in the present for reducing domination. If we assume, as is plausible, that later generations will be able to use resources more efficiently than earlier ones (perhaps because they will have greater knowledge and more advanced technology), then the higher present-day domination will be more than offset by the lower levels of domination in the future. Indeed, this consideration suggests that the present generation should conserve as much as it possibly can—that is, accept the highest level of domination it can imaginably tolerate—because there will exist, by assumption, a distant future generation (thousands of years from now, perhaps) efficient enough to recoup any cost the present generation might now impose on itself. What is worse, every succeeding generation is in precisely the same position as the present one, at least until it becomes apparent how many generations there will be. Attempting to minimize the sum total domination in this way in effect leads us to an infinite deferral of consumption.[37]

A better interpretation of JMD runs as follows. Suppose there exists some level of non-renewable resource consumption that is indefinitely sustainable.[38] By consuming no more than this, the present generation can ensure that the next generation will have the ability, at least, to achieve a similar overall level of non-domination. By consuming somewhat less, the present generation can ensure that the next generation might achieve even more than this without upsetting sustainability. Along these lines, it is most plausible to interpret JMD in a way that directs us to minimize present-day domination, so far as

---

[37] The infinite deferral paradox was noticed by Rawls (1971, pp. 286–7) to be a feature of utilitarianism (if interpreted in the same way).

[38] This might seem to be impossible by definition, if there are supposed to be an indefinite number of generations, and if non-renewable resources are, indeed, non-renewable. Here I assume that at some possible level of moderate consumption, technology would keep pace indefinitely (by improving efficiency, developing substitutes, and so on).

this is consistent with maintaining or else further reducing that level of domination in the future. This entails minimizing present-day domination to the extent that we are able, given no more than a sustainable level of non-renewable resource consumption.

Observe that, so formulated, each generation lies under exactly the same directive, and that this directive is expressed as an obligation owed to the immediately succeeding generation. That these are important advantages will be clear after the discussion in Section 6.4.3.

6.4.3 The population problem

In Section 6.4.2, I assumed that each successive generation would have exactly the same number of members. But decisions we make today might affect not only the well-being of people in the future, but also how many future people there will be. This can cause surprising difficulties for any conception of social justice.

One potential difficulty was noted earlier. If we were to interpret JMD as a non-personalist conception, it would seem that we could reduce the sum total domination merely by reducing the number of people who will live (on the assumption that all people will be subject to at least some small degree of domination). This option was rejected, however. Something cannot be better or worse, from a social justice point of view, unless there is someone it is better or worse for. Therefore, unless reducing (or increasing) the population will indirectly affect the well-being of those persons who will live no matter which policy we choose, a personalist conception of social justice must remain agnostic.

This leads to another difficulty. It is not merely the *number* of people who will live that our present decisions might affect: they might also affect *which* persons will live. If we make one policy decision rather than another, different people will meet and have different children. This effect is of course small in the short run, but it gets larger and larger with each passing generation. Since a personalist theory of social justice can compare alternative possibilities only with respect to the persons they have in common, comparative judgments of social justice become harder—and, eventually, impossible—the further we project into the future. This has been called the *non-identity problem*.[39] The significance of the non-identity problem can be seen as follows.

First, let us suppose that the level of non-renewable resource consumption permitted to each generation has already been fixed by our previous

---

[39] Following Parfit (1984, ch. 16).

argument. In other words, no matter how large or small the nth generation turns out to be, it will have only the fixed quantity x_n of resources available for its consumption. We might also suppose, as was implied in Section 6.4.2, that having greater available resources per capita will enable a greater per capita reduction in domination, and vice versa.[40] Now consider two policy options available to the present generation: on the first, the nth generation from now will have 500 million members, and on the second 1 billion. Under the second policy, therefore, we might imagine that the nth generation will be subject to considerably more domination than under the first (since it will have only half as many resources per capita available for reducing domination). Does it then follow that the first policy is more just? Not necessarily. In order to establish this, we must ask who the second policy is unjust for. Certainly, it is not unjust for the extra 500 million people, since they would not have existed had we adopted the first policy. (I assume here that, even if their domination would be severe, they would nevertheless live lives worth living.) But notice that it might not be unjust even for the first 500 million people: if the nth generation is sufficiently distant from the present generation, these 500 million will not be the same 500 million who would have lived had we adopted the first policy. A personalist conception of social justice can thus only make short-run comparative judgments. (Hence the advantage of an indefinitely reiterated short-term obligation, like the one proposed at the conclusion of Section 6.4.2.)

With these considerations in mind, let us see how JMD might view population policy. Again, I assume that the level of non-renewable resource consumption permitted to each generation has been previously fixed, but this time I drop our earlier assumption that generations are discrete and sequential. Instead, let us imagine a (still highly simplified) model of over-lapping generations. In each time period, there will be three living genera-tions: the present generation, which is assumed to be making any policy decisions; the previous generation, which has retired and thus is at least partly dependent on the present generation; and the next generation, com-posed largely of dependent children. Notice that, in this model, the present generation is assumed to be the only generation engaged in productive activity—converting consumed non-renewable resources into goods such as non-domination—during a given period.

The present generation faces several options with respect to population size. It can adopt policies or institutions that will tend to (proportionally) increase, decrease, or maintain the current population level in the future.

---

[40] This assumption is given further attention in Chapter 7.

Here, we may confidently suppose that the effects of such decisions will not change the membership of the next generation, since (per assumption) they have already been born, and thus already have fixed identities. This makes things considerably easier.

Suppose that the present generation adopts a policy that tends to increase the population in the future. While this does not change the composition of the next generation, it might affect its level of well-being and, indeed, the well-being of the present generation. This is because in the next period (when the present generation retires, and the next comes of age) both will be sharing the fixed pool of available resources with a larger number of people overall. By our earlier assumption that having greater available resources per capita will enable a greater per capita reduction in domination, this will be worse for everyone. Thus, it would seem, a decreasing population must be better.

Should we then aim to reduce population as much as possible? (Presumably, of course, there will be non-justice considerations against reducing population beyond a certain point; these I leave aside for the moment.) Before reaching this conclusion, we must take into account another issue. Productive activity is required in order to make use of the available resources in reducing domination, and in our simple model of overlapping generations, only the middle generation is engaged in such activity. It follows that we must take into consideration the ratio of productive to dependent members of a society at any given time. When the population is declining at a proportional rate, this ratio is less favorable than it would be if population were constant, as can be seen in Table 6.1. This effect must counterbalance, to some extent, the advantage of having more non-renewable resources per capita available for consumption, and thus argues against the population-reducing policy.

Which policy is best from the point of view of minimizing domination will thus depend on the relative strengths of these various considerations, which cannot be determined without a much more sophisticated model. While

Table 6.1

	Previous generation (I)	Present generation (II)	Next generation (III)	Ratio of II to I + III
Steady population	100	100	100	1: 3.00
Population declining by 20% per generation	100	80	64	1: 3.05

carrying out this exercise in detail might be an interesting project, it is obviously beyond the scope of this study. The important point is that, even if we interpret JMD as a personalist conception of social justice, it will not be indifferent with respect to the population size, and its recommendations are likely to be within reasonable bounds.

6.5 FINAL STATEMENT OF THE CONCEPTION

Having presented an argument for justice as minimizing domination and, in the process, having elaborated on many points of detail, it is perhaps worth providing a final statement of the conception by way of concluding this chapter:

> (JMD) Societies are just to the extent that their basic structure is organized so as to:
>
> [a] minimize the expected sum total domination experienced by their members in the present generation, so far as this is consistent with
>
> [b] maintaining or else further reducing the expected sum total domination that will be experienced by their members in the next generation,
>
> [c] counting the domination of each person in all generations equally.

As stated here, is JMD complete? In my view, it is complete as a conception of social justice, but not as a conception of justice. It is not a complete conception of justice because, as noted earlier, it does not address questions of global, transitional, or interpersonal justice. (I discuss these topics briefly in Chapter 7.)

Even if extended to cover these latter topics, however, JMD would not be a complete moral philosophy. This is for the obvious reason that justice is not the only thing we care about. For example, we also care about fairness in the distribution of goods. In Chapter 5, it was suggested that we might also care about family intimacy and privacy. Nor is this all. We might also care about the growth of knowledge; about our sense of community; about the fate of the environment; and many other things besides. We care about so many things, because so many things contribute to human flourishing. Sometimes, promoting one of these goods will not conflict with promoting the others. But this is not always the case. When the promotion of different goods does conflict, we have to make difficult trade-offs among them. How should these trade-offs be made?

A complete moral philosophy would not only specify and define all the goods relevant to human flourishing, but also provide an account of their relative importance and weights. It is not my aim in this study, however, to outline a complete moral philosophy. In any case, moral philosophy is not, in my view, sufficiently advanced at present to carry out this project. Justice is an important value, to be sure, but it is not the only valuable thing; indeed, it is not necessarily the *most* important thing. We might have, for example, humanitarian obligations more fundamental than our obligations of justice. Earlier it was assumed that we were discussing social justice in the context of a reasonably well-developed and prosperous society; in many societies not meeting this condition, however, substantial portions of the population lack adequate nutrition, shelter, medical care, and other basic needs. When people's very subsistence is at stake, social justice is of secondary importance.[41] But this priority may not be absolute. Similarly, while social justice, in its turn, is arguably more important than fairness or efficiency, it does not trump these, or other, values absolutely. At the margin, it may be worth trading off some justice in order to secure greater fairness or efficiency (and, at the margin, it may be worth trading off some humanitarian obligations in order to secure greater justice). Beyond very general assertions like this, however, we must be content—at least for the foreseeable future—with the fact of reasonable pluralism, that is, with the fact that different people will come to different conclusions as to where the exact balance between these competing values should lie.

Many contemporary political theorists and philosophers attempt to circumvent this difficulty by focusing on the *procedures* we might use for resolving such disputes, while remaining officially agnostic with respect to the substantive disputes themselves. It is not my view that this strategy can succeed. Briefly, this is because different procedures inevitably favor different outcomes, and so our choice of procedures cannot help but be informed by our underlying views about the disputes themselves.

Fortunately, reasonable pluralism does not, in my view, present as serious an obstacle as it might appear. This is because, even if we are uncertain how important justice is relative to subsistence, efficiency, fairness, and so on, there is nevertheless considerable progress to be made in simply clarifying what justice as such demands in any given context. This is, indeed, a prereq-

---

[41] Of course, levels of subsistence can be affected by basic structures, and to this extent basic structures can be evaluated on humanitarian, as well as social justice, grounds. Our humanitarian obligations are broader, however, than our obligations of justice: when someone is starving or otherwise in urgent need of rescue, it does not matter what our institutional relationship with them happens to be.

uisite of our making responsible choices with respect to the trade-offs we do indeed face. Moreover, at least some of the time, there will be strategies permitting advances in justice without significant costs in terms of the other things we care about: clarifying what justice as such demands in such cases facilitates these advances, even when we do not know how to balance justice against other important values at the margin. For these reasons, we should not let the fact of reasonable pluralism discourage us from working out what a conception of social justice like JMD would demand on its own.

7

Applications of Minimizing Domination

Societies are just to the extent that their basic structure is organized so as to minimize the expected sum total domination experienced by their (present and future) members, counting the domination of each member equally. Suppose we accept this view. What are its implications? This chapter considers the implications of justice as minimizing domination in three areas of persistent debate among contemporary political theorists and philosophers, namely, the demands of distributive justice, the appropriate bounds of toleration and accommodation, and the value of democracy.

By no means do these topics exhaust the potential applications of the theory; I will not discuss, for example, the applications of JMD to questions of personal privacy, family, or gender equality.[1] In a study of this scope, one must pick and choose, and I have selected the three aforementioned topics because they represent what might be thought of as hard cases. The first two have not been discussed extensively in the civic republican literature, and my approach specifically might be thought indifferent to distributive justice, and hostile to multiculturalism. The third has been discussed thoroughly in the literature, but my revisions of some common civic republican views might seem to undermine the obvious republican argument for democracy, and thus deprive civic republicanism of one of its more attractive selling points. Accordingly, my aim here is to demonstrate the power of JMD as a conception of social justice by showing that it can engage each of these issues in an interesting and compelling manner.

7.1 DISTRIBUTIVE JUSTICE

The expression distributive justice can be used in either a broad or a narrow sense. There is a loose sense in which all questions of justice are questions

---

[1] The aim of minimizing domination should be quite congenial to many feminist projects, however.

about the distribution of things we care about—benefits and burdens, rights and obligations, opportunities, and so on. From this point of view, the terms justice and distributive justice are more or less interchangeable.[2]

This section is concerned with the distributive justice in a narrower sense: it discusses only the distribution of entitlements to socioeconomic goods and services such as income and wealth, education and training, medical and other sorts of care, etc. (hereafter referred to as "the distribution of goods" for short). Note that, strictly speaking, it is always entitlements to things, and not things themselves, whose distribution is at issue; when properly understood, this does not affect the main debates. Also note that my discussion leaves aside the distribution of public offices and civil or political rights, since most conceptions of social justice (JMD included) offer different guidelines for distributing the latter.[3] Understood in this narrower sense, distributive justice is one application (among others) of a general theory of social justice.

Since JMD is concerned only with minimizing domination, it follows that distributions of income and wealth, education and training, medical and other sorts of care, and so on, are only of instrumental concern. In this respect, as in many others, JMD is similar to utilitarianism. Progressives as well as others inclined to regard serious socioeconomic inequality and poverty as unjust have not always been satisfied with the instrumental utilitarian arguments for distributive justice. It is far from clear that the best argument for reducing inequality and poverty is that the sum total happiness will be increased by doing so, especially since people might adapt their preferences to suit their circumstances, regardless of whether we reduce poverty and inequality or not.

Will it likewise be a problem that any argument for distributive justice derived from JMD must necessarily be instrumental? In my view, it will not. The aim of minimizing domination provides powerful reasons for regarding serious socioeconomic inequality and poverty as unjust, and compelling grounds for doing something (indeed, something in particular) about them. Since JMD is not a welfarist theory, many of the standard objections to utilitarianism will not apply here, as we shall see.

---

[2] Walzer (1983), for example, uses the terms in this interchangeable way.

[3] On some conceptions, this difference is built into the principles of social justice themselves. In Rawls's theory, for example, the distribution of civil and political rights is governed by the first principle of justice rather than by the difference principle. On other conceptions, like JMD, the difference arises in the process of applying the principles.

7.1.1 The general problem

Loosely speaking, the problem of distributive justice can be divided into two main questions. The first, obviously, is why serious socioeconomic inequality or poverty should be regarded as unjust. Sometimes it is thought that equality needs no justification, whereas inequality does. If this were true, then the first question would not need an answer. That it is not will be obvious once we reflect for a moment on the second question.

The second question concerns the appropriate characterization of what would count as a just distribution of goods. This question has several interrelated dimensions. One issue concerns whether, in assessing a given distribution, we should look at the bundles of goods themselves, or rather at what each person is able to accomplish with his or her bundle, or how happy each person is with his or her bundle. Roughly speaking, these views represent the resource, functioning, and welfare accounts of distributive justice, respectively. Another issue concerns whether a given distribution is just when each person's share of resources (or level of functioning or welfare) is the same, or when it is above a certain threshold, or when the smallest share (or lowest level) is as large (or high) as possible, or something else. These views represent the equality, sufficiency, maximin, and so on accounts of distributive justice.[4] Yet another issue concerns whether it is the actual equality, sufficiency, and the like of shares of resources, levels of functioning, etc. that we should focus on; or rather the *opportunity* to secure an equal share of resources, sufficient level of functioning, etc. that is important. Nearly everyone would agree that some opportunity element must be included in any plausible account of distributive justice, but there is considerable disagreement about how and where to draw the line between those choices people should be responsible for and those they should not.

Contemporary political theorists and philosophers have built up a formidable and sometimes arcane literature addressing these various problems.[5] Often, the strategy in this literature is to postpone answering the first question so as to focus narrowly on some aspects of the second. Judging by the failure of those contributing to this literature to arrive at any sort of consensus, this

---

[4] Less plausible accounts include the pure entitlement view that any given share (or level) is just if it was secured without violating anyone's rights, and what might be called the "aristocratic" view, that a distribution of shares (or levels) is just if the largest share (or level) is as large (or high) as possible.

[5] Since this literature is far too large to cite comprehensively, I will note here only a few signal contributions: Rawls (1971, 1982), Nozick (1974), Nagel (1977), Sen (1980, 1992), Dworkin (2000, esp. chs. 1–2), Roemer (1985, 1996), Scanlon (1986, 1997), Frankfurt (1987), Arneson (1989), G. A. Cohen (1989), Temkin (1993, 2003), Parfit (1995), and Anderson (1999).

strategy has not been entirely successful. The reason for this, in my view, is that working out an answer to the second question obviously hinges on our solution to the first. Whether it is more important for people to have an equal opportunity to secure resources, for example, or a sufficient level of actual functioning, or something else, clearly depends on our reasons for caring about distributive justice in the first place.[6] Our aim, therefore, should be to answer the first question first; having done this, I try to show that an answer to the second question follows easily.

Accordingly, let us reflect on the connection between justice and the distribution of goods. On the theory of social justice I have proposed, the connection is straightforward: a distribution of goods will be just when it arises from the operation of those political and social institutions or practices most likely, given our present knowledge and expectations, to minimize domination in the long run.[7] The issue, then, is simply one of determining which institutions and practices are most likely to do this.

It is useful in this respect to start with some baseline for comparison, and an obvious candidate is the common-sense libertarian ideal of a perfectly free market and minimal state. The libertarian baseline is a good one for several reasons. First, it represents (superficially, at any rate) what many people would regard as the simplest and most efficient set of social policies and institutions for governing the distribution of goods. Second, it represents the most serious challenge to the view (shared by many progressives) that severe inequality and poverty are unjust even when they arise from purely voluntary exchanges in a perfectly free market.

7.1.2 Assessing the libertarian baseline

In one respect, at least, the libertarian baseline will look rather good from a domination-minimizing point of view. This is because of all the political and legal systems we might adopt, a minimal state narrowly limited in its aims to protecting personal and property rights and enforcing contracts would pose the least possible danger of itself subjecting the members of its

---

[6] This point is nicely argued in Scheffler (2003).

[7] Note that the justice of a distribution is strictly procedural here: it is a question of what the ground rules, so to speak, of society should be, and not the actual pattern of holdings arising from those rules. Nozick (1974, pp. 153–64), attacks what he calls "patterned" accounts of distributive justice, of which he, incorrectly, takes Rawls's account to be a leading example. For a discussion and cogent reply to Nozick on this point, see Pogge (1989, ch. 1).

society to domination.[8] Unfortunately, we achieve this assurance only at the cost of introducing considerable domination in other domains. The argument to this effect will have several steps.

The first is to point out that, like many other socioeconomic goods, one's freedom from domination can be voluntarily exchanged. For example, a person might trade away contractual protections against the arbitrary power of his employer for higher pay; in patriarchal societies, women might prefer dependency on a husband's arbitrary will to remaining unmarried, given all the social and economic consequences that accompany the latter; people might sell themselves into slavery in exchange for protection; and so on. In other words, there is nothing special about the good of non-domination that necessarily places it outside the system of market exchange, broadly understood.

Now to be sure, most people (as I have argued) regard their freedom from domination as a particularly important good, and so we would not expect many to trade it away lightly. But there are other especially important goods to consider as well. People have what might be called *basic needs*—for an adequate level of nutrition and health, minimal clothing and shelter, an education sufficient to function in their community, and so on. In order to satisfy these basic needs, a person must have entitlements to the goods or services that doing so requires. If someone needs a life-saving heart bypass operation, for example, then she must have either the money to pay for it, or else an insurance plan that covers it, or else a publicly funded entitlement to receive it, or else some other equivalent. When it comes to basic needs, reasonable people do not typically regard failing to meet them as an option, and it follows that they might even be willing to trade away their freedom from domination—highly valued as that may be—in order to do so. Thus, a poor laborer living in the early days of unregulated market capitalism might accept employment on extremely disadvantageous terms, if his choice was between this employment and starvation.

The exact point at which reasonable people begin to trade away their freedom from domination in order to meet their basic needs will of course vary according to the time, place, and individuals in question. The minimum acceptable level of education, for example, differs widely according to the culture and level of economic development in a given community. The costs and risks an individual is prepared to bear in order to avoid domination

---

[8] This is not to say, of course, that less minimal states will necessarily inflict greater domination—only that there is a somewhat greater risk that they might. Because of this increased risk, less than minimal states might have to be more carefully designed than minimal ones (see Section 7.3.3).

might vary according to her particular preferences. And so on. This is not important for the argument here. What is important is the general fact that reasonable people may be willing to accept higher levels of domination rather than fail to meet their basic needs, and this remains true even if we believe that the specific meaning of basic needs is dependent on the particular context.

A different way of putting this is to point out that severe poverty renders people vulnerable to domination. Because we do not regard the satisfaction of basic needs below some minimum level as optional, when unable to satisfy them on our own we become dependent on the charity of those with the ability to do so for us. "Private charity breeds personal dependence," Michael Walzer writes, "and then it breeds the familiar vices of dependence: deference, passivity, and humility on the one hand; arrogance on the other."[9] On the arbitrary power conception developed in this study, domination must be understood structurally, not in terms of how things happen to turn out. It follows that being dependent on a person or group who has the power to arbitrarily withhold the goods or services necessary to meet one's basic needs, whose satisfaction one does not regard as optional, amounts to domination. The fact that the person or group in question happens to charitably supply them, if indeed they do, is neither here nor there. The point is that, as Thomas Scanlon suggests, severe inequalities "give some people an unacceptable degree of control over the lives of others."[10]

For the second step of the argument, let us return to the proposed libertarian baseline and imagine that we let a perfectly free market run for several generations. Naturally, there will be winners and losers. Some people will make bad choices—such as investing in a business that fails, or choosing a career in an industry that moves overseas; and some will suffer bad luck—such as developing a debilitating medical condition, or losing their home in a tornado. Conversely, others will make good choices or enjoy good luck—they will invent an incredibly popular new product, or happen to be born with highly valued natural talents. Thus, even if we start out with equal shares of goods, socioeconomic inequalities will inevitably arise. Moreover, these inequalities will continue to accumulate, both over the course of individual lives and, more significantly, from one generation to the next.

Now some of these accumulated inequalities might be fair or deserved, and others might not be. Which inequalities are fair or deserved depends on what the correct account of personal responsibility turns out to be, and for many accounts of distributive justice, figuring this out matters quite a bit. For an

---

[9] Walzer (1983, p. 92).
[10] Scanlon (1997, p. 44). See also Goodin (1988, ch. 6), Pettit (1997, pp. 159–60), and Barry (2005, pp. 24–5) for somewhat analogous arguments.

account of distributive justice derived from JMD, by contrast, figuring this out turns out not to matter much at all, as will be apparent shortly. What does matter is that, as these socioeconomic inequalities (fair or unfair, deserved or undeserved) accumulate over time, many people will eventually face the prospect of having to trade away some of their freedom from domination in order to meet what they regard as their basic needs.

Now the argument advanced so far might seem to be open to what we can call a *paternalism objection*. Roughly speaking, the objection runs as follows. Let us grant that freedom from domination, as I argued in Chapter 5, is a particularly important good, and thus that, to the extent that we are able to reduce domination, we lie under a prima facie moral obligation to do so, other things being equal. But what if those subject to domination accept that condition of their own volition (in order to satisfy basic needs, or for some other reason)? At this juncture, some libertarian-minded readers might be tempted to insist that any effort to reduce the resulting domination must fail to respect the autonomy of responsible individuals. Is it not paternalistic to second-guess the choices of those who, after all, only want to do the best they can for themselves, given whatever circumstances they happen to face? Perhaps.

Suppose, for the sake of argument, that we do have good reasons for respecting the choices that people make (including those choices driven by economic necessity), and thus that reducing the choices available to them would represent a failure to respect their autonomy. What difference will this make? In Chapter 6, I suggested that while our direct aim should always be the reduction of domination, sometimes the most practical means of achieving this aim lies in expanding opportunities, thus making it easier for people to avoid domination if they so desire. Whenever this is the case, we can reduce domination and respect people's autonomy at the same time. In such cases, the paternalism objection (even supposing it is valid) makes no difference, so our obligation to minimize domination must be decisive. The relevant question, then, is whether we can reduce the domination arising out of serious socioeconomic inequality and poverty simply by expanding opportunities. I will argue that we can.

7.1.3 An unconditional basic income

Under libertarian policies and institutions, people would arguably experience little domination at the hands of the state, but (I have argued) the inexorable accumulation of socioeconomic inequality would lead, through the ordinary operation of the market system, to considerable domination in the private sphere. Might some other configuration of policies and institutions yield less domination overall? Let us consider some alternatives.

Domination arises through the free market primarily because people can trade away their freedom from domination. Thus, a natural response might be to prohibit the relevant sorts of exchanges. Trading freedom from domination for other goods would then become what Walzer calls a "blocked exchange."[11] To some extent, this is already done in contemporary American law, which prohibits slavery and does not enforce unconscionable contracts, for example.[12] No doubt, these laws prevent some gross abuses, but the blocked-exchange strategy cannot serve as a general solution. There are several reasons for this. For one thing, any attempt to expand the list of blocked exchanges beyond a few relatively uncontroversial instances will probably fall afoul the paternalism objection noted earlier. But even supposing we overcome our aversion to paternalism, there is another and more significant difficulty: namely, that new and more subtle means of converting material advantage into domination will always be discovered and exploited. In the long run, it is unlikely that public policy could ever keep pace with, much less anticipate, such innovations—except perhaps with a regulatory structure so dense and intrusive as to raise serious objections on other grounds. Most significantly from our point of view, any state powerful enough to accomplish this Herculean task would itself undoubtedly become a great source of domination.

A second natural response also fails. Rather than regulate the points of exchange, we might attempt to regulate the relevant social relationships themselves. For example, various workplace regulations, reforms in family law, and so forth, might aim to reduce the arbitrariness with which potential agents of domination can exercise power over their dependents. In preventing some gross abuses, this second response might also be useful; as in the case of the first, however, and for the same reasons, it is unlikely to provide a general solution.

Suppose instead we approach the problem from the other end. People might trade away their freedom from domination for any number of reasons, but on the plausible assumption that the great majority value their enjoyment of non-domination highly, few will do so except when necessary to meet their basic needs. (The exact threshold at which individuals in a given community begin to do this will vary, of course, depending on local views regarding basic needs and the value of non-domination. This does not affect the general

---

[11] Walzer (1983, pp. 100–3).

[12] Slave contracts are prohibited by the 13th Amendment to the US Constitution; unconscionable contracts are unenforceable under §2–302 of the Uniform Commercial Code.

argument.) Obviously, then, the most reliable and least intrusive way to discourage people from trading away their freedom from domination is have the public meet the basic needs of those unable to do so for themselves. Not having to trade away their freedom from domination in order to meet their basic needs, few would probably choose to do so, thus considerably lowering the aggregate domination experienced. Moreover, unlike either the blocked exchange or the regulatory approach, this approach would continue to respect the choices that people make, and thus not fall afoul the paternalism objection.[13] Given these advantages, it is worth considering whether some configuration of policies and institutions could accomplish this without introducing new forms of domination as against the libertarian baseline.

Broadly speaking, there are two ways to publicly meet the basic needs of those unable to do so on their own. The first is to adopt a *means-testing* approach. For example, we could set up a program or bundle of programs that would address individuals' basic need requirements on a case-by-case basis. If someone were unable to meet her nutritional needs, for example, she could appeal to the public nutrition agency, which would then supply the shortfall; if she were unable to meet her health needs, she could appeal to the public health agency, and so on. Alternatively, we could set up a defined income minimum that would roughly correspond to a level of income deemed sufficient to meet all reasonable basic needs. Individuals whose income fell short of the defined minimum would receive a public handout equivalent to the difference. The advantage of either of these means-testing methods is that the public pays to meet the basic needs of only those who cannot do so on their own. But this advantage is also a potential flaw, for it is doubtful whether means testing can be carried out in a suitably non-arbitrary manner: practical experience suggests that state welfare agencies must inevitably employ extensive bureaucratic discretion in carrying out such policies, and that the particular vulnerability of persons in need of public assistance renders the usual sorts of constraints on such discretion more or less ineffective.[14] From a domination-minimizing point of view, it will not do to replace the arbitrary charity of private individuals and groups with the arbitrary charity of state welfare agencies, for this would merely substitute one form

---

[13] Moreover, this might have the added benefit of eventually obviating the need for many other sorts of paternalistic protections as well: workers can comfortably hold out for safe jobs on fair terms if they do not have to worry about meeting their basic needs in the meantime. Of course, there would still need to be protections against fraud and so forth, but Occupational Safety and Health Administration-style workplace regulations and minimum-wage requirements might become unnecessary.

[14] Persons needing public assistance generally lack the political resources necessary to ensure that their interests are given a fair hearing.

of domination for another.[15] We would then want to know whether, compared against the libertarian baseline, a means-tested basic needs guarantee eliminates (from the economic sphere) as much domination as it introduces (in the public sphere). In my view it probably would, but this remains an open question. Fortunately, we do not have to answer it.

The second approach would ensure that everyone's basic needs are met through the public provision of an *unconditional basic income*, such as that proposed by Van Parijs and others.[16] This unconditional basic income might take the form of cash, or else a combination of cash and vouchers for certain defined benefits (health care, education, and so on); and the cash portion of the unconditional basic income might be delivered either through regular government handouts, or else through some version of a negative income tax. Although important, resolving these issues is not essential for the argument at hand.[17] What is essential is that we understand the basic income grant to be unconditional, both in the sense that everyone receives the same basic income regardless of means, and in the sense that everyone receives it automatically, without having to satisfy some sort of participation or contribution requirement.[18] "Everyone" here refers, in principle, to all those persons—citizens or otherwise—affected by the institutions and practices of the relevant basic structure; in practice, however, an unconditional basic income system may be difficult to administer without at least some sort of residency requirement (but see Section 7.4.4).

With an assured basic income of the sort described, it is less likely that people would face the prospect of having to trade away their freedom from

---

[15] In addition, means testing can often be intrusive and humiliating: Young (1990, pp. 53–5), Wolff (1998), and Barry (2005, pp. 209–11). While these are not, in my view, considerations of social justice per se, they do raise independent and significant moral concerns.

[16] See Van Parijs (1995, 2004), Walter (1989), Groot (2002), Pateman (2004), Wolff (1998), and Barry (2005).

[17] Roughly, my own view is that the unconditional basic income ought to consist of a voucher for health insurance, a voucher for education through high school, and a guaranteed retirement income, together with the cash residual delivered as monthly checks to individuals, not households. The cash portion of children's basic income could be put in trust until they reach majority, at which point they could use it to pay for college or something else. The unconditional basic income would replace most other public welfare programs, and eliminate the need for much workplace regulation and the minimum wage. Many details, obviously, remain to be worked out: interested readers are referred to the technical discussions in *Basic Income Studies* (www.bepress.com/bis).

[18] Note that the plan described contrasts with other proposals (e.g., White [2003]; Dagger [2006]) that would require people to demonstrate that they are willing to participate in the workforce or contribute to society in some other way. While the lack of a participation requirement might seem controversial, it should be less so once it is recognized that the value of the basic income grant will not necessarily be sufficient to cover all basic needs. More on this will be discussed shortly.

domination in order to meet some basic needs. On the empirical assumption that people value non-domination rather highly, less domination would thus arise in the private sphere. Note that this remains true, even if the value of the basic income grant is not sufficient by itself to cover all basic needs: the larger the grant, the less domination we would expect to see, but even a small grant would *reduce* domination at the margin. (This observation is significant for the discussion later.) At the same time, since an unconditional basic income lacks any sort of means test or participation requirement, it would be non-arbitrary in its operation, and so little domination would be newly introduced in the public sphere. Thus, from a domination-minimizing point of view, the unconditional basic income is clearly superior to the libertarian baseline.[19]

7.1.4 Setting the level of the grant

How great should the value of the unconditional basic income grant be? This is a more difficult problem than one might expect. Before addressing it, however, let me briefly return to a point made near the opening of this discussion. There I asserted that the problem of distributive justice can be divided into two main questions. The first concerns why socioeconomic inequality and poverty should be regarded as unjust. Now, we have a clear answer: socioeconomic inequality and poverty are unjust because they compel reasonable people to trade away their freedom from domination in order to meet their basic needs.

Notice, however, that in developing our answer to the first question, we have also answered the second—namely, how a just distribution of goods should be characterized. From a domination-minimizing point of view, the distribution of goods will be just when it arises from the operation of those political and social institutions and practices most likely to minimize the sum total domination. The configuration of institutions most likely to do this, I have argued, is a free market together with an unconditional basic income. In my view, this is enough. In other words, provided that each person receives an unconditional basic income, whatever distribution of goods arises subsequently through the operation of the free market can be regarded as just.[20] Since, on my view, the justice of a distribution of goods hinges on the

---

[19] There may be other arguments, pragmatic and normative, for an unconditional basic income, of course; here I am only interested in the argument from JMD.

[20] To say that this resulting distribution would be just no matter how unequal is not to say that it could not be objected to on other grounds. Severe inequality might pose dangers to institutional stability, for instance; if so, we might have prudential grounds for engaging in more extensive redistribution. I am grateful to Cécile Laborde for pressing me on this point.

distribution of those goods themselves, and not on the levels of functioning or welfare provided by those goods, the account is resource based. Since the unconditional basic income will help most those who are least advantaged (and most vulnerable to domination), this account of distributive justice is a version of prioritarianism. And finally, since the market determines distributions beyond the basic minimum, there is considerable scope under the unconditional basic income policy for individual responsibility and opportunity.[21]

Now let us return to the thorny question of determining an appropriate level for the unconditional basic income. What portion of any given society's total income should be devoted to providing an unconditional basic income? (It is useful to express the problem in this way because the specific amount individuals will receive at any given time might depend on their age and health status, and the amount they will receive over their lifetime on how long they live and how healthy they have been.) An initially appealing answer might be—just enough to cover each person's basic needs, and no more. Unfortunately, this answer will not work. Consider Figure 7.1. The vertical axis in this figure represents units of subjective welfare w_i for some representative person i; the horizontal axis represents units x of socioeconomic goods or domination. Assume that these units have been defined so that one unit of goods can be exchanged for one unit of domination, and vice versa. The curve

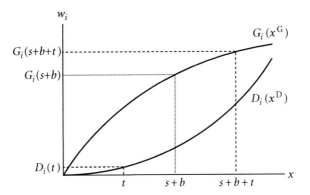

Figure 7.1

[21] Of course, not all inequalities arising out of the market are necessarily fair, and (as discussed in Chapter 6) societies may also aim to reduce some of this unfairness over and above the demands of social justice. Some inequalities, however, are fair—for example, those arising out of different income-versus-leisure preferences—and the unconditional basic income policy certainly provides room for these.

G_i indicates the welfare i derives from a given amount x^G of goods. Notice that this curve is concave, representing diminishing marginal returns: this captures the intuition that once our basic needs are met, the welfare gains we derive from ever-greater amounts of socioeconomic goods are fewer and fewer. The curve D_i indicates the welfare loss i derives from being subject to a given level x^D of domination. This curve is convex, capturing the intuition that low levels of domination are relatively tolerable, while greater levels are less and less tolerable. (This is equivalent to saying that non-domination, like other goods, is subject to diminishing marginal returns.) A reasonable person, we might suppose, will attempt to maximize $G_i(x^G) - D_i(x^D)$, that is, their welfare gains from goods, minus their welfare losses from domination.

Now imagine that we provide a comfortable basic income level b. Let us further suppose that i's income from other sources is s, and that i is not presently subject to any domination. Her welfare is thus given by $G_i(s + b)$, as indicated in Figure 7.1. Will she remain content with this income? She will not. Non-domination, by assumption, can be exchanged for other goods: trading away some of her non-domination, she might increase her income still further. Indeed, given our assumptions, we should expect her to do precisely this, up to the point where her marginal welfare gain from additional income t equals her marginal welfare loss from additional domination. In Figure 7.1, this point is at $s + b + t$, where the slope of $G_i(s + b + t)$ equals the slope of $D_i(t)$. It should, thus, be clear that no matter how high we set the level of the unconditional basic income, reasonable people may nevertheless voluntarily trade away some of their non-domination.[22] No level of basic income is enough, so to speak.

However, it should also be clear that the higher we set the level of the unconditional basic income, the less non-domination i will trade away, other things being equal.[23] This is because at higher levels of income, the marginal welfare gain from further increases that could be secured through trading away non-domination is smaller (i.e., the slope of G progressively decreases). If we are interested in minimizing aggregate domination, the conclusion therefore is straightforward: JMD demands that we set the unconditional

---

[22] This would not be true if people had lexical preferences for income sufficient to cover basic needs, freedom from domination, and additional income, in that order. In future work, I hope to show that basic needs are not like this—that is, that there is no clearly defined basic needs threshold, so preferences cannot be lexically ordered in this way.

[23] At least, this is true so long as we hold total national income constant, and ignore possible incentive effects of funding the basic income. Note, however, that by obviating the need for a minimum wage, eliminating "welfare traps," and so on, an unconditional basic income might well be an efficiency improvement over existing state welfare systems.

basic income as high as we possibly can, so as to reduce avoidable domination to its lowest possible level.

This might seem implausibly generous at first, but we must consider future generations as well as our own (see Chapter 6). Accordingly, the highest possible basic income should be understood to mean the highest *sustainable* one: in other words, the present generation should choose a basic income level such that succeeding generations can choose the same level, or greater.[24]

To sustain a given level of unconditional basic income, we must take into account two important constraints: first, domestic market constraints on our ability to raise the basic income without depressing economic incentives in the long run; and second, global market constraints on our ability to remain competitive with other nations. These constraints ensure that the unconditional basic income will not be exceedingly generous. Indeed, it is important to observe that the grant provided by the highest sustainable basic income might not be large enough by itself to cover all of its recipients' basic needs. This is not a defect in the argument, since (as observed earlier) even a small grant will reduce domination at the margin. Justice demands that we reduce domination so far as we can, but there is no assurance that we can eliminate it altogether. How much we can reduce domination in this case depends on how high a basic income we can (sustainably) afford, and this can only be determined through trial and error by economists and policy makers.[25] When we have done everything we are able to do, social justice cannot demand that we do more.

7.2 TOLERATION AND ACCOMMODATION

Any conception of social justice will tolerate many social and individual practices, and also, if strictly applied, discourage or prohibit many others. Even explicitly un-liberal conceptions, for example, will tolerate at least those practices that further justice as understood by that conception. Conversely, even the most liberal conception cannot, as a practical matter, tolerate every

---

[24] This is also the conclusion reached, on different grounds, by Van Parijs (1995). Note that the highest sustainable basic income is *not* equivalent to Rawls's difference principle, because the position of the least advantaged could be further improved over an unconditional basic income through means testing.

[25] As a rough guide, however, the United States is currently supporting, one way or the other, the equivalent of a per person annual basic income valued at roughly US$7,200. Considering that other nations are even more generous, this much at least might be regarded as sustainable.

conceivable practice simultaneously. The relevant question is always where to draw the line, and it is a question that must be faced by all conceptions of social justice, liberal and otherwise.

Suppose that some conception of social justice would, if uniformly applied in every case, place burdens on a given social and individual practice. If we wish to defend the practice and relieve this burden, we can make two different sorts of argument. On the one hand, we can argue that the conception of social justice in question is (partly or entirely) invalid *because* it would burden a practice (or practices) that ought not be burdened. On the other hand, we can argue that, although the conception of social justice is in general valid, it ought not be strictly applied in these (and perhaps other) cases, due to some broader countervailing considerations. Only the latter would genuinely be an argument for toleration or accommodation. Also notice that issues of the latter sort would arise even if we resolved the first question to our satisfaction—that is, even if we arrived at an agreement on the best conception of social justice. The issues of toleration and accommodation are thus perfectly general ones that can be addressed in general terms, with respect to any candidate conception of social justice. Here, of course, I address them specifically from a domination-minimizing point of view.

7.2.1 Permissible and impermissible practices

To begin with, let us suppose that there are some valid non-justice considerations in favor of encouraging a diversity of social and individual practices, other things being equal. These *reasons of toleration* might, for example, be the considerations offered by J. S. Mill, which tend to show that there are significant welfare benefits in permitting a wide a range of "experiments in living."[26] How weighty are these reasons? Specifically, should we regard them as having *greater* weight than the aim of minimizing domination? This is difficult to say. In what follows, I assume that encouraging a diverse range of practices as such has some positive benefits, but that these benefits are usually not so great as to outweigh the importance of reducing domination when these two aims happen to conflict. It is not my view that this is always true, only that it is true in most cases. At the margin, it may be worth trading off some small degree of non-domination in order to secure a much greater

---

[26] Mill (1859, esp. ch. 3). His arguments are primarily directed to demonstrating the benefits of tolerating diverse *individual* practices; we might easily extend his arguments, however, to show the benefits of tolerating diverse *social* practices as well: see, for example, Kukathas (1997).

degree of diversity. (And also, of course, there may be cases in which the two aims do not conflict, and so we are not forced to choose.)

Suppose that JMD were uniformly applied in every case. Which practices would then be tolerated or accommodated, and which would be discouraged or prohibited?[27] There are three scenarios worth considering.

First, there is presumably a wide range of social and individual practices that simply involve no domination. In such cases, JMD would *permit* toleration and, by our earlier assumption that we have further (non-justice) reasons for encouraging diversity, all these practices should indeed be tolerated.[28] In a few cases, the benefits of diversity might be strong enough to warrant positive accommodation—that is, subsidizing or otherwise propping up (possibly at some expense) practices that would otherwise disappear. Again, provided that these practices do not themselves involve any domination, this sort of positive accommodation would face no objection from JMD.

Second, there is presumably also some range of social and individual practices that do involve domination, either directly or indirectly. The practice of holding slaves is obviously a direct instance of domination. Other practices, however, while not themselves direct instances of domination, might nevertheless present effectively insuperable barriers to reducing or eliminating some instance of domination, and thus indirectly involve domination. The social practice of closing most employment opportunities to women, for example, is not itself necessarily an instance of domination (or at least not if the exclusion is systematic and non-arbitrary in its application); however, it is an effective consequence of doing so that most women will be severely dependent on their husbands, and thus subject to greater domination in the family. JMD cannot tolerate practices directly or indirectly involving domination. Indeed, if strictly applied in every case, JMD would require eliminating such practices, so far as this is pragmatically feasible, despite the fact that this may lead to some reduction in diversity. This simply follows from our assumption that the aim of reducing domination should take priority over the aim of encouraging diversity.[29]

---

[27] Note that, if JMD were strictly applied, any prohibitions would be implemented in a non-arbitrary manner, and thus not introduce new domination as such. This will rarely be the case, of course, but for the sake of getting our intuitions clear, I ignore this fact, and assume that any new domination introduced would be of small enough account as to not figure into our calculations.

[28] Provided, of course, there are not other (non-justice) considerations against toleration. These too will be ignored here, for the sake of focusing on the central question.

[29] In some cases, a practice (not itself an instance of domination) indirectly supports or buttresses domination *without* presenting an insuperable barrier to its elimination. The system of property rights in a society that practices slavery might be an example of this. Here we might eliminate slavery, while retaining property rights. Toleration would be permissible in such cases.

Finally, there might be a third range of social and individual practices that do not (directly or indirectly) involve domination themselves, but which are the by-product, so to speak, of domination. The practices of chivalry and noblesse oblige might not themselves involve any domination, for example, and indeed might fairly be regarded as admirable or beneficial in themselves. These practices are, however, let us say, the by-products of feudalism. Having dismantled the various practices of domination associated with feudalism— which JMD cannot tolerate—it may well be that the culture of chivalry and noblesse oblige will also fade and, eventually, disappear. This prospect we might regard with some regret. Fortunately, even if a practice is the by-product of domination, it is permissible to tolerate it under JMD—provided, of course, that it does not (as in the case of closing opportunities to women) present an insuperable barrier to the elimination of the underlying practices of domination. Unlike in the first range of cases, however, it would not be permissible to positively accommodate such practices, even in the interest of promoting diversity, if doing so would require retaining the practices of domination that are their source of vitality.[30]

This is where JMD would draw the line between permissible and impermissible social and individual practices, if uniformly applied in every case. Note that JMD is reasonably permissive, in the sense that it is prepared to tolerate at least—and in some cases positively accommodate—any practice, no matter how unconventional or (to some) distasteful, provided that it does not directly or indirectly involve domination. The real issue of toleration, however, has yet to be addressed: whether, in some particular cases, the participants in a burdened social or individual practice might have legitimate grounds for relief from the otherwise uniform application of these general rules.

7.2.2 Grounds for toleration or accommodation

Broadly speaking, legitimate grounds for relief from a uniform application of JMD might be either internal or external to the broader aim of minimizing domination. Internal grounds arise when it turns out that empirical conditions are such as to *require* the local toleration (or even, possibly, positive accommodation) of social or individual practices, specifically in

---

[30] To give another example: it is often complained that a more extensive provision for basic needs (such as an unconditional basic income grant would provide, for example) would have the consequence of reducing the admirable social practice of charity. This may indeed be regrettable, but it is not a good reason for failing to eliminate the domination associated with serious inequality or poverty.

order to avoid or reduce greater domination elsewhere. External grounds arise when it turns out that non-justice considerations are, on the whole, more important than the aim of promoting freedom from domination. Here I discuss internal grounds first and in depth, mentioning external grounds only briefly afterward.

Why might local toleration or accommodation be not merely permissible, but actually required on grounds internal to JMD? As has frequently been observed, practices often hold subjective value for their participants. This is quite apart from the fact (when there is such a fact) of their being good or bad from an objective normative point of view. A practice has subjective value for a person if his or her life would go less well were the practice to disappear. Social and individual practices might hold weak or strong, positive or negative, subjective value for a wide range of people. For example, a practice might hold a weak subjective aesthetic value for a large number of people who believe the world is a more interesting place for having that practice in it; and it might simultaneously hold a small negative aesthetic value for another large number of people who believe, on the contrary, that the practice is distasteful. Practices usually hold somewhat stronger subjective value for those individuals directly affected by them, even if they are not participants; they will value such practices positively or negatively depending on whether they happen to like those effects or not. What is most important for our purposes, however, is the fact that practices often hold substantial and positive subjective value specifically for the *participants* in those practices.[31]

There are many reasons why social and individual practices might hold positive subjective value for their participants. First, participants might value a practice simply out of habit, and the unpleasant chore of learning a new way of doing things. Second, they might value a practice because it benefits them or serves their interests in some way (men might value various patriarchal practices for this reason). Third, they might value a practice ideologically, in the sense that it plays some significant role within a distinctive conception of the good or comprehensive doctrine (keeping kosher, for example, holds this sort of value for many Jews). Fourth, with respect to social practices, people might value the associational benefits of participating in a shared practice together with other people—the sense of community, so to speak. Fifth, participation in a practice might partly contribute to one's sense of identity (part of what it means to be Jewish, for example, might include "being a

---

[31] Often, but of course not necessarily: it is possible for a social practice (at least) to persist despite its being detested by its very participants, for example, when eliminating the practice would require overcoming substantial collective-action problems. This will be rare, however.

person who keeps kosher"), such that, if the practice were to disappear, its participants would lose to some degree their sense of self-respect.[32]

These are not mutually exclusive reasons, of course; indeed, they will often overlap and reinforce one another in various ways. And to reiterate, these are reasons that the participants in a practice might themselves subjectively value it positively, in the sense that their lives would go worse in some respect if the practice were to disappear. These are not necessarily reasons for believing that a social or individual practice *actually does* have value, from an objective normative point of view. Slavery in the American South was pre-eminently a terrible and unjust social practice, but this is consistent with its having been subjectively valued positively by those who practiced it. (Why else would they have fought so hard to preserve it?)

It follows from the empirical fact that social and individual practices often carry positive subjective value for their participants that there might be situations in which JMD requires toleration or accommodation. Here I discuss two such situations, though there may be additional cases as well.

The first situation has been remarked on by others, though not from within the same theoretical framework.[33] Suppose that a group of persons participate in a number of overlapping and interconnected shared social practices. These practices carry positive subjective value for their participants, as we have seen; indeed, the combined value of these practices might be greater than the value of each considered separately, through a sort of interaction effect. Now suppose that some of these practices come under a severe burden. This might be, for example, because the persons in question are recent immigrants living in a country where the dominant societal culture does not value those practices; or it might be for other reasons. In response to perceived hostility from the outside, however, the members of that group might *strengthen* their commitment to their internal practices, so as to defend their sense of shared identity. The difficulty arises when those practices happen to be ones involving domination: an example might be immigrant groups in the United States whose practices are more severely patriarchal here than they were in the group's country of origin. In this case, of course, we would have no interest in tolerating or accommodating those particular practices that subject individuals to domination. But it might turn out that combating those particular practices would be easier if the burden on other practices shared by the same group were lessened. In this

---

[32] This last reason was argued most famously by Taylor (1994), but there is now an extensive literature arguing more or less the same point.

[33] Raz (1994, pp. 170–1); Spinner-Halev (2001).

situation, it would seem, the goal of reducing domination overall requires some measure of toleration or positive accommodation.

This is the first situation in which the goal of domination reduction might itself require toleration or positive accommodation. The second is quite different. Again, we start from the observation that existing practices often carry positive subjective value for their participants. Now in certain situations, this might create a certain vulnerability. Consider the following parallel: imagine a worker who has been trained for work in a particular sort of industry that subsequently goes into irreversible decline. It is true that the worker could retrain for work in a new industry, but this might not be very easy to do. Her training investment in the first industry is a sunk cost, so to speak. This makes her economically vulnerable to exploitation: if the hurdles to retraining are great enough, she might voluntarily choose to trade away some of her freedom from domination in order to obtain work with whatever skills she already has. If we are interested in reducing domination, we might want to temporarily prop up the declining industry until we are able to ease this danger. Note that our doing so has nothing to do with any intrinsic value we place in the industry itself, but strictly with our desire to protect workers from domination.

Sometimes a group of people sharing many overlapping and interconnected social practices distinct from those of the broader society can find themselves in an analogous position. We might think of a group of unassimilated recent immigrants as analogous to a group of specialized workers in a declining industry: just as a specialized worker cannot easily change industries, recent immigrants cannot always assimilate without substantial effort. Cultural differences are sunk costs, so to speak, and as such they can be exploited by others. For example, persons who do not speak English cannot easily become American citizens, making them vulnerable to domination in a variety of ways. People employing non-English-speaking workers, for example, wield tremendous arbitrary power over them. This being the case, reducing the domination of recent immigrants might entail special public measures to help overcome the problem of sunk cultural costs. These measures might take the form of special exceptions to general laws, public legal assistance, and so on. As in the case of protected industries, it should be clear that these measures stem from a desire to reduce domination, and not from an inclination to protect some intrinsically valuable culture.

Often, of course, measures of this sort are not taken. On the contrary, it is in the interest of those who would dominate recent immigrants to exacerbate their sunk cultural costs as much as possible, raising the barriers to assimilation. This is quite common.[34] One way of doing this is by placing a great weight on involuntary characteristics such as race or ethnicity by fostering discrimination: in a sense, this creates an unrecoverable sunk cost.

In these two situations, then, the aim of minimizing domination itself may actually *require* toleration or accommodation. (Obviously, whether it does or does not depends on the empirical details of each particular case, and it is beyond the scope of our discussion here to go into such details.) These are grounds internal to JMD. As mentioned earlier, however, there might also be external grounds for toleration or accommodation. This possibility arises from the fact, discussed several times in this study, of moral pluralism. Justice is very important, but it is not the only important thing, and at the margin it might make sense to live with less justice in order to secure more of some other good. One other good relevant in this context is the above-mentioned value of diversity. Another might arise from considerations of humanity—in particular, from the humanitarian concern that we do not force people into freedom from domination before they are psychologically and emotionally comfortable with it. It is especially important in the latter case, of course, not to use this as an excuse for inaction. If people are not comfortable with the prospect of non-domination, one should strive to change this fact through education and consciousness raising. However, this does not detract from the point that considerations of humanity might, in the near term, argue for easing the strictures of JMD.

7.3 DOMINATION AND DEMOCRACY

Many have felt that there must be some connection between democracy and the aim of reducing domination. We can see this especially when we consider that, historically, political liberty was often understood as non-domination (see Chapter 5), and that democracy was often advocated on political liberty grounds.[35]

---

[34] Indeed, in some cases, such tactics might be encouraged by elites with those minority groups themselves, when they have incentives to increase the dependency of a captive clientele. I am grateful to Brian Barry for pointing out this possibility.

[35] Indeed, this argument for democracy on the grounds of political liberty might be seen as the defining, signature theme of classical republicanism from Machiavelli to Madison. (Of course, in this tradition, the term "republic" or "commonwealth" was generally preferred. The term "democracy" was reserved for referring more narrowly to democracies without constitutional or other restraints.)

This section considers the application of JMD to the question of political and legal institutional design—or, more or less equivalently, to the distribution of public offices and civil or political rights. (Offices and rights, of course, must be instantiated in political and legal institutions to be effective; thus, to completely describe a political and legal institutional structure is, in effect, to specify how political rights and public offices are distributed.) We might term the application of principles of social justice to such issues an account of *political legitimacy*. Thus, on the view advanced in this study, we should regard a state as legitimate to the extent that its configuration of political and legal institutions, as compared with feasible alternative configurations, will tend to minimize the domination that it inflicts on those persons subject to its authority.[36] So what sorts of political and legal institutions best advance the aim of minimizing domination? That is, what states can best be regarded as legitimate? My answer, not surprisingly, is the traditional one: namely, democratic ones.

Suppose we provisionally define democracy here in a very loose sense as "rule by the people" or popular sovereignty. Since there are many ways in which to implement popular sovereignty (more or less direct, more or less egalitarian, etc.), democracy so defined will have many possible forms. It follows, then, that there are two different sets of issues to be discussed. The first: What is the value of democracy, from a domination-minimizing point of view? The second: What form of democracy, in particular, best suits the aim of minimizing domination? I discuss both issues here in turn.

7.3.1 How are democracy and non-domination connected?

Many people, as I have said, believe that there must be some connection between democracy and the aim of reducing domination. Some have expressed this by defining domination in such a way that the connection between the two is analytic.

We discussed one particularly explicit example of this in earlier chapters. Iris Young defines domination as "institutional conditions which inhibit or prevent people from participating in determining their actions or the conditions of their actions." She adds, for emphasis, that "social and political

---

[36] This raises the possibility that legitimacy and social justice, so defined, might conflict: perhaps a somewhat less than fully legitimate state could succeed, where a fully legitimate state would fail, in removing some substantial instance of domination in the private sphere. In this case, we would have to balance our commitment to narrow political legitimacy against our broader commitment to social justice. I will leave such possibilities aside for the time being, however.

democracy is the opposite of domination."[37] In Chapter 4, I discussed the shortcomings of this as an adequate conception of domination; here, we may leave such complaints aside. In the present context, what is relevant is that defining domination and democracy as opposites renders the connection between them trivial. Depending on our aims, doing so may also be self-defeating. If our aim is to advocate democratic political and legal institutions, then it does not contribute to our aims to define domination as a lack of democracy, and then go on to point out that in promoting democracy we would also be reducing domination (so defined).

Others have connected democracy and the aim of reducing domination in a less direct manner. Suppose we adopt the arbitrary power conception of domination proposed in this study, but that we define arbitrariness along the lines suggested by Pettit. "The capacity to interfere on an arbitrary basis is," he writes, "the capacity to interfere in a person's life without regard to their perceived interests"; or it is the capacity to interfere without being "forced to track the interests and ideas of the person suffering the interference."[38] An imbalance of power, on this view, would constitute domination to the extent that its exercise is not forced to track the collectively avowed interests of the various parties affected. Democratic institutions, quite naturally, are the instrument by which this sort of tracking is secured, and domination thereby avoided.

Now this last claim can be interpreted in two different ways. On the one hand, we might say that tracking the collectively avowed interests of a group of persons just means responding to its collective will as expressed via the suitably democratic procedures. On this reading, the connection between democracy and the aim of minimizing domination is analytic, albeit some-what indirectly so. In other words, domination has been defined in such a way that it could not be reduced without expanding democracy and, concurrently, expanding democracy is, by definition, reducing domination. The difficulty with this indirect approach is the same as the difficulty with the direct one: namely, that an analytic argument (direct or indirect) adds no substantive weight to our argument for democracy, assuming we want to make such an argument.

On the other hand, we might interpret the claim somewhat differently, as saying that democratic political and legal institutions are the institutions most likely, as a matter of contingent empirical fact, to track the collectively avowed

---

[37] Young (1990, p. 38).
[38] Pettit (1999, p. 165 and 1997, p. 55, respectively). See also Skinner (1998, pp. 26–7), Pettit (2001, pp. 138–9, 156–8), Richardson (2002, pp. 47–55), Maynor (2003, pp. 37–9), and Bohman (2008, pp. 207–8).

interests of a group of persons—thereby reducing arbitrariness and, *eo ipso*, domination as well. This drives a non-analytic wedge, so to speak, between the analytic steps in the argument that could, in principle, be tested empirically. Suppose it is tested, and discovered sound. It follows that, if minimizing domination is our aim (as I have argued it should be), we would have compelling substantive reasons for promoting democracy. This is the right sort of argument to make, in my view, but difficulties remain. In order to really test the empirical claim that democratic institutions are the ones most likely to track the collectively avowed interests of a group of persons, we would need some independent measure of collectively avowed interests. Unless we propose to lay out a comprehensive account of the common good, it is difficult to see how we could avoid falling back on the analytic strategy, in which collectively avowed interests are simply the upshot of a collective will expressed through the suitably democratic procedures.

It was partly for this reason that, in Chapter 4, I eschewed the substantive democratic interpretation of arbitrariness in favor of a strictly procedural one. On my preferred view, social power is arbitrary to the extent that its exercise is not externally constrained by effective rules, procedures, or goals that are common knowledge to all the persons or groups concerned. Since democracy as such does not enter into this conception of domination, it is left absolutely clear that a substantive argument connecting the aim of reducing domination to the value of democracy is necessary. (Or it is necessary, at any rate, if we want to argue for democracy on the grounds of social justice; democracy might serve other values as well, of course, but such considerations are beyond the scope of discussion here.)

7.3.2 The value of democracy

Given, then, the conception of domination laid down in Part I, why should we believe that broadly democratic political and legal institutions are the institutions most likely to minimize domination? It is not obvious that they are. This can be seen most easily by considering:

> *JMD Dictator*. Imagine an absolute dictator, who has all the political power and authority that it is, practically speaking, possible to have. Suppose she is sincerely committed to minimizing domination, and that she employs the full measure of her authority in aiming to do so.

Our challenge is to explain why democracy would do a better job than the JMD Dictator in achieving our aim of reducing domination. Since it is difficult to imagine another configuration of political and legal institutions likely to be as successful in reducing domination as the JMD Dictator, if we can demonstrate democracy's advantages over the JMD Dictator from this point of view, it follows (by transitivity) that democracy must also have advantages over any other option as well. This is, roughly, the strategy adopted by Mill in arguing for democracy, except of course that the advantages he was interested in are not explicitly advantages in terms of reducing domination.[39]

As a preliminary, three observations are in order. First, since we have not yet considered which of the many forms of democracy is best, the pro-democracy argument must be presented in fairly general terms, relying on features that all forms would presumably have in common. Second, we should exclude the possibility that a JMD Dictator might try to reduce domination indirectly, by devolving political authority on the people. This might be, of course, her best strategy for reducing domination, but if so, then the argument for democracy is already won, since the JMD Dictator succeeds in her aims only by transforming the dictatorship into a democracy anyway. Third and finally, I compare alternatives on the assumption that we are discussing reasonably long-term or equilibrium states, not transitional states. If indeed democracy turns out to be superior as an equilibrium state, nothing necessarily follows with respect to the complicated question of how best to transition from non-democratic to democratic regimes.

Now let us turn to the main issue. Initially, the most obvious argument against the JMD Dictator might run as follows: domination, on the conception developed in this study, arises whenever persons or groups are dependent on some other person or group who can exercise arbitrary power over them. But this is precisely the situation of citizens in a society governed by a JMD Dictator. Power is arbitrary, as we have seen, unless its exercise is externally constrained by effective rules, procedures, or goals that are common knowledge to all concerned. Thus, a slave master might be constrained in the treatment of his slaves by his own sense of natural duty and fairness, or a psychological predisposition for being nice, but these are merely internal constraints. Unless a constraint on the exercise of power is somehow externally enforceable, it does not count. Clearly, the JMD Dictator is much like a benevolent slave master in this respect. Even if her overriding aim is to reduce domination, her efforts will (in a sense) be self-defeating, since her dictatorship itself—by its very nature—will constitute a form of domination.

This argument is sound so far as it goes, but insufficient. It is true that the JMD Dictatorship would itself be a great source of domination. But this fact

[margin handwritten note: externally enforceable vs internal constraints]

---

[39] See Mill (1861, esp. ch. 3).

alone is not decisive. It is not decisive, first, because the question remains whether the domination constituted by the dictatorship itself would be greater overall than would all the other various forms of domination, considered in aggregate, that our JMD Dictator might be able to reduce or eliminate. For example, our JMD Dictator might be more successful in introducing an unconditional basic income than a democracy would have been, and this would reduce the incidence of domination in the economic sphere. Might not this reduction more than make up for the domination constituted by the dictatorship itself? Perhaps, or perhaps not: this is, at any rate, an open question.

Even if it does not, however, the issue is still not settled. This is because democratic government might also, just as well as a dictatorship, constitute a form of domination. In a democracy, the "will of the people" exercises social power over each citizen considered individually, and if that power is not externally constrained, it counts as arbitrary from the latter's point of view. When this is the case, the purported disadvantage of the JMD Dictator vis-à-vis democracy might not be a (relative) disadvantage at all. Of course, in most democracies, popular majorities are effectively constrained by institutionalized constitutional rights, the rule of law, and so on—but then again we might attempt to place similar constraints on a JMD Dictator. Our argument would then hinge on showing that these constraints would necessarily be less effective with respect to the latter than to the former. As it happens, there are plausible grounds for believing this is the case (as we shall see), but here we have become entangled in a discussion of what form of democracy would be best, and that question has been postponed.

There is another, more direct line of argument to be pursued first. This is what might be called the *civic virtues* argument. In outline, the idea is, first, that we are most likely to succeed, practically speaking, in our aim of minimizing domination if both citizens and public officials are generally imbued with an appropriate set of reasonably robust civic-minded dispositions; and second, that democratic political and legal institutions are far more likely to cultivate such civic-minded dispositions than are the political and legal institutions of a JMD Dictatorship.

Before further discussing the details of this argument, I should hasten to make two clarifications. The first is that the argument for civic virtues here is strictly instrumental. It is not claimed that the possession and exercise of these civic virtues, whatever they turn out to be, is a human good for its own sake.[40]

---

[40] This argument has been made, of course, by the civic humanists. But it is not the view advanced in this study (nor, for that matter, is it the view of civic republicans such as Pettit and Skinner).

It is good for people to possess civic virtues only insofar as those virtues will instrumentally bring about a reduction in the overall level of domination in society. The second clarification is that the civic virtues in question need not be particularly demanding. Indeed, on my view, they probably are not. Certainly, they do not include anything like the requirement that citizens identify themselves and their interests with the community as a whole in any particularly strong sense. Since the term 'civic virtue' sometimes has a demanding connotation, I generally employ the expression civic-minded dispositions in its stead.

How might the widespread cultivation of civic-minded dispositions improve our prospects for minimizing domination? There are many possible connections to be drawn here, but I will focus on two.

The first arises from the intimate connection between the aim of minimizing domination and securing the rule of law. Imagine for a moment that there were no system of criminal and civil law. In the absence of such a system, citizens would not know where they stood with one another; their interrelations would be governed by mere force—that is to say, by the arbitrary whim of the momentarily stronger party. In order to enjoy some degree of nondomination, therefore, it is absolutely essential to introduce a domestic legal system: only then is it possible for fellow citizens to enjoy some measure of independence from arbitrary power in their mutual relations. In the classical republic tradition, this view was commonly expressed as the "Empire of Law" ideal—the notion that in a free republic laws, and not men, rule.[41] Of course, this cannot ever be literally true, but it can be approximated in a sort of artificial way, such that citizens experience their everyday lives more or less *as if* it were true in their society. Accomplishing this requires, however, that the law be widely regarded as clear, predictable, and legitimate. This, in turn, is possible only when there is a generally high level of compliance with the law, and when legal rules are embedded in a shared network of informal social meanings. Put another way, achieving the rule of law requires a fairly robust respect for the law on the part of both citizens and public officials. Respect for the law is thus an instrumentally valuable civic-minded dispositions.

The second connection between civic-minded dispositions and our prospects for minimizing domination arises from a quite different difficulty. This is the fact that, no matter how carefully designed, the operation and functioning of

---

[41] Recall that, in this tradition, liberty was understood as non-domination. Thus, we can easily understand the claim that, as Blackstone (1765, p. 122), for example, puts it, "laws, when prudently framed, are by no means subversive but rather introductive of liberty" and thus "where there is no law, there is no freedom." The expression "an Empire of Laws" derives from a passage in Livy (*Hist.*, II.1), and was popularized especially by James Harrington in his *Oceana*.

government in a complex society necessarily entail considerable discretion on the part of public authorities. There are two especially prominent instances of this. To begin with, it is clear that no matter how detailed and carefully crafted it is, a system of explicit rules and regulations cannot possibly cover all contingencies and circumstances. It follows that discretionary authority must inevitably be left in the hands of courts, public agencies, and administrative bureaucracies. Even apart from this, there additionally remains extensive discretion in the hands of legislatures to set public law and policy in the first place: a daily changing system of rules is not much better than having no rules at all. If discretionary authority of either sort is not to count as arbitrary, it is essential that it be externally constrained by common-knowledge procedures and goals. For these external constraints to be effective, citizens and public officials must be willing and able to exercise some degree of discretionary oversight. Thus, the second sort of instrumentally valuable civic-minded disposition is the disposition to keep tabs on discretionary public authorities, and to undertake oversight interventions when necessary. This includes the general responsibility of citizens to stay informed and participate in elections on a regular basis.

The argument is not complete, of course, unless we can further show that a JMD Dictator will be less effective than a democracy at cultivating the required civic-minded dispositions. The reasons for believing that this is the case, however, are fairly obvious, and have been expounded on at length by Tocqueville, Mill, and many others. In brief, they boil down to the observation that the opportunity to exercise at least some degree of genuine influence and control over political and legal outcomes—for example, by sitting on juries and by participating in electoral politics—is the only really effective motivation for developing civic-minded dispositions. The historical record (and common sense) shows that top-down efforts to promote civic-mindedness will never be as effective as the practical experience of living in a society with the genuinely democratic institutions.

Let me reiterate that these are contingent, empirical claims. Though eminently plausible, in my view, they could be shown false. In that event, JMD would support and regard as legitimate whatever configuration of political and legal institutions is indeed shown best able (in their equilibrium state) to minimize the sum total domination.

7.3.3 The best form of democracy

Earlier, we provisionally defined democracy as popular sovereignty. But there are many forms of democracy. Which, then, should we favor (or regard as most legitimate)? This topic is too broad. I focus on only one dimension of it here, namely: Would our aim of minimizing domination be better served by maximal democracy, or by some sort of constitutionally constrained democracy?[42]

Under maximal democracy, the political authority of popular majorities would not be subject to constitutional limits. If, however, the exercise of political authority must be subject to externally effective constraints to not constitute domination, what then is to prevent a maximally democratic government from itself constituting a source of domination? Let us suppose that, under present and foreseeable conditions, sovereign states cannot be effectively constrained in the required external manner by international institutions like the United Nations, human rights conventions, and so on. Realistically speaking, any effective constraints on political authority must somehow originate from within a given society itself. How is this possible?

Constitutionalism, properly understood, is the solution. Roughly, the idea is that a constitutional specification of basic rights and political procedures serves as the focus of an equilibrium in citizen–government relations, in which electoral incentives and, as a last resort, active resistance (more on this later) serve as the sanctions on governments that might otherwise be tempted to exercise political authority arbitrarily. In other words, the constitution serves in a dual role: first, it specifies constraints on the government's arbitrary powers—which constraints, if given effective external support, would prevent that political authority from itself constituting domination; at the same time, the constitution acts as a coordination device for the citizens, enabling them to overcome the collective-action problem that would otherwise hinder their ability to provide the very support needed.[43] It follows, of course, that our aim of minimizing domination would be better served by constitutional, and not maximal, democracy: only a constitutional democracy would not itself constitute a source of domination.

(Might a JMD Dictatorship be placed under constitutional constraints in a similar manner? In principle, the answer is probably yes, though for the reasons discussed earlier we might still prefer a constitutional democracy to a constitutional dictatorship. Historically speaking, there were many reasonably stable and, at least to some extent, effectively limited monarchies. As was often pointed out by the classical republicans and other critics, however, it has been the inevitable tendency of such monarchs to strive against, evade, and

---

[42] Pettit (1997, ch. 6, 1999, pp. 172–88), endorses the latter view, for example, whereas Bellamy (2007, esp. chs. 4–5), vigorously defends the former.

[43] This argument is drawn from Hampton (1994) and Weingast (1997). The basic intuition may also be found, I would argue, in Harrington (1656), though, of course, it is not nearly so explicit.

undermine those limits whenever possible.[44] Having once accepted the principle of single-person rule, it is often difficult to resist following the logic of that principle out in every sphere of political and legal authority. This suggests that constitutional government will be most stable when based on popular sovereignty, and this may be a further argument for democracy.)

Having presented the case for constitutionalism from the point of view of minimizing domination, it might be instructive to contrast this view with a very different argument proposed by some deliberative democrats and others.[45] Suppose we regard a deliberative political process as genuinely democratic if and only if that process conforms to certain procedural requirements, as given by a list. Deliberation is not democratic unless everyone is free to express his or her views, for example; thus, freedom of expression must be on the list. Similarly, perhaps, an equal weighting of each participant's considered opinion. And so on. This being the case, enforcing the requirements on our list—even against the will of popular majorities, when necessary—can be understood as effectively making political processes *more* democratic, not less. Many political and legal theorists have found this argument extremely persuasive. Indeed, at times it has seemed to provide the primary rationale for American Supreme Court jurisprudence.[46] If this argument worked, it would derive constitutionalism from the value of democracy itself in a particularly satisfying way. Unfortunately, it does not work.

The difficulty with the deliberative-democratic approach lies in a mismatch between the bundle of constitutional rights we believe social justice demands on the one hand, and the bundle of rights presupposed by the deliberative process itself on the other. Obviously, the argument appears strongest when applied to basic political rights and liberties such as free expression, assembly, the right to vote, and so on. But many basic rights that social justice seems to require cannot easily be accounted for in this manner. Consider the right of personal privacy. Now of course, we need not essentialize any particular construction of personal privacy, for privacy rights have often had the effect of obscuring, and thereby sheltering, considerable injustice (the most notorious instance, of course, being traditional Anglo-American family law, which has long protected the domination of married women by their husbands, and children by their parents). But surely one would expect any satisfactory account of social justice to entail at least *some* rights to personal privacy,

---

[44] Classic arguments to this effect can be found in Nedham (1656), Milton (1660), and many others; for further discussions, see Lovett (2005).

[45] See, for example, Ely (1980), J. Cohen (1989, 1996), Habermas (1996, 1998), Holmes (1995), and others.

[46] Here, I refer to the activities of the Warren and Burger Courts, especially as interpreted by Ely (1980) in light of the famous fourth footnote in *United States v. Carolene Products* (1938).

once these are appropriately specified—rights to reproductive choice, for example, or same-sex marriage rights. But what sort of argument could possibly tie these rights to the necessary preconditions of a genuinely democratic political process? It is not obvious that any could.[47]

Now deliberative democrats might complain that domination minimization provides only an instrumental argument for democracy, and indeed this is correct. In fact, JMD does not even require that democracy be *maximized* in order to satisfy the demands of social justice. Relatively little democracy might suffice to cultivate the necessary civic-minded dispositions and to provide the necessary bulwark for constitutional restraints on political authority—or, at any rate, this might be true once democracy has been firmly established as an equilibrium state. JMD thus offers what can fairly be called a "minimalist" conception of democracy in the spirit of Machiavelli: the basic idea is simply that it is safer in the long run to entrust ultimate political authority with the people, who are mainly interested in not being subject to domination, rather than with the elites, who would subject others to domination.[48]

7.4 REALIZING JUSTICE AS MINIMIZING DOMINATION

Our discussion of democracy was based on a comparison of political regimes in their static or equilibrium states. But political regimes, and indeed societies more generally, are not always in equilibrium. On the contrary, it is precisely our hope that societies will advance toward greater and greater social justice.

In this section I consider various problems connected with moving from a less to a more just society: that is to say, I discuss how we should best *realize* justice as minimizing domination. For reasons that become clear shortly, these problems are particularly thorny, because they necessarily take us beyond the scope of social justice, into the realms of interpersonal, transitional, and global justice. Reflecting on these themes, thus, reveals more precisely the limits of social justice. Each of these is an extensive topic in its own right, of course, and cannot possibly be addressed comprehensively in a

---

[47] Habermas (1993, pp. 59–60) admits as much with respect to the issue of abortion. Attempts have been made, of course, to work out such an argument (see especially J. Cohen [1996]). It is strange, however, to think that the case for privacy hinges on its being a necessary precondition to democratic participation.

[48] An account of the argument for democracy similar in spirit can be found in Shapiro (2003, esp. ch. 2), except that his conception of domination is wholly inadequate. See also Lovett (2005).

study of this scope. Here they are discussed only insofar as each relates narrowly to the realization of social justice, where this is understood as the minimization of domination.

7.4.1 Reform, resistance, and rebellion

To get our ideas clear, it may help to introduce some simplifications. The most useful of these will be to imagine a rather crisp distinction between the various feasible equilibrium states for a society on the one hand, and the possible routes of transition among them on the other. From the point of view of JMD, we are concerned only with the aggregate levels of domination experienced over time. Let us assume that transitions from one equilibrium state to another, being temporary, carry finite transition costs in terms of the domination individuals would be subject to in the process. By contrast, let us assume that while in equilibrium, societies indefinitely accrue levels of domination, for as long as they remain in that state. Thus it should be obvious that, in the long run, the most important thing is to arrive at the equilibrium state accruing the smallest overall level of domination, as this comparative benefit will (eventually) outweigh even the most costly transitions. The more interesting issues, then, lie in the choice of means—the different feasible routes of transition—for arriving at the desired end of a maximally just society.

Transitions can be effected either internally or externally. Internally, the members of a given society themselves can aim to move their society from less just to more just equilibrium states. Externally, actors outside a given society (neighboring states, international organizations, etc.) can aim to do the same thing. The latter topic falls under the heading of global justice, and it will be discussed later. Here the focus is on the internally effected transitions. Broadly speaking, transitions can be internally effected either through ordinary political action—voting and running for office, for example—or else through resistance. We should note, of course, that the line between ordinary political action and resistance is entirely relative to a given society's laws and policies: for example, when public assemblies are not legal, assembling in public is an act of resistance. Ordinary political action is thus simply defined as all those sorts of reform-minded activities permissible within the framework of the existing basic structure of the society. Correspondingly, resistance is defined as any reform-minded activity not permissible within the framework of the existing basic structure.

Possible modes of resistance, in turn, can be usefully distinguished into three types. The first is what might be called passive resistance or conscientious refusal: this occurs when a person merely refuses to obey or comply with a command, as for example, when a person refuses to present himself for military service when drafted. The second is what might be called active non-violent resistance or *civil disobedience*: this occurs when a person (often, though not necessarily, in concert with others) performs public, non-violent acts contrary to law or political authority, usually with the intention of engaging public sympathy.[49] The third is what might be called active violent resistance or *rebellion*: this occurs when a person (often, though not necessarily, in concert with others) takes up arms, and is prepared—if necessary—to use them, against the prevailing social and political order.

In comparing these alternate strategies (ordinary political action versus the various sorts of resistance) for effecting transitions between equilibrium states, many considerations apply. Among these: first, the fixed costs (in terms of domination), if any, attendant on a particular strategy; second, the probability that the strategy will indeed succeed in bringing about the desired transition; and third, the length of time carrying out each particular strategy is likely to take. With respect to the last of these, a speedier transition is presumably, other things being equal, better than a slower one, in that the benefits of society's being in a more just equilibrium state begin to accrue sooner. Thus, while resistance may have greater fixed costs than ordinary political action, these costs might in some cases be compensated for if resistance brings about a greater social justice more quickly.

Under what conditions, if any, are these appropriate strategies for effecting transitions? We can address this question from two different directions: on the one hand, we can consider the conditions under which persons or groups have the *right* to adopt one or more of these strategies; on the other hand, we can consider the conditions under which persons or groups have the *obligation* to do so. In later addressing the question from the second direction it will become apparent why these are not equivalent, and indeed, why there is some considerable gap between them.

With respect first to the rights of persons or groups, it should be obvious that the difficult problem is resistance. Ordinary political action is, by definition, legally permissible within the framework of the existing basic structure of a given society, and surely we would want to grant the members of that society a right to employ all such legally permissible means in advancing the cause of social justice. But should they additionally have the right to advance the cause of social justice through resistance? This depends. Consider two equilibrium states available to a given society: in its current state, the basic structure includes some substantially unjust social institution or practice,

---

[49] These first two sorts of resistance are discussed and defined in greater detail by Rawls (1971, pp. 363–71).

whereas in another possible state it does not. First, we must estimate the probability that this injustice could be reformed through ordinary political action and, if so, how long this is likely to take. This establishes a benchmark for comparison. Generally speaking, the scope of legitimate resistance is reduced when ordinary political action is more likely to be efficacious: the bar for legitimate resistance is thus probably much higher in democracies than it is under non-democratic regimes.

Second, we must consider the fixed transition costs that accrue to each of the various modes of resistance. When it comes to the two non-violent types of resistance, these costs are almost entirely limited to their deleterious effects on the rule of law. Since maintaining the rule of law can be expected, in the long run, to further the aim of minimizing domination (reasons for believing this were discussed in Section 7.3.2), these effects may to some extent restrict the right to engage in resistance. But in the case of conscientious refusal, any harm to the rule of law is trivial. It follows that people should have the right, under nearly any conditions, to advance the cause of social justice through passive resistance. (Whether people are *obligated* to do so in a particular case will depend on further considerations, as discussed in Section 7.4.2)

Civil disobedience might be expected to have a somewhat greater deleterious effect on the rule of law, but this effect is still probably small.[50] Thus, provided we reasonably expect civil disobedience to effect a speedier transition to a more just equilibrium state than ordinary political action, the bar for legitimate civil disobedience can probably be met. It would thus be permissible to engage in civil disobedience on behalf of, say, a guaranteed public provision of basic needs, even in a democracy such as the United States, given the difficulty in bringing about such reforms through ordinary political action. This relatively low threshold for permissible civil disobedience stems from the fact that JMD does not entail any direct obligation to obey the law or political authority as such: the only reasons for not engaging in civil disobedience on behalf of social justice stem indirectly from the (minor) negative side effect such activities might have on the maintenance of the rule of law.

The third level of resistance, however, is another story. The negative impact of violent rebellion on the general maintenance of personal security through law and order is obviously severe; what is worse, this negative impact is nearly always further exacerbated by the efforts of political and legal authorities to suppress it. Considering these effects, the bar to rebellion must be set very high indeed. I can imagine two situations in which it could possibly be met. The first arises in societies subject to autocratic regimes, especially when such

---

[50] Rawls (1971, pp. 373–5), notes that the effect might be greater if too many groups engage in civil disobedience simultaneously. In this case, the groups should, he thinks, take turns.

regimes are highly stable (as were, e.g., the old feudal orders of Europe). In cases of severe domination, when there is no reasonable chance of ordinary political action leading to reform, violent resistance may be a permissible option. The great social revolutions of France, Russia, and so on might be examples of this scenario. The second situation arises in societies where reasonably democratic political regimes are in danger of transitioning to autocracy. Examples might be the destruction of the Wiemar democracy by the Nazis, or the military coups in Argentina, Chile, and so on. In this type of situation, violent resistance in defense of democracy might be permissible, given that a failure to resist at the outset would foreclose the possibility of reform through ordinary political action in the future.

7.4.2 The duty of justice

So far, we have considered only when persons or groups have the right to engage in efforts aimed at advancing the cause of social justice. Having the right to do something does not, however, necessarily entail having an obligation to do it. Thus, we must next consider the question of our personal obligations to effect internal transitions from less to more just equilibrium states.

What does justice demand of us personally? Let us say that a conception of direct interpersonal justice is an account of those moral obligations that we have as individuals arising out of what might be called the *duty of justice*.[51]

> (DJ) Individuals have a prima facie obligation to act (by themselves, or in concert with others) so as to bring about and maintain social justice, so far as they are able.

The duty of justice describes only a part of our obligations as individuals. Clearly, human beings have many additional obligations—both to themselves (obligations of prudence), and to others (obligations of morality). It follows that the duty of justice may conflict with these other obligations. If we ask whether a person should further social justice at some cost or risk to herself, we are asking how to balance the duty of justice against her prudential obligations; if we ask whether a person should further social justice even when this would harm or injure someone else, we are asking how to balance the duty of justice against her other (non-justice) moral obligations. These are extremely difficult questions to answer.

---

[51] This term is obviously due to Rawls (1971, p. 115).

In the comments that follow, I assume that the duty of justice is not an absolute one, and thus that it can be outweighed by competing obligations. Fortunately, however, there are many cases in which the duty of justice does not conflict with our other obligations. For example, if we live in a reasonably just society, the duty of justice will usually require only that we comply with the demands placed on us by the basic structure of our society—that is, that we "play by the rules."[52] In most (though not all) cases, compliance with a reasonably just social order will not conflict with our other moral or prudential obligations. Also, there are many cases in which the duty of justice simply does not arise—namely, when we are not (as individuals) in a position to further social justice. In such cases, obviously, a balancing of the duty of justice against our other obligations will not be necessary.

What sort of obligation is the duty of justice? Moral philosophers often distinguish between what are sometimes called general or *universal* interpersonal obligations on the one hand, and special or *agent-relative* interpersonal obligations on the other. The former are obligations that presumably always have force, regardless of the particular relationship between the relevant individuals. Thus, people lie under a duty not to harm others without sufficient reason, regardless of who the potential victim is, or what the relationship between them happens to be. The latter, by contrast, are obligations that arise only with respect to specific parties under special conditions. Thus, if Andrea promises to give $100 to Bob, her duty to keep this promise can be discharged only by her, and only with respect to him: it is not discharged by her giving $100 to Carla, for example, nor by Carla's independently giving $100 to Bob.

An especially significant set of agent-relative interpersonal obligations are what might be called our *associational duties*. If I join a club, I thereby acquire a special set of agent-relative obligations with respect to the other club members (and they, in turn, with respect to me). Indeed, this is essentially what it means to be in a club: if no agent-relative obligations adhered to membership, then membership would be meaningless, and joining the club pointless.

On one view, the duty of justice is an agent-relative associational duty that arises from our membership in a particular society. This, for example, is what Rawls believes: society is a system of mutually beneficial cooperation, he

---

[52] The traditional view of justice as "giving each their due" (e.g., as expressed in Plato and Aristotle) more or less corresponds to this requirement, on the assumption that existing political and social institutions and practices are already just, or at any rate, not amenable to change. The topic of social justice specifically arises only once we begin to regard our shared institutions and practices as an object of choice: only then does it become relevant to ask what rules we should be playing by.

argues, and the duty of justice arises specifically through our participation in that system.[53] Thus, any obligations imposed on us by the duty of justice are owed by us specifically to our fellow participants—that is, to the members of our society, and not to persons in other societies.[54]

Certainly, there are agent-relative associational duties that arise from our membership in a particular society; earlier (in Chapter 6) I suggested that duties of fairness might be one example: part of what it means for a people to constitute a community is for them to agree to collectively share risks and burdens according to their own ideas of solidarity. In my view, however, the duty of justice is not one of them. It is rather a universal interpersonal obligation: each of us has, in principle, an obligation to ensure that people everywhere live under just institutions and practices.[55] One advantage of this view is that it can account more easily for any obligations of justice we have with respect to future generations and persons in societies other than our own. It often strains the imagination to think of (temporally and geographically) distant persons as engaged in a system of mutually beneficial cooperation with us; fortunately, the universal view does not require that we do this. There are other advantages as well, but since these topics have been discussed extensively by others, I will not elaborate. Instead, I will concentrate on the specific obligations imposed by the duty of justice, insofar as they relate to advancing the cause of social justice.

Some of the obligations imposed by the duty of justice are *direct*, others *indirect*. Among the former is the fairly obvious direct obligation to avoid subjecting others to domination. This would entail, if one lived in a society permitting slavery for example, an obligation not to hold slaves.[56] For the most part, however, the obligations imposed by the duty of justice will be indirect. This is because we will not best succeed in minimizing the sum

---

[53] Rawls (1971, esp. pp. 108–17). Note this is consistent with his observation that the duty of justice should be viewed as a "natural" duty, that is, not one itself derived from some sort of voluntary agreement. This is because any voluntary agreement necessarily presupposes some pre-existing obligation to abide by agreements in general: in order to avoid infinite regress, we must begin with a natural duty.

[54] Some of the details and consequences of this view are grappled with in Scheffler (2001) and Nagel (2005). One oft-discussed consequence is that any obligations of global justice must be regarded as obligations between whole "peoples," and not individuals: see Rawls (1999).

[55] Note that, with respect to a given institution or practice, this obligation is specifically *owed to* all those persons (including persons in future generations) affected by that institution or practice, whether they are fellow citizens or not.

[56] This obligation might conflict with other moral obligations, however. Traditional family law was such that the condition of marriage was, for women, a condition of domination. In many cases, however, since women faced dismal choice scenarios, marriage was nevertheless their best option. In refusing to marry, therefore, a man might make his prospective wife worse off overall than she would otherwise be.

total domination by imposing on each individual the obligation to weigh every option he or she faces, in every situation, according to its expected impact on this sum. The far more efficacious strategy is to work out in advance, as best we can, which configuration of political and social institutions and practices can best be expected to minimize the sum total domination, and then impose on each individual the much simpler obligation to comply with this preferred configuration. In doing so, individuals act to minimize the sum total domination indirectly, thus discharging their obligations under the duty of justice.

This, of course, is the complete story only in societies with largely just basic structures. Few, if any, societies answer to this description. Rather, individuals usually live under a mix of reasonably just and (marginally or substantially) unjust political and social institutions and practices. The degree to which an institution or practice is unjust is simply the degree to which some feasible alternative configuration of institutions or practices might secure a lower sum total domination. The duty of justice does not impose an obligation to comply with an unjust institution or practice as such: on the contrary, it imposes an obligation to aim, so far as one is able, to bring about the best alternative. Considering then the four sorts of reform-minded activity discussed earlier, clearly our obligations depend on a complicated weighing of the good we can do versus the costs to ourselves and others of doing so. On the assumption that ordinary political action imposes few costs or risks to anyone, the duty of justice generally imposes on people the obligation to avail themselves of such means in aiming to realize more just institutions and practices. Resistance involves substantially greater dangers, however. On the assumption that we have prudential obligations to ourselves as well as moral obligations to others, our obligation to engage in resistance is considerably weaker. This entails a substantial gap between our obligations and our rights.

7.4.3 Transitional justice

When it comes to the transition from one equilibrium state to another, it is not always the case that all the principles of social justice will continue to apply without modification or qualification. This is because conceptions of social justice are designed for more or less stable, ongoing societies, and thus we have no reason to believe, a priori, that such theories will work equally well when the continuity of social and political institutions or practices has been decisively broken.

The expression "transitional justice" generally refers in the literature to the set of problems that arises in the wake of a transition from a substantially unjust society to a relatively more just one.[57] Most discussions in the literature are specifically focused on the transition from an autocratic to a democratic form of government, but we might also consider other major transitions, as, for example, from a slave-holding to a non-slave-holding society. Notice that the issues here are fundamentally issues of the present—namely, what justice requires of us here and now with respect to the fact that, in the recent past, our social or political institutions were substantially unjust. The difficulty is that, in the immediate wake of a transition, there are likely many people around who were complicit in the earlier injustice, and indeed who engaged in conduct that, under the new dispensation, is prohibited and (perhaps) punishable. The temptation is very strong, especially on the part of those who suffered under earlier injustice, to call these persons to account.

There is, however, a commonly heard argument against doing this. The new and more just regime is, presumably, committed to the value of the rule of law. Absolutely central to the idea of the rule of law is the principle that there can be no punishment without prior law. But, when the previous acts of injustice were performed, many of them were perfectly legal, or perhaps even expressly commanded by the previous authorities. To punish them now (even if those acts, undertaken after the transition, would be criminal) clearly violates this principle to which the new regime is strongly committed. Of course, many acts of injustice under the previous regime may indeed have been contrary to law (though tolerated) even under that regime, and *these* acts might legitimately be prosecuted now with the fullest vigor. But for the rest, so the argument goes, we must now take our stand with the principles of the rule of law.

This argument might seem quite congenial to the theory of social justice advanced in this study. In several places (most recently, earlier in this chapter), I have argued that the rule of law is essential to the aim of reducing domination. Nevertheless, this is not the most important consideration from the standpoint of JMD. The rule of law is, within this theory, instrumentally valuable to an ongoing society. In that context, it provides citizens a stable and predictable basis on which to build lives largely free from domination. But if, in other contexts, domination could be greatly reduced by means that involved violating the rule of law, doing so might be permissible. What then is the appropriate framing of the problem?

From the point of view of minimizing domination, there are two central considerations. The first is what sort of policy is most likely, with respect to transitions in general, to move societies as quickly as possible from less just to

---

[57] See, for example, Kritz (1995), Nino (1996), and Elster (2004).

more just equilibrium states. The greatest resistance to such transitions will almost certainly come from those implicated in domination. Our goal should thus be to structure incentives so as to soften their resistance as much as possible, and thus encourage a transition as quickly and as easily as possible. The right incentive structure is the one that will be harsh with respect to persons who resist transition and defend domination, and lenient with persons who do not resist transition and relinquish their position as agents of domination voluntarily. Such an incentive structure might recommend offering general amnesty to those implicated in the earlier injustices, provided they agree to a peaceful transition.

Notice that this policy may involve violating rule of law principles with respect to the prosecution of those who resist the transition. Those who suffered under the previous unjust regime will likely be cheered by this prospect. At the same time, they may complain that such a policy does not go far enough, insofar as a general amnesty will leave many injustices unpunished. Here it is important to take account of the second central consideration with respect to minimizing domination: namely, which (present) policies will maximize the chances that, on arriving at a more just equilibrium state, it will hold and prove stable. Pragmatically speaking, stability in the near term may depend crucially on the support of precisely those persons who suffered under the previous unjust regime, and who now demand and expect some sort of accountability. If these demands cannot be adequately met by prosecuting those persons not covered by the amnesty, we face a serious dilemma to which there is no obvious resolution.

7.4.4 Global justice

To this point, I have discussed only internally affected transitions. But societies can be moved from less to more just equilibrium states through external pressure as well. To what extent do states, international organizations, and so on (hereafter, "international actors") have rights or obligations to further social justice around the world? This question raises enormously complex issues of global justice that a study of this scope cannot hope to address comprehensively. Therefore, I will touch on only a few relevant points.

International actors, like individual persons, have rights and obligations arising out of a duty of justice.[58] They also, again like individual persons, have

---

[58] This, of course, is shorthand: the rights and obligations of international actors must really be proxies for the underlying rights and obligations of their constituent members. Nevertheless, it is often useful shorthand, and it will be used as such here.

(potentially) competing prudential and moral obligations. An example of the former might be the obligations of a state to pursue its security interests; an example of the latter might be the duty of any international actor to relieve suffering in humanitarian disasters around the world.

The duty of international justice is distinct from these: it is, roughly, the obligation of international actors to further just global institutions and practices. The latter—which might be referred to as the basic structure of global society—include the rules governing the recognition and autonomy of states; the complex nexus of international trade agreements, global capital markets, international lending institutions, etc.; the various practices and conventions of just war; and so on. Different configurations of the basic structure of global society might be regarded as more or less just, and international actors have some obligation to bring about and maintain just configurations, so far as they are able. Accordingly, a conception of *global justice* is the international analogue of a conception of social justice—that is, it is an account of the referent of an international actor's duty of justice, much as a conception of social justice is an account of the referent of an individual's duty of justice.

A complete account of global justice is, of course, beyond the scope of this study; here I am interested in the topic only insofar as it relates to the realization of social justice, where this is understood as the minimization of domination. Clearly, the realization of social justice, so understood, can be encouraged or discouraged by global institutions and practices. For example, two especially significant sources of domination in many societies are autocratic political regimes and severe socioeconomic poverty. With respect to the first, the ease with which people might substitute democratic for autocratic regimes has often been strongly influenced by their security environment: historically speaking, democracies have often had grave difficulties surviving harsh interstate competition with their democratic political institutions intact.[59] Global institutions and practices that tend to establish and maintain peace and order will thus greatly enhance the prospects for reducing domestic domination.[60] Successful transitions to democracy might also be hindered by how global institutions view the recognition and autonomy of states. For example, the virtually unlimited rights of states as such (regardless of the governing regime's character) to borrow in global capital markets and exploit domestic natural resources may present domestic political actors with an

---

[59] This "republican security dilemma" is analyzed in Deudney (2006).

[60] To the extent that democracies are, in fact, less inclined to go to war with one another, this might provide another instrumental argument for democracy.

irresistible temptation to attempt autocratic coups.[61] Since autocratic government is a significant source of domestic domination, international actors lie under an obligation to promote and maintain global institutions and practices that will tend to discourage the creation of autocratic political regimes, and encourage and support democracies.

With respect to severe socioeconomic poverty, it is again the case that global institutions and practices have a significant role to play. For example, it was argued earlier that a public basic-needs provision is the best way to prevent people from trading away their freedom from domination, but the globalization of capital and labor markets may seriously undermine unilateral domestic efforts to meet the basic needs of those individuals unable to do so on their own. It follows that international actors have an obligation to advance whatever global institutions and practices will best assist efforts to alleviate socioeconomic poverty around the world.[62] The difficulty, of course, lies in determining what sorts of feasible institutions and practices are most likely to do this. Even if desirable, a globally funded and administered unconditional basic income (adjusted for the variable costs of living around the world) would no doubt simply be unfeasible. A more pragmatic, though still difficult, strategy would be to calculate first what a global unconditional basic income should be, and then attempt to mimic its effects through a combination of domestic initiatives, foreign aid, and other policies. Unfortunately, a detailed discussion is far beyond the scope of this study.

Finally, there is the question of whether the duty of international justice extends not only to the advancement of just global institutions and practices, but also to *interventions*—that is, the promotion of just domestic institutions and practices around the world. Granting that a society should aim to ensure both that its own domestic basic structure and the basic structure of global society are as just as possible, to what extent should it also aim to ensure that the domestic basic structures of *other* societies are as just as possible? This is, roughly speaking, the international analogue of the question of toleration discussed earlier, and in principle our answers should be the same: JMD cannot tolerate practices directly or indirectly involving domination, and it should make no difference whether the practice happens to reside in one society rather than another. Justice, on this view, would seem to license considerable intervention. However, we must always take into account countervailing considerations. On the one hand, interventions might often be self-defeating: if, for example, an intervention aimed at eliminating one sort of domination succeeded only at the cost of provoking autocratic reactions or

---

[61] See Pogge (2002, esp. ch. 6).

[62] Laborde (2010) arrives at a similar conclusion.

seriously destabilizing international order, there might well be a net increase in the sum total domination. On the other hand, the duty of international justice must always be balanced against the other moral and prudential obligations of international actors. Justice matters a great deal, but it is not the only thing that matters. In light of these considerations, our hopes must often rest on the prospects for internally effected transitions in the direction of greater social justice.

8

Conclusion

The term "domination" can assume many different meanings in contemporary political and social theory literature. Most often, perhaps, it is used to mean an imbalance in social power, especially when conjoined with some measure of dependency. This I have referred to as the imbalance of power conception of domination. Less often, but still not uncommonly, the term is used in connection with various forms of preference or belief manipulation, or, more generally, with any sort of systematic advantaging of one person or group at the expense of another. These I have referred to as the hegemony and outcome-based conceptions of domination, respectively. In Part I, I argued that each of these conceptions should be rejected in favor of the *arbitrary power* conception of domination, on the grounds that it best answers to our desiderata of being both useful and general, while also fitting reasonably well with our considered intuitions. On this preferred view, domination should be understood as the condition experienced by persons or groups whenever they are dependent on a social relationship in which some other person or group wields arbitrary power over them. According to this conception, it does not matter whether the subject of domination is dependent objectively or merely subjectively, whether the agent of domination chooses to actively exercise her social power or not, nor indeed whether the agent benefits materially from her position of domination (though many agents do). Although the arbitrary power conception developed in this study is structural, I have nevertheless insisted that there must be actual human agents in any genuine instance of domination. In the strictest sense of the term, we cannot experience domination at the hands of practices, institutions, or ideas alone, though each of these may certainly contribute to whatever domination does exist.

The arbitrary power conception is meant to be a strictly descriptive account of the situations or states of affairs that count as domination. Although this conception makes no reference to the normative features of domination, any fully satisfactory theory of domination must have two parts: in addition to a descriptive account of the sort offered in Part I, it must also include a normative account of what we should do about whatever instances of domination we actually encounter in the world. In Part II, I have outlined a rough normative account of domination along these lines. I have argued that non-domination is an important good connected with human flourishing, and, thus, that the political and social institutions and practices of any society should be designed so as to minimize domination. This conception of social justice, dubbed *justice as minimizing domination*, demands the public provision of an unconditional basic income, policies of special toleration and accommodation to protect groups otherwise vulnerable to domination, and constitutionally constrained, democratic political and legal institutions. If we are willing to define political liberty or freedom as non-domination, then this conception of social justice can be seen as the core of an attractive and progressive civic republican political doctrine.

My approach in this study has been theoretical. Entirely absent is what would constitute the third main part of a complete account of domination—namely, an empirical investigation of the causes of domination on the one hand, and its effects on the other. These important topics I leave to others more qualified to address them. Many other related and important issues have been partially or fully left aside. For example, the theory of human action that provided the background for analysis in Part I and the theory of human flourishing that supported the normative claims of Part II were both merely assumed. Although these and many other significant analytical gaps and theoretical implications no doubt demand further development, if what I have done is enough to suggest the attractions of a progressive political doctrine taking freedom from domination as its central value, then I will regard this study largely as a success.

In the introduction, I suggested that one reason for being interested in a progressive civic republican political doctrine is its potentially broad rhetorical appeal. This study, however, has been addressed to specialists. It is not, I would imagine, the sort of thing lay readers (even reasonably progressive ones) would find especially inspiring. There is a perfectly reasonable explanation for this. Every political doctrine has two faces, so to speak. The public face of common-sense libertarianism, for example, is very appealing to a wide audience. It starts from a small set of intuitively compelling premises about the singular value of personal liberty, the inviolability of individual rights, and so on, and yields concrete political implications. But the scholarly face of common-sense libertarianism is something else entirely: when pressed by professional political theorists and philosophers, it is seen to lack depth and to face insurmountable difficulties. Liberal contractualism, by contrast, has remarkable theoretical depth. It has been resilient for a reason: however well or poorly it fares with the general public, it always finds strong support among specialists impressed by its conceptual power. Unfortunately, the public face of liberal contractualism is not as attractive—or at any rate, not to a wide public audience. It is difficult for many to see how the value of both individual liberty and socioeconomic redistribution could be united in a single, consistent political doctrine.

My hope is that a progressive civic republican political doctrine might succeed in being attractive from both points of view. On the one hand, it draws theoretical depth from, among other things, its structural affinities with utilitarianism. This ensures its resiliency in scholarly debate. From this point of view, indeed, I have argued that justice as minimizing domination has important advantages over liberal contractualism: it dispenses with the cumbersome apparatus of the social contract model, for example, and is thus freed from many of the challenges that such models face with respect to intergenerational and global justice. On the other hand, a progressive civic republican political doctrine can also be presented in a way that is appealing to a wide public audience. Particularly, if we define political liberty or freedom as nondomination, civic republicanism can draw on a rich and powerful rhetorical tradition that resonates strongly with many people, and many Americans in particular. Such a doctrine captures our sense that freedom and justice must run together; it also makes possible an argument for socioeconomic redistribution in direct and compelling terms. It thus has the potential to respond to the challenge presented by the common-sense libertarianism.

This study has focused on developing the scholarly face of civic republicanism. Its aim has been to show that, suitably interpreted, the idea of social justice as minimizing domination can withstand critical theoretical scrutiny. Developing the public face of civic republicanism is a task that remains to be done.

APPENDIX I

The modern English terms "domination" and "to dominate" have their roots in Roman law. The comparatively old Latin word *dominus*, meaning literally "master of a house (*domus*)," entered into the language of law at some time after the Twelve Tables as *dominium*, where it eventually came to designate the important but elusive concept of ownership.[1] Roughly, ownership consisted of a twofold relationship: it represented the absolute title to a thing (*res*) held by the property owner as against any competing claims to possession on the one hand, and the unlimited right of enjoyment held by the property owner over the thing he owned on the other.

Later in the republican period, the term acquired a more distinctly political, as opposed to narrowly legal, sense. This new sense arose quite smoothly out of the old. Like most other ancient peoples, the Romans practiced slavery and, as a matter of law, slaves were regarded as *res mancipi*—analogous to what we call real property or real estate. In theory then, the unlimited rights of the property holder in general included unlimited rights over his slaves in particular. The free citizens of Rome could thus be regarded— gliding over some complications—as those male heads of household (*paterfamilias*) who were not slaves, that is, who were not under the *dominium* of anyone.[2] As it is sometimes put, the Romans came to regard the ideas of *libertas* and *civitas* as being equivalent.[3]

When the Republic came on hard times, some (presciently) feared for the loss of their traditional political freedoms if Rome were to fall under the sway of a despotic ruler. Already in the habit, perhaps, of describing free citizens as persons who were not slaves, it was natural in articulating this danger to draw the obvious analogy: if the Republic collapses, we freemen of Rome will cease to be citizens and become rather like slaves, under the *dominatio* (domination) or *dominatus* (absolute power) of a despotic ruler— a *dominus* (master). Cicero was among the most avid users of the concept of domination in this political sense. For example, writing of democracy, he comments

> But if the people hold to their own rights, they deny that there is anything more outstanding, more free, more blessed. . . . [T]his commonwealth . . . is the only one properly so named; and so it is usual for the "concern of the people" to be liberated from the domination (*dominatione*) of kings and aristocrats, and not for kings or the power and wealth of an aristocracy to be sought by a free people.[4]

---

[1] See Noyes (1936, pp. 78–9) and Tucker (1985, p. 81).

[2] Among the many complications, there were also foreigners (*peregrini*), free persons who were not heads of household and therefore were under the *potestas* of a *paterfamilias*, emancipated former slaves (*libertini*), and so on. See Nicholas (1962, esp. part 2).

[3] Wirszubski (1968, pp. 1–4).

[4] *De re publica*, I.48, this translation Zetzel (1999, p. 21). Cf. *De re publica*, I.67 and *Contra Verres*, I.35.

(Note the explicit contrast of domination and liberty.) With respect to monarchy as a form of government, Cicero comments

> It is...a genuinely good form of commonwealth; but it verges on the most terrible type. As soon as this king turned to a more unjust form of <u>mastery</u> (*dominatum*), he immediately became a tyrant; no animal can be imagined that is more awful or foul or more hateful to gods and men alike.[5]

Speaking of Caesar shortly after his assassination, Cicero comments

> Why trouble to list minor crimes—forged legacies, business deals, fraudulent sales? For here you have someone who actually aspired to be absolute monarch of Rome, indeed <u>master</u> (*dominusque*) of the whole world.[6]

These terms were similarly used in this sense by other writers with republican sympathies. For example, Sallust puts the following in the mouth of a tribune:

> Sharing as they all do the same desires, hatreds, and fears, they stick closely together; if they were honest men, you would call it friendship, but these are just a gang of criminals. If your love of liberty were as ardent as their craving for <u>power</u> (*dominationem*), the republic would surely not be violated as she now is.[7]

The historian Livy, narrating a Senate debate regarding some pro-plebian reforms that took place in the early Republic, has one reformist rhetorically ask the senators:

> Finally tell me this: does the ultimate power in the state belong to you or to the Roman people? When we finished with the monarchy, was it to put <u>supreme authority</u> (*dominatio*) into your hands or to bring political liberty to all alike?[8]

In this and other passages, Livy explicitly regards domination and liberty as opposites. Even later, in the writings of Tacitus, we find passages such as the following:

> To safeguard his <u>domination</u> (*dominationi*), Augustus made his sister's son Marcellus a priest and curule aedile—in spite of his extreme youth.[9]

In short, by the opening of the imperial period, *dominus, dominatio*, and their various cognates have moved beyond the narrow domain of law into the language of general politics.

---

[5] *De re publica*, II.47–48, this translation Zetzel (1999, pp. 47–8). Cf. *De re publica*, I.43, I.61, *De officiis*, II.2, and *Tusculanae disputationes*, V.57–8.

[6] *De officiis*, III.83, this translation Grant (1971, p. 191). Cf. *De re publica*, I.69, II.46 and *Tusculanae disputationes*, I.48.

[7] *Bellum jugurthinum*, XXXI.16, this translation Handford (1963, p. 67).

[8] *Ab urbe condita*, IV.5, this translation Sélincourt (1971, p. 274). Cf. *Ab urbe condita*, III.39, VI.18.

[9] *Annales*, I.3, this translation Grant (1996, p. 32). Cf. *Annales*, III.26, XII.4.

As opposition to the imperial system faded, however, so did the negative connotation of these terms. *Dominium* retreated into the language of law, where it came to designate theoretically absolute ownership (*dominium perfectum*), one extreme end on the continuum of property rights.[10] Because the Empire, in a sense, could be viewed as the property of the Emperor—in principle, he had the absolute right to interfere in any affair within his domains—*dominus* became a natural auxiliary title adopted by some emperors (though Augustus and Tiberius notably declined it).[11] This more or less politically neutral meaning of the terms persisted through the Middle Ages and into the early modern period, especially among those working in the natural law tradition.

The term domination and its cognates seem to have entered English usage mainly along two parallel tracks during the Renaissance, in both instances probably transmitted from Latin through medieval French.[12] On the one hand, the term "domination" referred to rule, sway, or control, and especially to that of a monarch over his kingdom: as in "kynges and prynces haue domynacions and lordships" (1483); or "the lordship and domination over thys yle" (1585). The associated verb "to dominate"—to rule or hold sway over—arose somewhat later, in the early seventeenth century. Henry Cockeram's *English Dictionarie* (1623) defines "domineere" as "to beare rule or great sway." On the other hand, the terms "dominion" and sometimes "domination" were used interchangeably to refer to a territory under rule: Shakespeare, for example, refers to the "subiectes of his saide dominacion of Wales" in *Henry VIII*. A clear division of labor between the two terms "domination" and "dominion" was not standardized until the eighteenth century. John Locke, for example, sometimes uses dominion to mean domination ("slaves . . . are by the right of nature subjected to the absolute dominion and arbitrary power of their masters"), and domination to mean dominion ("the spreading domination of the two great empires of Peru and Mexico").[13]

Although both "domination" and "to dominate" were in general English use during the seventeenth century, neither initially carried a necessary negative connotation, as can be seen from the examples earlier. The contemporary sense of the word with its negative connotations was more or less fixed by the end of the eighteenth century. Thus, John Walker's *Critical Pronouncing Dictionary* (1791) defines domination as "power, dominion; tyranny, insolent authority," and similarly the *Pronouncing Dictionary of the English Language* (author unknown, 1796) defines it as "power, dominion; tyranny."

---

[10] See Tuck (1979, pp. 10–13). Note the frequent use of the term in *Institutes* (I.3.2, I.5.2, *passim*).

[11] Suetonius, *De vita Caesarum*, II.53, III.27.

[12] For what follows, see OED, 2nd edn, s.v. "domination," "dominate," and "dominion." A third, less relevant, use emerging in the same period refers to the fourth order of angels—for example, Milton, *Paradise Lost*, V.601: "Here all ye Angels, Thrones, Dominations, Princedoms, Virtues, Powers." For developments outside English, not discussed here, see Richter (1995, ch. 3).

[13] Locke (1690, §85, p. 45) and Locke (1960, §105, p. 56), respectively.

APPENDIX II

In this appendix, I experiment with some formal models of social relationships characterized by domination. Before laying out the basic model, let me remark briefly on its scope. Relationships of domination can be considered from at least two points of view. On the one hand, we can examine the *dynamics* of domination—the history of how relationships of domination come into being, the ways in which they change over time, and the conditions under which they ultimately break down. On the other hand, we can examine the *statics* of domination—the internal experience of those parties to such relationships under relatively stable conditions. Both are worthy of investigation. My own interests and scholarly competence, however, incline toward the latter. Thus, the formal models offered here are static models.

AII.1 The basic model

To a large extent, the architecture for a formal model of domination was determined by the conception developed in Part I. To begin with, domination was defined as a social relationship between two or more persons or groups. Thus, our formal model must have at least two actors—the agent and the subject of domination—who will be named player 1 and player 2, respectively. (Later the model is expanded to allow for more than two players.) Depending on the situation imagined, these players might represent a slave master and a group of slaves, the class of nobles and the class of peasants, a husband and a wife, an employer and a group of employees, a colonial power and one of its colonies, and so forth. To avoid gratuitous abstraction in what follows, let us suppose that player 1 is a foreperson at some factory with relatively unregulated working conditions, and that player 2 is a wage laborer under her supervision.

These players are assumed to act purposefully, as if they are pursuing certain goals or ends; moreover, these goals or ends are assumed to be at least minimally rational (i.e., complete and internally consistent). The nature of these assumptions has already been discussed, and will not be expanded on here. We must here, however, provide our players with more substantive aims. Obviously, this will restrict somewhat the generality of our model, for real persons and groups have a wide variety of goals and ends, many of which deviate from the substantive aims that will be assigned to our representative players. This should not concern us overmuch. Whenever people face real-world situations in which what they want to do depends on what others are going to do, they make assumptions regarding one another's goals and ends. They could hardly do otherwise. Often these assumptions are wrong, in which case people sensibly adjust their actions as best they can, but some sort of assumptions are unavoidable. In this sense, we are doing no more than an ordinary person would have to do when faced with domination.

Let us assume that the goals or ends of the players are in conflict. In particular, those subject to domination typically have control over some (not necessarily material) social good valued by the agents of domination. The latter's aim will be to extract as much of this good from the former as possible, and conversely, the former player's aim will be to surrender as little as possible.[1] For example, if player 2 represents a slave and player 1 a slave master, then the valued social good might be productive labor; if player 2 represents the peasant class and player 1 the class of nobles, the valued good might be feudal dues; if player 2 represents a wife and player 1 her husband, the valued good might be some combinations of household and sexual services. In some cases, an agent of domination may only want deference and status recognition, but there will always be something that she wants from the subject (or else there would be no conflict to speak of).

In our model, the level of the wage laborer's *effort* is the valued good under contention. Let the set E of possible levels of effort be a compact and convex range on the real line from some minimum $\underline{e}$ to some maximum $\bar{e}$. Both players have preferences over E. Let us suppose the foreperson receives utility from the wage laborer's effort according to a strictly quasi-concave function $u_1(e)$ continuous on E, with an ideal point at e_1; and similarly, suppose that the wage laborer receives utility from his effort according to a strictly quasi-concave function $u_2(e)$ continuous on E, with an ideal point at e_2. To keep things as simple as possible, we might concentrate on the interval in E from 0 to 1, assume that $e_1 \geq 1$ and that $e_2 \leq 0$, and assign the players linear loss utility functions. The foreperson's utility function would thus be $u_1(e) = 1 - | e_1 - e |$, and that of the wage laborer is $u_2(e) = 1 - | e_2 - e |$. In other words, as the wage laborer's effort increases, his utility goes down, while that of the foreperson goes up.

A point of clarification may be in order here, because it might appear as though specifying these utility functions involves stronger assumptions than it really does. In particular, are we asserting that people desire to work as little as possible—suggesting some unwarranted assumption about human laziness? In fact, we are not. Rather, we might suppose that the effort in question is *surplus* effort, over and above what a wage laborer would offer voluntarily at a given wage and under given employment conditions. Thus, we can interpret the assumption $e_2 \leq 0$ to mean that the wage laborer would not want to offer any extra effort than he believes he should at the wage level and under the employment conditions in question. This is perfectly reasonable, and not at all suggesting laziness. (Depending on the situation we are interested in, we can always adjust our interpretation of the valued good under contention so as to correspond to the appropriate surplus value.[2] Under slavery, for example, we might suppose any effort is surplus effort.) The foreperson's aim is thus to extract as much

---

[1] As Scott and Foucault each contends in their own way, relations of domination are always relations of resistance. See, for example, Scott (1985, esp. chs. 2–3; 1990, p. 45) and Foucault (1990, pp. 95–6).

[2] The choice of language here is usefully reminiscent of Marx. Without too much terminological violence, as discussed in Chapter 5, we can say that domination nearly always involves exploitation. Of course, this deviates from traditional Marxism, which sees exploitation only in the marketplace, and not, say, within families.

surplus effort as possible, over and above whatever the wage laborer would willingly provide, given the terms of his employment. It is precisely in the nature of domination to place agents in a position to extract more valued goods from subjects than the latter would willingly offer.

As we have seen, domination arises under social relationships structured in a particular way. Social structures can be captured to some extent in game-theoretic formal models, through a specification of the game's rules. The main structural features are these: first, the subject must be dependent on the social relationship to some degree; second, the agent must have some power over the subject; and third, this power must be arbitrary. The basic model will simplify these features drastically, and focus on the second feature in particular (subsequent refinements will incorporate the others). Accordingly, let us suppose that the foreperson has some social power over the wage laborer, enabling her to coerce some particular level of surplus effort e_c. (Recall from Chapter 3 that to coerce someone is to change what they would otherwise prefer to do by raising the costs of some options relative to others: perhaps the fore person has the power to unilaterally fire the laborer, dock his wages, or otherwise make things uncomfortable for him.) By definition, $e_c > 0$. Furthermore, because the wage laborer would not want to exert a greater level of surplus effort than the foreperson can coercively extract, we can set $e_c = 1$. We can, thus, interpret the assumption that $e_1 \geq 1$ as meaning that the foreperson would ideally prefer to receive at least as much surplus effort as she can coercively extract, and perhaps more. Our normalization of the model on the $[0, 1]$ interval within E has thus been given a meaningful interpretation at both ends.

Finally, let us define the players' strategies.[3] The basic model of domination has only two stages. In the first stage, the wage laborer decides how much surplus effort to offer the foreperson. In formal notation, his strategy space $S_2 = \{s_2 \in R_+ \mid \underline{e} \leq s_2 \leq \bar{e}\}$. Given our normalization of the model on an interval in E, we may simply say that a strategy s_2 for the wage laborer is just a number between 0 and 1. In the second stage, the foreperson decides whether or not to exercise her coercive social power over the wage laborer. The foreperson's possible actions are thus limited to "coerce" and "don't coerce," but as this is a sequential model, she may condition her choice of action on the level of surplus effort offered in the previous stage. Thus, a complete strategy s_1 for the foreperson specifies for each possible level of surplus effort the wage laborer could decide to offer whether or not she will respond by coercing him. For example, a strategy might be "coerce if he offers less than 0.69 units of effort, and don't coerce if he offers more." Formally, her possible strategies are functions mapping the set of possible offers into a discrete action set, that is, $s_1: S_2 \rightarrow A$, where $A = \{a \in 1$ ("coerce"), 0 ("don't coerce")$\}$; and her strategy space S_1 is the compact and convex set of all such mappings.

After the foreperson moves, the game ends. If the foreperson coerces the wage laborer (if $a = 1$), then $e = e_c = 1$; and otherwise (if $a = 0$), $e = s_2$, that is, the level of surplus effort offered by the wage laborer in stage one. Now, we might naturally

---

[3] I will not permit mixed strategies for either player.

suppose that the experience of being coerced itself is at least slightly unpleasant. Accordingly, let us revise the wage laborer's utility function slightly, as follows:

$$u_2(e, a) = 1 - |e_1 - e| - ap \qquad (1)$$

where $e_2 \leq 0$, where a takes the value of 1 if the foreperson coerced the wage laborer and 0 otherwise, and where $p \in R_+$ captures the negative utility associated with the experience of being coerced. Similarly, we might suppose that it is at least somewhat costly for the foreperson to exercise her coercive powers. This cost must be interpreted very broadly. In particular, it can be assumed to include at least:

- the material costs of coercing the wage laborer (effort, time spent, resources expended, etc.),
- the social costs (others may disapprove of the use of coercion),
- the psychological costs (the foreperson might feel badly about using coercion),
- less the social benefits (others might approve of using coercion), and
- less the psychological benefits (the foreperson might enjoy using coercion).

By assuming that exercising coercive powers is at least somewhat costly, we are only assuming that the negative utility of the first three items outweighs the positive utility of the last two. If this were not the case, the foreperson would actually enjoy coercing the wage laborer, and thus would do so regardless of the level of effort he offered. Pure sadists aside, therefore, our assumption is reasonable. Now the foreperson's utility function becomes:

$$u_1(e, a) = 1 - |e_1 - e| - ac \qquad (2)$$

where $e_1 \geq 1$, where a takes the value of 1 if the foreperson coerced the wage laborer and 0 otherwise, and where $c \in R_+$ such that $c < 1$ represents the utility cost associated with coercing the wage laborer. (Note that if c were greater than 1, the foreperson would never coerce the laborer because she could never recoup the costs from the latter's surplus effort; she would, in short, have no *credible* power over him.) The basic model assumes that the values of p and c are common knowledge, as are the utility functions represented in equations (1) and (2), and of course all the rules of the game.

This completes our specification of the basic model. What does it predict will happen? Clearly, this is a strategic situation in which what either player wants to do will depend on what the other is doing. The standard solution concept for such models is the Nash equilibrium, described in Chapter 4. To review, a Nash equilibrium exists whenever no one wants to unilaterally change his or her strategy, given the strategies adopted by others; this solution concept carries no assumptions regarding the Pareto optimality, efficiency, symmetry, or equity of the result (and indeed, in the final version of the model later in this chapter, the outcome is suboptimal, inefficient, asymmetric, and inequitable). The Nash equilibrium strategies in the basic model are:

$$s_1^* = \begin{cases} a = 0 & \textit{if } s_2 \geq 1 - c \\ a = 0 & \textit{if } s_2 < 1 - c \end{cases} \text{ and } s_2^* = 1 - c \qquad (3, 4)$$

Proof: Using backward induction, suppose after stage one that $s_2 \geq 1 - c$. In this case, player 1 would not want to coerce, because $1 - \mid e_1 - s_2 \mid \geq 1 - \mid e_1 - 1 \mid - ac$, and we may assume that she does not want to coerce if perfectly indifferent.[4] But suppose that $s_2 < 1 - c$ after stage one: in this case she would want to coerce, because $1 - \mid e_1 - 1 \mid - ac \geq 1 - \mid e_1 - s_2 \mid$. Thus, for any possible s_2, the optimal strategy for player 1 is given by s_1^* above. Now consider some $s_2 < s_2^*$: given, s_1^*, player 2 will be coerced in stage two. Since $1 - \mid e_2 - 1 \mid - ap < 1 - \mid e_2 - s_2^* \mid$, player 2 strictly prefers s_2^*. Likewise, consider some $s_2 > s_2^*$: given s_1^*, player 2 will not be coerced in stage two. Nevertheless, since $1 - \mid e_2 - s_2 \mid < 1 - \mid e_2 - s_2^* \mid$, player 2 still strictly prefers s_2^*. Therefore, s_2^* represents his optimal strategy, given what he expects player 1 to do. □

In prose, the foreperson will only coerce the wage laborer if her gains in terms of extra surplus effort extracted outweigh the costs of coercing. Knowing this, and preferring not to be coerced, the wage laborer will offer a level of surplus effort just high enough to make the foreperson not want to coerce him, but not higher.

Of course, not every aspect of the domination experience is captured using the Nash equilibrium concept, and therefore our formal model necessarily emphasizes certain aspects of that experience at the expense of others. Only if one demands the impossible from a formal model—namely, that it stands as a perfect substitute for the complete descriptive and normative analyses offered in the main part of this study—would one regard these limitations as a problem. But of course we should not demand this. And in any case, even with this rather bare-bones formal model, some interesting points are worth noting. First, in equilibrium, we never actually see the foreperson exercising her coercive powers over the wage laborer, but nevertheless the mere fact that she has this power results in her receiving some surplus effort. This handily accords with a point made in Chapter 5 regarding the tendency of those suffering under political domination to make anticipatory concessions: The wage laborer suffers under domination despite the fact that he is never actually interfered with.[5] It also supports our decision in Chapter 2 to understand domination structurally. Second, if we take the level of surplus effort offered by the wage laborer as a measure of the degree to which he is dominated, then his domination is related to the willingness of the foreperson to exercise her coercive powers: that is, the more reluctant she is to exercise these powers, the less surplus effort she is able to extract. This stands to reason. But as we shall see, this particular result depends on his being aware of the foreperson's state of mind.

AII.2 Modeling arbitrariness

This section expands the basic model to incorporate the element of arbitrariness. Unfortunately, the Nash equilibrium concept cannot capture the true nature of

---

[4] We could assume player 1 coerces when she is perfectly indifferent, in which case player 2's optimal strategy would be defined by the ugly expression $s_2^* = \lim_{\varepsilon \to 0} \{1 - c + \varepsilon\}$. Since there is no real material difference between these two results, the assumption made in the proof is warranted to avoid pointless mathematical complexity.

[5] Cf. Scott (1990, esp. chs. 1–3), Wartenberg (1990, pp. 121–6), and Pettit (1997, pp. 63–4).

arbitrariness directly, but there is a trick by which we may capture one aspect of the experience indirectly. Recall that having an arbitrary power over someone means being able to exercise that power without being externally constrained by the effective rules, procedures or goals that are common knowledge. From the point of view of the person subject to domination, this experience is somewhat analogous to a situation in which one simply does not know the internal rule, procedure, or goal actually being followed by the power-holding agent. Obviously, these situations are not equivalent, but the experience of either is somewhat similar from the subject's point of view. Now the internal rule, procedure, or goal actually being followed by an agent of domination is just his or her Nash equilibrium strategy: thus, if we hide the agent's strategy from the subject, we thereby indirectly capture some part of the experience of being subject to arbitrary power.[6]

Fortunately, this is fairly easy to represent in our model. The foreperson's Nash equilibrium strategy, as shown earlier, is determined by the value of c, the overall cost of her actually coercing the wage laborer. Therefore, let us suppose that the wage laborer does not know what this cost is, and thus that he does not know what level of surplus effort he needs to offer in stage one in order to avoid being coerced in stage two. This turns the basic model into what is called an *incomplete information game*. The standard technique for modeling incomplete information is to introduce a new stage of the game, prior to the two stages of the basic model, and to add an artificial player called "nature," who randomly selects a cost c from some range C in this prior stage. We then suppose that nature's move is known to the foreperson, but hidden from the wage laborer (everything else remains common knowledge, as in the basic model).[7] Some readers might prefer a less contrived interpretation—which can be rendered mathematically equivalent—as follows. Let $ĉ$ represent the foreperson's fixed, underlying material costs, which are known to (or at least can reasonably be estimated by) the wage laborer; and let an error term $\varepsilon \in R$ such that $-k \leq \varepsilon \leq k$ represent the foreperson's variable psychological costs (what side of the bed she woke up on that morning, and so forth), which are not known to the wage laborer. Then simply define $c = ĉ + \varepsilon$. This second interpretation will be mathematically equivalent to the first, if $c\ddot{o}$ is the median value of C, and if $ĉ - k$ and $ĉ + k$ are the lower and upper bounds of C, respectively.

In order to solve this incomplete information game, it is less important that we know how ε is actually determined—or, on the alternate interpretation, how nature

---

[6] This indirect approach will only work so long as this is a one-shot game, unless the foreperson's strategy is determined randomly in each new iteration of the game (in which case all iterations would look the same); otherwise, the Nash equilibrium concept will drive the foreperson to reveal her strategy over time. Note, however, that repeated games are notorious for having multiple Nash equilibria.

[7] This technique for modeling incomplete information derives from the work by John Harsanyi. There is some dispute as to whether these should be called games of *imperfect*, as opposed to incomplete, information: the former is, strictly speaking, more accurate, but common usage seems to have settled on the term "incomplete information." For discussion, see Binmore (1992, pp. 501–11).

selects a cost $c \in C$. Far more important is defining what the wage laborer's *beliefs* regarding the expected value of c are likely to be. One way or another, he will have to decide what level of surplus effort to offer, and in order to do this he cannot avoid forming such beliefs. It cannot be an objection to our formal model, therefore, if we attribute reasonable expectations to the wage laborer accordingly. By our earlier assumptions, we can define the range of possible costs $C = \{c \in R \mid 0 \leq c \leq 1\}$. If the wage laborer does not have any additional information to go on, it might be reasonable for him to suppose that any one value in this range is as likely as any other. Formally, we would say that he believes c to be a real number randomly drawn from a uniform distribution on the interval C. Fortunately, the mathematics of the model are kept as simple as possible by this assumption.

Apart from this, the basic model will be left as is. The wage laborer's strategy space is the same as before, $S_2 = \{s_2 \in R_+ \mid \underline{e} \leq s_2 \leq \bar{e}\}$, keeping in mind that we have normalized the model on the interval $[0, 1]$ in E. The foreperson's strategy space is now conditional both on the wage laborer's as well as on nature's move—that is, the randomly determined cost of exercising coercion. For example, her strategy might be, "if my costs are c, then coerce the wage laborer if he offers a level of effort less than $1 - c$, and otherwise don't." Formally, then, S_1 becomes the compact convex set of all mappings $s_1: S_2 \times C \rightarrow A$, where $A = \{a \in 1$ ("coerce"), 0 ("don't coerce")$\}$. Again, employing the Nash equilibrium solution concept, we find that the equilibrium strategies are:

$$s_1^* = \begin{cases} a = 0 & \text{if } s_2 \geq 1 - c \\ a = 0 & \text{if } s_2 < 1 - c \end{cases} \text{ and } s_2^* = \min\left\{\frac{1 + p}{2}, 1\right\} \tag{5,6}$$

Proof: Using backward induction, first note that player 1's situation in stage two is no different than in the basic model; thus the proof of equation (5) is the same as that of equation (3). Now consider player 2's situation in stage one, given s_1^*: his optimal strategy will be to maximize the expected utility function $Eu_2 = \text{prob}\{a = 1\} \cdot (1 - \mid e_2 - e_c \mid -p) + \text{prob}\{a = 0\} \cdot (1 - \mid e_2 - s_2 \mid)$. There are three cases: for any $s_2 < 0$, the prob$\{a = 1\}$ is 1; for any $s_2 \geq 1$, the prob$\{a = 0\}$ is 1; and for any $0 \leq s_2 < 1$, the prob$\{a = 0\}$ is the prob $\{s_2 \geq 1 - c\}$ which, since c is randomly drawn from a uniform distribution on the interval $[0, 1]$, is just s_2, and the prob$\{a = 1\}$ is $1 - s_2$. We assume that $e_c = 1$, that $e_2 \leq 0$. Given this, in the first case, $Eu_2 = e_2 - p$, and in the second case, $Eu_2 = 1 + e_2 - s_2$. Since $p > 0$, $s_2 = 1$ is always better for player 2 than any $s_2 < 0$; this eliminates the first case. In the third case, we find by substitution and simplification that $Eu_2 = e_2 - s_2{}^2 + s_2 - p + ps_2$. This function is maximized where its first-order partial derivative $\partial Eu_2/\partial s_2 = -2s_2 + 1 + p = 0$, and solving for s_2, we find that $s_2 = (1 + p)/2$. Thus if $p > 1$, player 2 cannot do better than $s_2^* = 1$, and otherwise $s_2^* = (1 + p)/2$. $\square$

The intuition behind this result can be explained as follows. In deciding what level of surplus effort to offer, the wage laborer must ask himself: "Given any level of surplus effort I might offer, what is the probability that I will not be coerced?" If, as we have supposed, he believes c equally likely to be any value between 0 and 1, then the probability of not being coerced is the same as the level of surplus effort he offers. That is, if the wage laborer offers $s_2 = 0.75$, there is precisely a 75% chance that $c > 1-s_2$, in which case the foreperson will not exercise her coercive powers, and a 25% chance that $c < 1-s_2$, in which case she will. Given this estimation, the wage laborer will offer a level of surplus effort balancing his various benefits and risks: offering more, he reduces the risk of being coerced, but only at the cost of engaging in more surplus effort than he desires; offering less, he engages in less surplus effort, but increases his risk of being coerced. Mathematically, it turns out that these costs and benefits are optimized at s_2*, as given earlier.[8]

Note that once the arbitrariness has been taken into account, the negative utility associated with suffering coercion p becomes a direct factor in determining the level of surplus effort offered. As we would expect, the wage laborer will offer more and more surplus effort as suffering coercion becomes more and more unpleasant. In the basic model, this was not a factor, because with perfect information the wage laborer could offer a level of surplus effort ensuring that he would not be coerced. With incomplete information, this is no longer possible: For any offer of surplus effort less than 1, there is some positive probability of his being coerced. Thus, unlike in the basic model, we may actually observe the foreperson exercising her coercive powers over the wage laborer—namely, whenever c turns out to be less than $1-(1 + p)/2$. Because exercising her coercive powers carries a deadweight cost for the foreperson, the Nash equilibrium in this version of the model is inefficient (i.e., not Pareto optimal).[9]

What are the utility payoffs at this equilibrium likely to be? In order to estimate this, we must make some additional assumptions about the *actual* probability distribution of c, and not just the wage laborer's *beliefs* about this distribution. Accordingly, let us suppose his beliefs are roughly correct—in other words, that c is, indeed, a real number randomly drawn from a uniform distribution on the interval C from 0 to 1.[10] In this case, we can estimate the outcome by substituting the wage laborer's Nash equilibrium offer of surplus effort from equation (6) into each player's respective expected utility function. For the wage laborer, we find the following for any $p \leq 1$:

$$Eu_2 = e_2 - \left(\frac{1+p}{2}\right)^2 + \left(\frac{1+p}{2}\right) - p + p\left(\frac{1+p}{2}\right)$$

If we let $e_2 = 0$ (i.e., if we assume the wage laborer would ideally prefer to put forward no surplus effort), this reduces to:

$$Eu_2 = \frac{p^2 - 2p + 1}{4} \tag{7}$$

---

[8] Note that it is assumed the wage laborer is risk-neutral, making the math much simpler. Changing this assumption would change the point prediction of the model, but not the general result.

[9] It follows that there may be gains to be had through bargaining that are not modeled here. But, of course, bargaining costs may preclude their being recovered, and in any case bargaining between unequal parties suffers from serious commitment problems.

[10] On this assumption, we can also determine the likelihood of observing the foreperson's use of her coercive powers. If $p = 0.25$ for example, coercion will occur with a probability of 37.5%.

In most (but not quite all) cases, the expected utility payoff for the wage laborer will be smaller than it is when the foreperson's power to coerce him is not arbitrary, as in the basic model. Recall from above the assumption that $p > 0$—in other words, that there is some negative utility associated with being coerced, however small—and note that for any $p > 1$, the wage laborer would simply offer $s_2 = 1$ (ensuring that he will not be coerced, whatever the value of c turns out to be). Given these bounds on the value of p, we find that so long as $c > 0.25$, the wage laborer will always do better when the foreperson's power to coerce him is not arbitrary. Some representative outcomes are displayed in Table A2.1. The most interesting discovery here is that even when the cost is 0.50 in the basic model—exactly the same as the expected cost in the model incorporating arbitrariness—the wage laborer does better knowing this cost in advance. In other words, the *mere fact of arbitrariness itself* has negative consequences for the wage laborer. Those suffering under political domination are forced to overcompensate in taking defensive measures against the arbitrary power, because such power is not externally constrained by the commonly known and effective rules, procedures, or goals.[11]

What about the foreperson's expected utility payoff in this model? Substituting the wage laborer's equilibrium strategy for any $p \leq 1$ into her utility function yields the following:

$$Eu_1 = \left(\frac{1+p}{2}\right)^2 - \left(\frac{1+p}{2}\right) + c\left(\frac{1+p}{2}\right) - c - e_1 + 2$$

If we let $e_1 = 1$ (i.e., if we assume the foreperson would ideally prefer the wage laborer put forward the maximum surplus effort he could be coerced to engage in), this becomes

$$Eu_1 = \frac{3 + p^2 - 2c(1 - p)}{4} \tag{8}$$

As we would expect, the foreperson usually does better having arbitrary power over the wage laborer. She always does better if in the basic model $c > 0.5$, or if in the model

Table AII.1

Utility cost of being coerced	Cost of coercion known			Cost of coercion not known
	$c = 0.25$	$c = 0.50$	$c = 0.75$	
$p = 0.05$	$u_2 = 0.25$	$u_2 = 0.50$	$u_2 = 0.75$	$Eu_2 = 0.23$
$p = 0.25$	$u_2 = 0.25$	$u_2 = 0.50$	$u_2 = 0.75$	$Eu_2 = 0.14$
$p = 0.50$	$u_2 = 0.25$	$u_2 = 0.50$	$u_2 = 0.75$	$Eu_2 = 0.06$

[11] Note that this is true *despite* the fact that we have made the wage laborer risk-neutral. If he were risk-averse, this effect would be even more pronounced.

incorporating arbitrariness $p > 1$. The intuition here is that when the cost of coercing the wage laborer is high, it is more important that the exact value of that cost be hidden from the wage laborer; and that when the negative utility of being coerced is high, the wage laborer will be at greater pains to prevent this from happening. Obviously, whenever the foreperson's actual cost of exercising coercive power is the same as the wage laborer's estimation of her expected cost, the foreperson does better if her actual cost is not common knowledge. In some other cases, however, the foreperson may prefer *not* having arbitrary power, just as (though more rarely) the wage laborer may prefer she *does* have arbitrary power. Let me explain.

In the basic model, the foreperson's utility payoff in equilibrium is $1-c$, while in the model incorporating arbitrariness, it is $(3 + p^2 - 2c(1-p))/4$. It follows that the foreperson will prefer having arbitrary power whenever:

$$1 - c < \frac{3 + p^2 - 2c(1-p)}{4}$$

Conveniently, this can be expressed as an indifference function $I_1: P \rightarrow C$ if we solve for c, like so:

$$c > \frac{1 - p^2}{2 + 2p} \tag{9}$$

At any given p, when c is greater than the value of equation (9), the foreperson would prefer having arbitrary power, and not when it is less. Similarly, the wage laborer's equilibrium utility payoffs in the two versions of the model can be compared thus:

$$c > \frac{p^2 - 2p + 1}{4} \tag{10}$$

At any given $p \leq 0$, when c is greater than the value of equation (10), the wage laborer would prefer that the foreperson did *not* have arbitrary power.

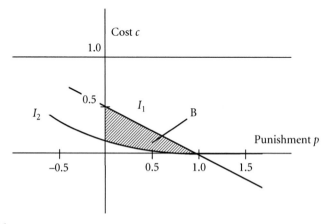

Figure AII.1

The two indifference functions given by equations (9) and (10) are plotted in Figure A2.1. This figure should be interpreted as follows. The horizontal axis represents the negative utility p associated with being coerced; by earlier assumption, $p > 0$. The vertical axis represents the cost c of coercing the wage laborer, keeping in mind that this cost is common knowledge in the basic model, but known only to the foreperson in the second model; by earlier assumption, $0 < c < 1$. The indifference curve I_1 is given by equation (9); north of this curve, the foreperson would prefer having arbitrary power, and south of it she would prefer it was not arbitrary. Similarly, the indifference curve I_2 is given by equation (10); north of this curve, the wage laborer would prefer the foreperson's power was not arbitrary, and to the south he would prefer that it was. (The explanation of this latter counter-intuitive possibility is that when the cost of coercing the wage laborer is very low, he is so badly off that he would prefer a riskier scenario with some chance of a substantially greater expected utility payoff. Thus, people in very desperate situations may consent to suffer under domination—a topic discussed in Chapter 5.) The shaded area B between these indifference curves represents those situations in which *both* players would prefer the foreperson's power was not arbitrary. The existence of this area is guaranteed by the fact that the second version of the model has a Pareto-inefficient Nash equilibrium outcome, which in turn is a direct result of there being incomplete information. Inefficiency is standard in incomplete information models. It stems from the fact that exercising coercive power carries a deadweight cost: when both players are perfectly informed, they act to ensure these costs are never incurred. In a parallel example, game theory models of worker strikes find that if both employers and employees are perfectly informed, strikes should never occur. Only when there is incomplete information will the employers and employees risk the deadweight costs incurred by an actual strike. An interesting conclusion that we are left with here is that there may be at least a few real-world situations in which both the agents and the subjects of political domination can be made better off by reducing the arbitrariness of the former's powers. For those who believe that the powerful will never agree to reform on moral grounds alone, this could be a hopeful result.

AII.3 Modeling dependency

This section expands the basic model again, this time so as to include the element of dependency. Recall from Chapter 2 that in nearly any social relationship, those suffering under domination will have some opportunities for exit: even slaves may attempt escape rather than stay put, medieval peasants may flee from the manor to the city, the wives of abusive husbands may seek divorce, and so on. How we define the range of exit options depends, of course, on the situation we are interested in modeling. In our model, the wage laborer's outside options might be defined as including some range of alternate job opportunities, plus the option of long-term unemployment (short-term unemployment being regarded as a transition cost). Let W represent the finite set of all such outside options known to the wage laborer, and w any given element of this set.

Naturally, nothing ensures that any of these opportunities for exit are particularly desirable. Let $\omega(w)$ represent the wage laborer's evaluation of taking opportunity w, all things considered—that is, his estimation of all the advantages and disadvantages of w, less the costs associated with making the transition itself. In some cases, the wage laborer may be able to estimate these values rather precisely, but this will not necessarily be the case: he may not know how long it will take to secure the new job, nor exactly what his prospects at that job are likely to be, and so on. Nevertheless, in deciding whether or not to take advantage of some opportunities, the wage laborer must inevitably make an educated guess, and we can suppose that this is what $\omega(w)$ represents.[12] Further, let $w^* = \arg\max\{\omega(w)\}$ for all $w \in W$, and let $\omega^* = \omega(w^*)$. In other words, ω^* represents the wage laborer's overall evaluation of his best exit opportunity. Obviously, from the point of view of our model, this is going to be the value we are interested in. For the sake of argument, assume that ω^* is common knowledge.

Two new stages will be added to the model. Just after nature randomly determines the value of cost c, the foreperson can determine and announce the value of p, the negative utility associated with being coerced. This might be interpreted as the foreperson's making it clear to the wage laborer just how much power she is granted under the terms of the employment agreement. (To keep things simple, let us assume that the foreperson must subsequently adhere to whatever terms she announces.[13]) Once this is done, the wage laborer decides whether or not to exit the social relationship and takes some $w \in W$. Naturally, we can assume he would take w^* if anything: if he does, the game ends, he receives the payoff ω^*, and the foreperson a payoff of 0. If he does not, the game continues as before: the wage laborer next selects a level of surplus effort e to offer the foreperson, and finally the foreperson decides whether or not to coerce the wage laborer. The two players' strategy spaces must be adjusted accordingly. A complete strategy for the foreperson is now an ordered pair of two mappings, $s_1 = (s_1{}^P\colon C \to P, s_1{}^A\colon S_2 \times C \to A)$, where $P = \{p \in R_+\}$ and $A = \{a \in 1$ ("coerce"), 0 ("don't coerce")\}. Her strategy space S_1 is the set of all such ordered pairs. A complete strategy for the wage laborer is now a mapping $s_2\colon P \to D$, where D is a set of ordered pairs $d = (d^W, d^E)$ where $d^W \in \{1$ ("exit"), 0 ("don't exit")\} and $d^E \in E$ is an offer of some level of surplus effort. His strategy space S_2 the set of all such mappings. If the foreperson coerces the wage laborer, then $e = e_c$; and if not $e = d^E$. In all other respects, the model remains as before. The complete game so modified can be given a simplified extensive-form representation as in Figure A2.2, with the players' payoffs indicated. In order to solve this game, some further assumptions will be needed. First, as was done earlier, let us set $e_1 = 1$, $e_2 = 0$, and $e_c = 1$. This enables the wage laborer to make a definite comparison between his current situation and his

[12] A more complex model, of course, might model this with incomplete information. Here, I assume any risk aversion on the wage laborer's part has been built in to the function $\omega(w)$.

[13] If this were not assumed, the announcement would be mere cheap talk, conveying no information to the wage laborer at all (thus, rendering the announcement useless). On a more elaborate model, the commitment problem could be made endogenous by allowing the foreperson to sink costs in some manner.

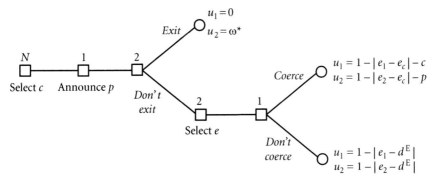

Figure AII.2

prospects under w^*. Second, we will assume, as we did in Section A2.2, that the wage laborer's expectations regarding the value of c are accurate. Given these assumptions, we find the Nash equilibrium strategies are as follows:

$$s_1^* = \begin{cases} \textit{if}\,\omega^* \leq 0, \text{then } p \geq 1 \text{ and} \begin{cases} a = 0 \ \textit{if}\,s_2 \geq 1 - c \\ a = 0 \ \textit{if}\,s_2 < 1 - c \end{cases} \\[2ex] \textit{if}\,\omega^* > 0, \text{then } p = \max\{1 - 2\sqrt{\omega^*}, 0\} \text{and} \begin{cases} a = 0 \ \textit{if}\,s_2 \geq 1 - c \\ a = 0 \ \textit{if}\,s_2 < 1 - c \end{cases} \end{cases} \tag{11}$$

$$s_2^* = \begin{cases} \textit{if}\,\omega^* > 0 \ \text{ and } \ p > 1, \text{ then } \ d^W = 1 \\[1ex] \textit{if}\,\omega^* > \dfrac{p^2 - 2p + 1}{4}, \text{ then } d^W = 1 \\[2ex] \text{otherwise}, d^W = 0 \ \text{ and } \ d^E = \min\left\{\dfrac{1+p}{2}, 1\right\} \end{cases} \tag{12}$$

Proof: Using backward induction, note that player 1's situation in the final stage is the same as in earlier models, so the proof of equation (3) applies in determining a; likewise, in the second to last stage, player 2's situation is also the same, so the proof of equation (6) applies in determining d^E, if $d^W = 0$. It follows that player 2's expected payoff for not exiting will be 0 if $p > 1$, and otherwise as given by equation (7). Thus, $d^W = 1$ if $\omega^* > 0$ in the former case, or if $\omega^* > (p^2 - 2p + 1)/4$ in the latter case. In either case, d^E can take any value. If neither condition holds, then $d^W = 0$ and $d^E = \min\{(1 + p)/2, 1\}$. Finally, we will determine the value of p. Given s_2^*, if $\omega^* \leq 0$ then player 2 will not exit no matter how high p is; player 1 will thus set $p \geq 1$ to ensure $d^E = 1$ under the threat of coercion. If $\omega^* > 0$, then player 2 may or may not exit, depending on p. Using the quadratic equation and solving the above inequality for p, we find that p must be less than $1 - 2\sqrt{\omega^*}$ to ensure that $d^W = 0$ (the irrelevant root is discarded). Now if $p > 1 - 2\sqrt{\omega^*}$ then $u_1 = 0$, but if $p \leq 1 - 2\sqrt{\omega^*}$ then, as per equation (8), $u_1 = (3 + p^2 - 2c(1-p))/4$, which is positive if $0 \leq p \leq 1$, and is maximized when $p = 1 - 2\sqrt{\omega^*}$. $\square$

This result may be interpreted as follows. On the one hand, if the wage laborer's best outside option w^* is very good, he will take it regardless of what the foreperson does; in this case, he is not dependent on the social relationship at all. On the other hand, if $\omega^* < 0$, then the wage laborer's best guess is that his outside options are all worse than his current prospects, at least once transition costs are factored in; in this case, his dependency on the social relationship is all but complete. The foreperson can then threaten the wage laborer with the most severe coercion imaginable, thus securing the maximum surplus effort possible. (Imagine that a surplus effort of $e = 1$ corresponds to working as much as humanly possible—every waking hour, every day of the week. When $\omega^* < 0$, the wage laborer has no outside option better than this.) Within this range, the dynamics of the social relationship are more nuanced: roughly speaking, the foreperson will threaten the wage laborer with enough coercion to extract some surplus effort, but no so much as to induce him to leave for his best outside opportunity.

Some representative payoffs in this version of the model are suggested in Table A2.2. Two points are worth noting here: First, the wage laborer's expected payoff in this model is equivalent to ω^*. This follows from the fact that the foreperson will optimally adjust the value of p such that the wage laborer is indifferent between remaining in the social relationship and exiting: setting p higher than this triggers the laborer's exit, while setting p lower than this deprives the foreperson of surplus effort she might extract. This result depends, of course, on ω^* being common knowledge; a more sophisticated version of the model would not have to make this assumption. Second, the wage laborer's expected payoff decreases with increasing dependency, while the foreperson's expected payoff increases. This is as we would expect, and it confirms the connection between dependency and the severity of domination discussed in Chapter 2.

One additional remark on this version of the model may be in order. Suppose a person works at his favorite job, all things considered; thus, all other employment opportunities are worse, relatively speaking. Does it follow that she suffers under domination? If it did, that would seem odd. Fortunately, it does not. As we have seen, dependency is a necessary, but not sufficient condition of domination. A person is dependent, in a sense, on a social relationship she prefers to any alternative, but she does not suffer under domination unless it is additionally the case that someone else in that social relationship happens to wield arbitrary power over her. If one valued the

Table AII.2

ω^*	p	e	Eu_2	Eu_1
0.200	0.106	0.553	0.200	0.529
0.100	0.368	0.684	0.100	0.626
0.050	0.553	0.777	0.050	0.715

benefits of a social relationship high enough to outweigh the costs of suffering under some degree of domination, then one might voluntarily agree to suffer under domination to that extent. This is the problem of consensual domination, which is discussed in Chapter 5.

AII.4 Modeling multiple subjects

Before concluding this appendix, I will consider one final modification of the basic model. In this version, there will be more than one subject of political domination. Let $n \geq 2$ be the number of wage laborers (players 2, 3, ..., $n + 1$), and let i represent any one of them. With appropriate interpretation, this version of the model can apply to any case in which those suffering under domination outnumber those inflicting it, and 1:n can be taken as the ratio between these two groups. Let us further suppose the foreperson can exercise her coercive powers over only one of these wage laborers in the final stage of the game.[14] Her strategy space is now correspondingly more complex. A complete strategy will be an ordered pair of two mappings, $s_1 = (s_1{}^P \colon C \to P, s_1{}^A \colon \{S_n\}$ $\times\ C \to A)$, where $P = \{p \in \mathbf{R}_+\}$, $\{S_n\}$ is the series of each wage laborers' respective surplus effort offer, and A is a set of ordered pairs $a = (a, i)$ where $a \in 0$ ("don't coerce") or 1 ("coerce"), and i is the wage laborer to be coerced if $a = 1$. The model will remain otherwise unchanged.

Even though the foreperson's power is limited as described, our earlier results will not necessarily change. Why might this be the case? Suppose for the moment that each wage laborer must decide on his level of surplus effort independently, without being able to coordinate with the other wage laborers. Also, let us ignore outside options for the moment. Under these conditions, each wage laborer will probably end up offering exactly the same level of effort as he would if he were facing the foreperson alone. This is because the foreperson could adopt the strategy of coercing whichever laborer puts forward the least surplus effort (and, let us suppose, choosing randomly among any set of laborers whose surplus effort levels are equally low).[15] By working slightly harder than his fellows, any individual wage laborer can avoid being coerced himself. The only possible equilibrium in this situation will thus see every wage laborer adopting the strategy $s_i{}^* = \min\{(1 + p)/2, 1\}$. This is because on the one hand, if any worker put forward less surplus effort, he would guarantee being coerced himself, while on the other hand, no worker can do better by offering more than he would if he faced the foreperson alone. So long as coordination among the workers is impossible, therefore, the foreperson can maintain tight control, even with quite limited powers of coercion.

But let us suppose the wage laborers manage to coordinate their strategies. In particular, suppose they can commit to each offering the same level of surplus effort, perhaps by agreeing to internally sanction one another in case of defection. This

---

[14] Again, I ignore repeated versions of the game here.
[15] Indeed, in equilibrium, her strategy must include this rule of thumb, for in this model the greatest gains to be had will always lie in coercing the worker offering the least surplus effort.

changes each wage laborer's individual estimate of the probability that he will be coerced at a given level of effort: roughly speaking, the more wage laborers there are, the lower each individual wage laborer's chance of being the one singled out for coercion. First, let us see how this changes the Nash equilibrium result in the model that includes arbitrariness but not dependency. Ignoring outside options, the new equilibrium strategies are:

$$s_1^* = \begin{cases} \text{if for all } i \in n, s_i \geq 1 - c, \text{then } \alpha = (0,0) \\ \text{otherwise}, \alpha = (1, i) \text{ such that } i = min\{s_i\} \end{cases} \tag{13}$$

$$\text{for all } i \in n, s_i^* = min\left\{\frac{2 + p - n}{2}, 1\right\} \tag{14}$$

Proof: Using backward induction, first note that player 1's situation in stage two is no different than in the basic model: she will always do better by coercing some $i \in n$ when at least one $s_i < 1 - c$. Furthermore, she will always do the best to coerce the player giving the lowest offer. When two or more players offer an equally low level of surplus effort, player 1 is indifferent, so we may assume she will select one of them to coerce randomly. Now consider player i's situation in stage one, given s_1^*: the optimal strategy for each will be to maximize the expected utility function $Eu_i = prob\{a = (1, i)\} \cdot (1-| e_i - e_c |-p) + (1-prob\{a = (1, i)\}) \cdot (1-| e_i - s_i |)$. Note that by assumption, s_i is the same for all $i \in n$. There will be three cases. As in the proof for equation (6), we can eliminate any $s_i \leq 0$. The $prob\{a = (1, i)\}$ for any given $i \in n$ when s_i takes a value between 0 and 1 is $(1-s_i)/n$. This fact, plus the assumption that $e_c = 1$, and that $e_i \leq 0$ for all $i \in n$, simplifies this to $Eu_i = 1 + e_i - s_i - (1 - 2s_i + s_i^2 + p - ps_i)/n$. This function is maximized where its first-order partial derivative $\partial Eu_i / \partial s_i = -1 - (2s_i - p - 2)/n = 0$, and solving for s_i we find that $s_i^* = (2 + p - n)/2$, if this is less than 1. Otherwise (in the third case), $s_i^* = 1$, as per the proof for equation (6). $\square$

Note that, as one would expect, when $n = 1$, equation (14) reduces to equation (6). Increasing the number of wage laborers n has the effect of lowering the level of surplus effort offered by each individual wage laborer. At equilibrium, player i's expected payoff in this version of the model can be determined by substituting her optimal strategy s_i^* into her expected utility function:

$$Eu_i = 1 + e_i - \left(\frac{2+p-n}{2}\right) - \left(1 - 2\left(\frac{2+p-n}{2}\right) + \left(\frac{2+p-n}{2}\right)^2\right.$$
$$\left. + p - p\left(\frac{2+p-n}{2}\right)\right)\frac{1}{n}$$

which if we let $e_i = 0$ simplifies to:

$$Eu_i = \frac{p^2 - 2pn + n^2}{4n} \tag{15}$$

Note that when $n = 1$, this simplifies into equation (7), as we would expect, and that for any $n \geq 2$, Eu_i increases with n. Thus, we find that coordination among a group suffering under domination can ameliorate the harshness of their situation.

Next, let us bring dependency back into the model, and assume the wage laborers have outside options. To keep things simple, assume that each individual wage laborer assigns exactly the same evaluation ω^* to his best outside option in W, and that all the other assumptions discussed in this section and in Section A2.3 continue to hold. The new equilibrium strategies are:

$$s_1^* = \begin{cases} \text{if } \omega^* \leq 0, \text{then } p \geq n \\ \text{if } \omega^* > 0, \text{then } p = \max\{n - 2\sqrt{\omega^* n}, 0\} \\[2mm] \text{if for all } i \in n, d_i^E \geq 1 - c, \text{then } \alpha = (0, 0) \\ \text{otherwise}, \alpha = (1, i) \text{ such that } i = \min\{d_i^E\} \end{cases} \tag{16}$$

$$\text{for all } i \in n, s_i^* = \begin{cases} \text{if } \omega^* > 0 \text{ and } p > n, \text{then } d_i^W = 1 \\ \text{if } \omega^* > \dfrac{p^2 - 2np + n^2}{4n}, \text{then } d^W = 1 \\[2mm] \text{otherwise}, d^W = 0 \text{ and } d^E = \min\left\{\dfrac{2 + p - n}{2}, 1\right\} \end{cases} \tag{17}$$

Proof: Using backward induction, first note that player 1's situation in the final stage is no different than in the previous model, so the proof of equation (13) applies in determining α. Likewise, in the second to last stage, player i's situation is the same as in the previous model, so the proof of equation (14) applies in determining d_i^E if $d_i^W = 0$. It follows that player i's expected payoff for not exiting will be given by equation (15) if $p \leq n$, and will be 0 otherwise. Thus, $d_i^W = 1$ if $\omega^* > (p^2 - 2np + n^2)/4n$ in the former case, or if $\omega^* > 0$ in the latter case. In either case, d_i^E can take any value. If neither condition holds, $d_i^W = 0$, and $d_i^E = \min\{(2 + p - n)/2, 1\}$. Finally, we determine the value of p. Given s_i^*, if $\omega^* \leq 0$, player i will not exit no matter how high p is, so player 1 will set $p \geq n$ to ensure that $d_i^E = 1$ under the threat of coercion. If $\omega^* > 0$, then player i may or may not exit, depending on p. Using the quadratic equation and solving the above inequality for p, we find that p must be less than $n - 2\sqrt{\omega * n}$ to ensure that $d_i^W = 0$ (the irrelevant root is discarded). Analogously to the proof of equation (11), player 1 will do best to set $p = n - 2\sqrt{\omega * n}$. $\square$

Generally speaking, we find that the foreperson will raise the penalty associated with being coerced in order to compensate for the increased number of wage laborers, but not so far as to induce them to take their outside options.

This concludes the appendix. These formal models correspond to arguments advanced in the main text. If domination is something we are interested in reducing (as argued in Part II), we see from these models that there are (at least) three methods of combating it. First, equations (12) and (17) suggest that we can reduce domination by reducing a subject's dependency—that is, by improving their outside option ω^*. This is argued in Chapter 2. Second, equations (6) and (14) suggest that we can reduce domination by reducing the agent's power—that is, by lowering the value of p—supporting what is argued in Chapter 3. Third and finally, as discussed in Chapter 4, Table A2.1 suggests that in most cases we can improve the condition of those subject to domination by forcing those who wield power to exercise such power according to known rules.

Bibliography

Adam, Barry D. 1978. *The Survival of Domination: Inferiorization and Everyday Life*. Elsevier Press.

Airaksinen, Timo. 1992. "The Rhetoric of Domination," *Rethinking Power*, Thomas E. Wartenberg, ed. State University of New York Press.

Allen, Amy. 1999. *The Power of Feminist Theory: Domination, Resistance, Solidarity*. Westview Press.

Althusser, Louis. 1979. *For Marx*. Ben Brewster, tr. Verso.

Altman, Andrew. 1990. *Critical Legal Studies: A Liberal Critique*. Princeton University Press.

Anderson, Elizabeth S. 1999. "What Is the Point of Equality?," *Ethics* 109: 287–337.

Anderson, Perry. 1974. *Lineages of the Absolutist State*. Schocken Books.

Arendt, Hannah. 1958. *The Human Condition*. The University of Chicago Press.

——.1968. *Totalitarianism: Part Three of the Origins of Totalitarianism*. Harcourt Brace.

——.1990. *On Revolution*. Penguin Books.

——.1993. "What Is Freedom?," *Between Past and Future: Eight Exercises in Political Thought*. Penguin Books.

Arneson, Richard J. 1989. "Equality of Opportunity for Welfare," *Philosophical Studies* 56: 77–93.

Barry, Brian. 1977. "Justice Between Generations," *Law, Morality and Society: Essays in Honor of H. L. A. Hart*, P. M. S. Hacker and Joseph Raz, eds. Clarendon Press.

——.1980. "Is It Better to Be Powerful or Lucky?," *Political Studies* 28: 183–94, 338–52.

——.1989. *Theories of Justice*. University of California Press.

——.1995. *Justice as Impartiality*. Oxford University Press.

——.2001. *Culture and Equality: An Egalitarian Critique of Multiculturalism*. Polity Press.

——.2002. "Capitalists Rule OK? Some Puzzles about Power," *Politics, Philosophy, and Economics* 1: 155–84.

——.2005. *Why Social Justice Matters*. Polity Press.

Bellamy, Richard. 2007. *Political Constitutionalism: A Republican Defense of the Constitutionality of Democracy*. Cambridge University Press.

Berlin, Isaiah. 1969. "Two Concepts of Liberty," *Four Essays on Liberty*. Oxford University Press.

Binmore, Ken. 1998. *Game Theory and the Social Contract, Vol. 2, Just Playing*. MIT Press.

Blackstone, William. [1765] 1979. *Commentaries on the Laws of England*, 4 vols. University of Chicago Press.

Boaz, David. 1997. *Libertarianism: A Primer.* The Free Press.

Bohman, James. 2004. "Republican Cosmopolitanism," *Journal of Political Philosophy* 12: 336–52.

——. 2008. "Nondomination and Transnational Democracy," *Republicanism and Political Theory*, John Maynor and Cécile Laborde, eds. Blackwell Publishers.

Bourdieu, Pierre. 2002. *Masculine Domination.* Richard Nice, tr. Stanford University Press.

Bowles, Samuel, and Herbert Gintis. 1992. "Power and Wealth in a Competitive Capitalist Economy," *Philosophy and Public Affairs* 21: 324–53.

—— ——. 1993. "The Democratic Firm: An Agency-Theoretic Evaluation," *Markets and Democracy: Participation, Accountability, and Efficiency*, Samuel Bowles, Herbert Gintis, and Bo Gustafsson, eds. Cambridge University Press.

Braithwaite, John, and Philip Pettit. 1990. *Not Just Deserts: A Republican Theory of Criminal Justice.* Oxford University Press.

Calvert, Randall L. 1995. "Rational Actors, Equilibrium, and Social Institutions," *Explaining Social Institutions*, Jack Knight and Itai Sened, eds. University of Michigan Press.

Carter, Ian. 2008. "How Are Power and Unfreedom Related?," *Republicanism and Political Theory*, John Maynor and Cécile Laborde, eds. Blackwell Publishers.

Cicero. [n.d.] 1971. *Selected Works.* Michael Grant, tr. Penguin Books.

——. [n.d.] 1999. *On the Commonwealth and On the Laws.* James E.G. Zetzel, tr. Cambridge University Press.

Cohen, G. A. 1983. "The Structure of Proletarian Unfreedom," *Philosophy and Public Affairs* 12: 3–33.

——. 1989. "On the Currency of Egalitarian Justice," *Ethics* 99: 906–44.

Cohen, Joshua. 1989. "Deliberation and Democratic Legitimacy," *The Good Polity*, Alan Hamlin and Philip Pettit, eds. Blackwell Publishers.

——. 1996. "Procedure and Substance in Deliberative Democracy," *Democracy and Difference*, Sheyla Benhabib, ed. Princeton University Press.

Cole, David. 1999. *No Equal Justice: Race and Class in the American Criminal Justice System.* W.W. Norton.

Coleman, Jules L., and Brian Leiter. 1993. "Determinacy, Objectivity, and Authority," *University of Pennsylvania Law Review* 142: 549–637.

Connolly, William E. 1983. *The Terms of Political Discourse*, 2nd edn. Princeton University Press.

Cowen, Tyler, and Derrek Parfit. 1992. "Against the Social Discount Rate," *Justice Between Age Groups and Generations*, Peter Laslett and James S. Fishkin, eds. Yale University Press.

Dagger, Richard. 2006. "Neo-Republicanism and the Civic Economy," *Politics, Philosophy, and Economics* 5: 151–73.

Daniels, Norman. 1979. "Wide Reflective Equilibrium and Theory Acceptance in Ethics," *Journal of Philosophy* 76: 256–82.

Davidson, Donald. 1980. *Essays on Actions and Events.* Clarendon Press.

Davis, Kenneth Culp. 1969. *Discretionary Justice: A Preliminary Inquiry*. Louisiana State University Press.

Deudney, Daniel. 2006. *Bounding Power: Republican Security Theory from the Polis to the Global Village*. Princeton University Press.

Dicey, A. V. [1915] 1982. *Introduction to the Study of the Law of the Constitution*. Liberty Fund.

Douglass, Frederick. [1855] 1969. *My Bondage and My Freedom*. Dover Publications.

Dowding, Keith M. 1991. *Rational Choice and Political Power*. E. Elgar Publishers.

——. 1996. *Power*. University of Minnesota Press.

Dworkin, Ronald. 1977. *Taking Rights Seriously*. Harvard University Press.

——. 1986. *Law's Empire*. Belknap Press.

——. 1990. "Foundations of Liberal Equality," *The Tanner Lectures on Human Values* 11: 3–119.

——. 2000. *Sovereign Virtue: The Theory and Practice of Equality*. Harvard University Press.

Edgeworth, F. Y. 1881. *Mathematical Psychics: An Essay on the Application of Mathematics to the Moral Sciences*. C. Kegan Paul and Co.

Elster, Jon. 1979. *Ulysses and the Sirens: Studies in Rationality and Irrationality*. Cambridge University Press.

——. 1983a. *Explaining Technical Change: A Case Study in the Philosophy of Science*. Cambridge University Press.

——. 1983b. *Sour Grapes: Studies in the Subversion of Rationality*. Cambridge University Press.

——. 1986. "Introduction," *Rational Choice*, Jon Elster, ed. New York University Press.

——. 1989. *The Cement of Society*. Cambridge University Press.

——. 2000. "Rationality, Economy, and Society," *The Cambridge Companion to Weber*, Stephen Turner, ed. Cambridge University Press.

——. 2004. *Closing the Books: Transitional Justice in Historical Perspective*. Cambridge University Press.

——. 2007. *Explaining Social Behavior: More Nuts and Bolts for the Social Sciences*. Cambridge University Press.

Ely, John Hart. 1980. *Democracy and Distrust: A Theory of Judicial Review*. Harvard University Press.

Emerson, Richard M. 1962. "Power-Dependence Relations," *American Sociological Review* 27: 31–41.

Epstein, Lee, and Jack Knight. 1997. *The Choices that Justices Make*. CQ Press.

Feinberg, Joel. 1993. "Psychological Egoism," *Reason and Responsibility: Readings in Some Basic Problems of Philosophy*, Joel Feinberg, ed. Wadsworth Publishing.

Ferejohn, John. 2001. "Pettit's Republic," *The Monist* 84: 77–97.

Flynn, Edith E. 1989. "Victims of Terrorism: Dimensions of the Victim Experience," *The Plight of Crime Victims in Modern Society*, Ezzat A. Fattah, ed. Macmillan.

Foucault, Michel. 1980. "Two Lectures," *Power/Knowledge: Selected Interviews and Other Writings: 1972–1977*, Colin Gordon, ed. Pantheon Books.

Foucault, Michel. 1988. "The Ethics of Care for the Self," *The Final Foucault*, James Bemauer and David Rasmussen, eds. MIT Press.

———. 1990. *The History of Sexuality, Vol. 1, An Introduction*, Robert Hurley, tr. Vintage Books.

———. 2003. *"Society Must Be Defended," Lectures at the Collège de France 1975–1976*, David Macey, tr. Picador.

Frankfurt, Harry G. 1971. "Freedom of the Will and the Concept of a Person," *The Journal of Philosophy* 48: 5–20.

———. 1987. "Equality as a Moral Ideal," *Ethics* 98: 21–43.

Freeman, M. D. A. 1983. *The Rights and Wrongs of Children*. Dover.

Friedman, Marilyn A. 2008. "Pettit's Civic Republicanism and Male Domination," *Republicanism and Political Theory*, John Maynor and Cécile Laborde, eds. Blackwell Publishers.

Frye, Marilyn. 1983. "Oppression," *The Politics of Reality: Essays in Feminist Theory*. The Crossing Press.

Gallie, W. B. 1956. "Essentially Contested Concepts," *Procedings of the Aristotelian Society* 56: 167–98.

Gauthier, David. 1986. *Morals by Agreement*. Clarendon Press.

Genovese, Eugene D. 1974. *Roll, Jordan, Roll: The World the Slaves Made*. Vintage Books.

Gert, Bernard. 1972. "Introduction," Thomas Hobbes, *Man and Citizen*, Bernard Gert, ed. Hackett Publishing.

Geuss, Raymond. 1981. *Idea of a Critical Theory: Habermas and the Frankfurt School*. Cambridge University Press.

Goodin, Robert E. 1988. *Reasons for Welfare: The Political Theory of the Welfare State*. Princeton University Press.

Gramsci, Antonio. 1971. *Selections from the Prison Notebooks*, Quintin Hoare and Goeffrey Nowell Smith, tr. International Publishers.

Groot, L. F. M. 2002. "Compensatory Justice and Basic Income," *Journal of Social Philosophy* 33: 144–61.

Habermas, Jürgen. 1971. *Knowledge and Human Interests*, Jeremy J. Shapiro, tr. Beacon Press.

———. 1975. *Legitimation Crisis*. Thomas McCarthy, tr. Beacon Press.

———. 1993. *Justification and Application: Remarks on Discourse Ethics*. Ciaran P. Cronin, ed. MIT Press.

———. 1996. *Between Facts and Norms: Contributions to a Discourse Theory of Law and Democracy*. William Rehg, tr. MIT Press.

———. 1998. "On The Internal Relation Between the Rule of Law and Democracy," *The Inclusion of the Other: Studies in Political Theory*, Ciaran Cronin and Pablo De Greiff, eds. MIT Press.

Hampton, Jean. 1994. "Democracy and the Rule of Law," *Nomos 36: The Rule of Law*, Ian Shapiro, ed. New York University Press.

Harrington, James. [1656] 1977. "The Commonwealth of Oceana," *The Political Works of James Harrington*, J. G. A. Pocock, ed. Cambridge University Press.

Hart, H. L. A. 1994. *The Concept of Law*, 2nd edn. Clarendon Press.

Harsanyi, John C. 1953. "Cardinal Utility in Welfare Economics and in the Theory of Risk-Taking," *Journal of Political Economy* 61: 434–5.

——. 1955. "Cardinal Welfare, Individualistic Ethics, and Interpersonal Comparisons of Utility," *Journal of Political Economy* 63: 309–21.

Hastie, Reid, and Robyn M. Dawes. 2001. *Rational Choice in an Uncertain World: The Psychology of Judgment and Decision Making.* Sage Publications.

Havel, Vaclav. 1992. "The Power of the Powerless," *Open Letters: Selected Writings 1965–1990*, Paul Wilson, ed. Vintage Books.

Hayek, Friedrick A. 1960. *The Constitution of Liberty.* University of Chicago Press.

Hayward, Clarissa Rile. 2000. *De-Facing Power.* Cambridge University Press.

Heath, Joseph. 2000. "Ideology, Irrationality, and Collectively Self-defeating Behavior," *Constellations* 7: 363–71.

Hegel, G. W. F. [1807] 1977. *Phenomenology of Spirit*, A. V. Miller, tr. Oxford University Press.

Held, David. 1980. *Introduction to Critical Theory.* Hutchinson.

Hobbes, Thomas. [1651] 1998. *Leviathan.* J. C. A. Gaskin, ed. Oxford University Press.

Holcombe, Lee. 1983. *Wives and Property: Reform of the Married Women's Property Law in Nineteenth-century England.* University of Toronto Press.

Holmes, Stephen. 1995. *Passions and Constraint: On The Theory of Liberal Democracy.* University of Chicago Press.

Horkheimer, Max, and Theodor W. Adorno. 1988. *Dialectic of Enlightenment*, John Cumming, tr. Continuum.

Isaac, Jeffrey C. 1987a. "Beyond the Three Faces of Power: A Realist Critique," *Polity* 20: 4–31.

——. 1987b. *Power and Marxist Theory: A Realist View.* Cornell University Press.

Jefferson, Thomas. [1788] 1975. "Notes on the State of Virginia," *The Portable Thomas Jefferson*, Merrill D. Peterson, ed. Penguin Books.

Kavka, Gregory S. 1986. *Hobbesian Moral and Political Theory.* Princeton University Press.

Kelly, Paul. 2005. *Liberalism.* Polity Press.

Kelman, Mark. 1987. *A Guide to Critical Legal Studies.* Harvard University Press.

Kelsen, Hans. 1967. *Pure Theory of Law*, 2nd edn., Max Knight, tr. Peter Smith.

Kittay, Iva Feder. 1999. *Love's Labor: Essays on Women, Equality, and Dependency.* Routledge.

Kritz, Neil, ed. 1995. *Transitional Justice: How Emerging Democracies Reckon with Former Regimes*, 3 vols. Institute of Peace Studies.

Kukathas, Chandran. 1997. "Cultural Toleration," *Nomos 39: Ethnicity and Group Rights*, Ian Shapiro and Will Kymlicka, eds. New York University Press.

Kymlicka, Will. 1990. *Contemporary Political Philosophy: An Introduction.* Oxford University Press.

Laborde, Cécile. 2010. "Republicanism and Global Justice: A Sketch," *European Journal of Political Theory*, 9: 48–69.

Larmore, Charles. 2004. "Liberal and Republican Conceptions of Freedom," *Republicanism: History, Theory, and Practice*, Daniel Weinstock and Christine Nadeau, eds. Frank Cass.

Lewis, David. 1969. *Convention*. Harvard University Press.

Livy. [n.d.] 1971. *The Early History of Rome*, Aubrey de Sélincourt, tr. Penguin Books.

Locke, John. [1690] 1980. *Second Treatise of Government*. Crawford B. Macpherson, ed. Hackett Publishing.

Lovett, Frank. 2001. "Domination: A Preliminary Analysis," *The Monist* 84: 98–112.

——.2002. "A Positivist Account of the Rule of Law," *Law and Social Inquiry* 27: 41–78.

——.2004. "Can Justice Be Based on Consent?," *Journal of Political Philosophy* 12: 79–101.

——.2005. "Milton's Case for a Free Commonwealth," *American Journal of Political Science* 49: 466–78.

——.2007. "Consent and the Legitimacy of Punishment: Response to Brettschneider," *Political Theory* 35: 806–10.

Luce, R. Duncan and Howard Raiffa. 1957. *Games and Decisions: Introduction and Critical Survey*. Wiley.

Lukács, Georg. 1971. *History and Class Consciousness: Studies in Marxist Dialectics*, Rodney Livingstone, tr. MIT Press.

Lukes, Steven. 2005. *Power: A Radical View*, 2nd. edn. Palgrave Macmillan.

Machiavelli, Niccolò. [1532] 1998. *The Prince*, Harvey C. Mansfield, tr. University of Chicago Press.

Marcuse, Herbert. 1955. *Eros and Civilization: A Philosophical Inquiry into Freud*. Beacon Press.

——.1964. *One-Dimensional Man: Studies in the Ideology of Advanced Industrial Society*. Beacon Press.

Markell, Patchen. 2008. "The Insufficiency of Non-Domination," *Political Theory* 36: 9–36.

Mason, Mary Ann. 1994. *From Father's Property to Children's Rights: The History of Child Custody in the United States*. Columbia University Press.

Maynor, John W. 2003. *Republicanism in the Modern World*. Polity Press.

McGinn, Colin. 1999. "Reasons and Unreasons," *The New Republic* May 24, 1999: 34–8.

Memmi, Albert. 1971. *Dominated Man: Notes Towards a Portrait*. Beacon Press.

Mill, John Stuart. [1859] 1998a. "On Liberty," *On Liberty and Other Essays*, John Gray, ed. Oxford University Press.

——.[1861] 1998b. "Considerations on Representative Government," *On Liberty and Other Essays*, John Gray, ed. Oxford University Press.

——.[1869] 1998c. "The Subjection of Women," *On Liberty and Other Essays*, John Gray, ed. Oxford University Press.

Miller, Peter. 1987. *Domination and Power*. Routledge and Keagan Paul.

Millgram, Elijah. 2000. "What's the Use of Utility?," *Philosophy and Public Affairs* 29: 113–36.

Milton, John. [1660] 1932. "The Readie and Easie Way to Establish a Free Common-wealth," *The Works of John Milton*, Vol. 6, William Haller, ed. Columbia University Press.

Moon, Donald. 1993. *Constructing Community*. Princeton University Press.

Montesquieu, Charles de Secondat. [1748] 1949. *The Spirit of the Laws*, Thomas Nugent, tr. Hafner Press.

Morriss, Peter. 2002. *Power: A Philosophical Analysis*, 2nd edn. Manchester University Press.

Murray, Charles. 1997. *What It Means to Be a Libertarian: A Personal Interpretation*. Broadway Books.

Nagel, Thomas. 1977. "Equality," *Tanner Lecture on Human Values*, delivered at Stanford University.

——.1991. *Equality and Partiality*. Oxford University Press.

——.2005. "The Problem of Global Justice," *Philosophy and Public Affairs* 33: 113–47.

Narveson, Ian. 2001. *The Libertarian Idea*. Broadview Press.

Nedham, Marchamont. [1656] 1767. *The Excellencie of a Free State*, Richard Baron, ed. London. Printed for A. Millar and T. Cadell.

Nelson, Daniel. 1995. *Managers and Workers*, 2nd edn. University of Wisconsin Press.

Nicholas, Barry. 1962. *An Introduction to Roman Law*. Clarendon Press.

Nino, Carlos S. 1996. *Radical Evil on Trial*. Yale University Press.

Norman, Richard. 1976. *Hegel's Phenomenology: A Philosophical Introduction*. St. Martin's Press.

Noyes, C. Reinold. 1936. *The Institution of Property: A Study of the Development, Substance, and Arrangement*. Longmans, Green, and Co.

Nozick, Robert. 1974. *Anarchy, State, and Utopia*. Basic Books.

Nussbaum, Martha C. 2000. *Women and Human Development*. Cambridge University Press.

Okin, Susan Moller. 1989. *Justice, Gender, and the Family*. Basic Books.

——.2002. "'Mistresses of Their Own Destiny': Group Rights, Gender, and Realistic Rights of Exit," *Ethics* 112: 205–30.

Osofsky, Gilbert, ed. 1969. *Puttin' on Ole Massa: The Slave Narratives of Henry Bibb, William Wells, and Solomon Northrup*. Harper & Row.

Parfit, Derek. 1984. *Reasons and Persons*. Clarendon Press.

——.1995. *Equality or Priority?* University of Kansas Press.

——.2002. "What We Could Rationally Will," *Tanner Lectures on Human Values*, delivered at University of California, Berkeley.

Pateman, Carole. 2004. "Democratic Citizenship: Some Advantages of a Basic Income," *Politics and Society* 32: 89–105.

Patterson, Orlando. 1982. *Slavery and Social Death: A Comparative Study*. Harvard University Press.

Pettit, Philip. 1982. "Habermas on Truth and Justice," *Marx and Marxisms*, G. H. R. Parkinson, ed. Cambridge University Press.

——.1989. "The Freedom of the City: A Republican Ideal," *The Good Polity*, Alan Hamlin and Pettit, eds. Blackwell Publishers.

Pettit, Philip. 1993. "Analytic Philosophy," *A Companion to Contemporary Political Philosophy*, Robert E. Goodin and Philip Pettit, eds. Blackwell Publishers.

——. 1996. "Freedom as Antipower," *Ethics* 106: 576–604.

——. 1997. *Republicanism: A Theory of Freedom and Government.* Clarendon Press.

——. 1999. "Republican Freedom and Contestatory Democratization," *Democracy's Value*, Ian Shapiro and Casiano Hacker-Cordon, eds. Cambridge University Press.

——. 2001. *A Theory of Freedom: From the Psychology to the Politics of Agency.* Oxford University Press.

——. 2004. "Discourse Theory and Republican Freedom," *Republicanism: History, Theory, and Practice*, Daniel Weinstock and Christine Nadeau, eds. Frank Cass.

Pocock, J. G. A. 1975. *The Machiavellian Moment: Florentine Political Thought and the Atlantic Republican Tradition.* Princeton University Press.

Podgorecki, Adam. 1996. "Totalitarian Law: Basic Concepts and Issues," *Totalitarian and Post-Totalitarian Law*, Podgorecki and Vittorio Olgiati, eds. Dartmouth Publishing.

Pogge, Thomas. 1989. *Realizing Rawls.* Cornell University Press.

——. 2002. *World Poverty and Human Rights.* Polity Press.

Posner, Eric A. 2000. *Law and Social Norms.* Harvard University Press.

Postema, Gerald J. 1982. "Coordination and Convention at the Foundations of Law," *Journal of Legal Studies* 11: 165–203.

Radin, Jane. 1989. "Reconsidering the Rule of Law," *Boston University Law Review* 69: 781–819.

Rahe, Paul A. 1992. *Republics Ancient and Modern: Classical Republicanism and the American Revolution.* University of North Carolina Press.

Rakowski, Eric. 1991. *Equal Justice.* Clarendon Press.

Rasmussen, Douglass B. 1999. "Human Flourishing and the Appeal to Human Nature," *Social Philosophy and Policy* 16: 1–43.

Rawls, John. 1951. "Outline of a Decision Procedure for Ethics," *Philosophical Review* 60: 177–97.

——. 1958. "Justice as Fairness," *Philosophical Review* 67: 164–94.

——. 1971. *A Theory of Justice.* Belknap Press.

——. 1982. "Social Unity and Primary Goods," *Utilitarianism and Beyond*, Amartya Sen and Bernard Williams, eds. Cambridge University Press.

——. 1993. *Political Liberalism.* Columbia University Press.

——. 1999. *The Law of Peoples.* Harvard University Press.

——. 2001. *Justice as Fairness: A Restatement*, Erin Kelly, ed. Belknap Press.

Raz, Joseph. 1979. *The Authority of Law: Essays on Law and Morality.* Clarendon Press.

——. 1985. "Authority, Law, and Morality," *The Monist* 68: 295–324.

——. 1986. *Morality of Freedom.* Clarendon Press.

——. 1994. *Ethics in the Public Domain: Essays in the Morality of Law and Politics.* Clarendon Press.

——. 1999. *Practical Reason and Norms*, 2nd edn. Oxford University Press.

Richardson, Henry S. 2002. *Democratic Autonomy: Public Reasoning about the Ends of Policy.* Oxford University Press.

Richter, Melvin. 1995. *The History of Political and Social Concepts: A Critical Introduction.* Oxford University Press.

Roemer, John E. 1985. "Equality of Talent," *Economics and Philosophy* 1: 151–87.

——. 1993. "A Pragmatic Theory of Responsibility for the Egalitarian Planner," *Philosophy and Public Affairs* 22: 146–66.

——. 1996. *Theories of Distributive Justice.* Harvard University Press.

——. 1998. *Equality of Opportunity.* Harvard University Press.

Ross, Alf. 1968. *Directives and Norms.* Routledge and Kegan Paul.

Rousseau, Jean-Jacques. [1762] 1987. "On the Social Contract," *The Basic Political Writings,* Donald A. Cress, tr. Hackett Publishing.

Rubin, Edward L. 1989. "Law and Legislation in the Administrative State," *Columbia Law Review* 89: 369–426.

Sallust. [n.d.] 1963. *The Jugurthine War and The Conspiracy of Catiline,* S.A. Handford, tr. Penguin Books.

Savage, Leonard J. 1972. *Foundations of Statistics.* 2nd edn. Dover Publications.

Scanlon, T. M. 1982. "Contractualism and Utilitarianism," *Utilitarianism and Beyond,* Amartya Sen and Bernard Williams, eds. Cambridge University Press.

——. 1986. "Equality of Resources and Equality of Welfare: A Forced Marriage?," *Ethics* 97: 111–18.

——. 1997. "The Diversity of Objections to Inequality," *The Ideal of Equality,* Matthew Clayton and Andrew Williams, eds. Palgrave Macmillan.

——. 1998. *What We Owe To Each Other.* Belknap Press.

Schauer, Frederick. 1991. *Playing by the Rules: A Philosophical Examination of Rule-Based Decision-Making in Law and in Life.* Clarendon Press.

Scheffler, Samuel. 1982. *The Rejection of Consequentialism.* Clarendon Press.

——. 2001. *Boundaries and Allegiances: Problems of Justice and Responsibility in Liberal Thought.* Oxford University Press.

——. 2003. "What Is Egalitarianism?," *Philosophy and Public Affairs* 31: 5–39.

——. 2006. "Is the Basic Structure Basic?," *The Egalitarian Conscience: Essays in Honour of G. A. Cohen,* Christian Sypnowich, ed. Oxford Univerity Press.

Schelling, Thomas C. 1960. *The Strategy of Conflict.* Harvard University Press.

Scott, James C. 1985. *Weapons of the Weak: Everyday Forms of Peasant Resistance.* Yale University Press.

——. 1990. *Domination and the Arts of Resistance: Hidden Transcripts.* Yale University Press.

Searle, John R. 2001. *Rationality in Action.* MIT Press.

Segal, Jeffrey A., and Harold J. Spaeth. 2002. *The Supreme Court and the Attitudinal Model Revisited.* Cambridge University Press.

Sen, Amartya. 1979. "Utilitarianism and Welfarism," *The Journal of Philosophy* 76: 463–89.

——. 1980. "Equality of What?," *The Tanner Lectures on Human Values* 1: 197–220.

——. 1983. "Poor, Relatively Speaking," *Oxford Economic Papers* 35: 153–68.

——. 1992. *Inequality Reexamined.* Harvard University Press.

——. 2002. *Rationality and Freedom.* Belknap Press.

Shapiro, Carl, and Jospeph Stiglitz. 1984. "Equilibrium Unemployment as a Worker Discipline Service," *American Economic Review* 74: 433–44.

Shapiro, Ian. 2003. *The State of Democratic Theory.* Princeton University Press.

Shapiro, Scott J. 2000. "Law, Morality, and the Guidance of Conduct," *Legal Theory* 6: 127–70.

Shklar, Judith N. 1998. "The Liberalism of Fear," reprinted in *Political Thought and Political Thinkers,* Stanley Hoffman, ed. University of Chicago Press.

Sidanius, Jim, and Felicia Pratto. 1999. *Social Dominance: An Intergroup Theory of Social Hierarchy and Oppression.* Cambridge University Press.

Sidgwick, Henry. [1907] 1981. *The Methods of Ethics.* Hackett Publishing.

Sidney, Algernon. [1698] 1996. *Discourses Concerning Government,* Thomas G. West, ed. Liberty Fund.

Skinner, Quentin. 1984. "The Idea of Negative Liberty," *Philosophy of History: Essays on the Historiography of Philosophy,* Richard Rorty, J. B. Schneewind, and Skinner, eds. Cambridge University Press.

——. 1991. "The Paradoxes of Political Liberty," reprinted in *Liberty,* David Miller, ed. Oxford University Press.

——. 1998. *Liberty before Liberalism.* Cambridge University Press.

Smith, Adam. [1776] 2000. *An Inquiry into the Nature and Causes of the Wealth of Nations,* Edwin Cannan, ed. Modern Library.

Spinner-Halev, Jeff. 2001. "Feminism, Multiculturalism, Oppression, and the State," *Ethics* 112: 84–113.

Spitz, Jean-Fabien. 1995. *La liberté politique.* Presses Universitaires de France.

Stewart, Angus. 2001. *Theories of Power and Domination: The Politics of Empowerment in Late Modernity.* Sage Publications.

Strawson, Peter. 1962. "Freedom and Resentment," *Proceedings of the British Academy* 48: 1–25.

Tacitus. [n.d.] 1996. *The Annals of Imperial Rome,* Michael Grant, tr. Pengiun Books.

Taylor, Charles. 1975. *Hegel.* Cambridge University Press.

——. 1992. "To Follow a Rule," reprinted in *Philosophical Arguments.* Harvard University Press, 1995.

——. 1994. "The Politics of Recognition," *Multiculturalism: Examining the Politics of Recognition,* Amy Gutmann, ed. Princeton University Press.

Temkin, Larry S. 1993. *Inequality.* Oxford University Press.

——. 2003. "Equality, Priority, or What?," *Economics and Philosophy* 19: 61–87.

Thompson, E. P. 1975. *Whigs and Hunters: The Origins of the Black Act.* Pantheon Books.

Tocqueville, Alexis de. [1835] 1990. *Democracy in America, Vol. 1,* Phillips Bradley, ed. Vintage Classics.

——. [1840] 1990. *Democracy in America, Vol. 2,* Phillips Bradley, ed. Vintage Classics.

Tuck, Richard. 1979. *Natural Rights Theories: Their Origin and Development.* Cambridge University Press.

Tucker, T. G. 1985. *Etymological Dictionary of Latin.* Ares Press.

Tully, James. 2005. "Exclusion and Assimilation: Two Forms of Domination in Relation to Freedom," *Nomos 46: Political Exclusion and Inclusion*, Milissa S. Williams and Stephen Macedo, eds. New York University Press.

Van Parijs, Philippe. 1995. *Real Freedom for All: What (If Anything) Can Justify Capitalism?* Clarendon Press.

———. 2004. "Basic Income: A Simple and Powerful Idea for the Twenty-first Century," *Politics and Society* 32: 7–39.

Vaughan-Evans, Laurie and Diane Wood. 1989. "Women as Victims," *The Plight of Crime Victims in Modern Society*, Ezzart A. Fattah, ed. Macmillan.

Viroli, Maurizio. 2002. *Republicanism*, Antony Shugaar, tr. Hill & Wang.

von Neumann, John, and Oscar Morgenstern. 1944. *The Theory of Games and Economic Behavior*. Princeton University Press.

von Wright, Georg Henrik. 1968. *An Essay in Deontic Logic and the General Theory of Action*. North-Holland Publishing.

Walter, Tony. 1989. *Basic Income: Freedom from Poverty, Freedom to Work*. Marion Boyars.

Walzer, Michael. 1983. *Spheres of Justice: A Defense of Pluralism and Equality*. Basic Books.

Wartenberg, Thomas E. 1990. *The Forms of Power: From Domination to Transformation*. Temple University Press.

Watson, Alan. 1989. *Slave Law in the Americas*. University of Georgia Press.

Weber, Max. [1904] 1977. "'Objectivity' in Social Science and Social Policy," *Understanding Social Inquiry*, Fred R. Dallmayr and Thomas A. McCarthy, eds. University of Notre Dame Press.

———. [1919] 1946. "Politics as a Vocation," *From Max Weber: Essays in Sociology*, H. H. Gerth and C. Wright Mills, tr. Oxford University Press.

———. [1922] 1978. *Economy and Society: An Outline of Interpretive Sociology*, Guenther Roth and Claus Wittich, eds. University of California Press.

Weingast, Barry R. 1997. "Democratic Stability as a Self-Enforcing Equilibrium," *Understanding Democracy: Economic and Political Perspectives*, Albert Breton et al., eds. Cambridge University Press.

White, Stuart. 2003. *The Civic Minimum: On the Rights and Obligations of Economic Citizenship*. Oxford University Press.

Wirszubski, CH. 1968. *Libertas as a Political Idea at Rome During the Late Republic and Early Principate*. Cambridge University Press.

Williams, Bernard. 1973. "A Critique of Utilitarianism," *Utilitarianism: For and Against*, J. J. C. Smart and Bernard Williams. Cambridge University Press.

Wittgenstein, Ludwig. 1958. *Philosophical Investigations*, 3rd edn., G. E. M. Anscombe, tr. Prentice Hall.

Wolff, Johnathan. 1998. "Fairness, Respect, and the Egalitarian Ethos," *Philosophy and Public Affairs* 27: 97–122.

Wood, Gordon S. 1969. *The Creation of the American Republic: 1776–1787*, University of North Carolina Press.

Young, Iris Marion. 1990. *Justice and the Politics of Difference*, Princeton University Press.

Index

Accommodation: *see* toleration

Action: defined 30; purposeful 30–3; rational vs. reasonable 32–3, 63–4; and paths of action or strategies 56–57; *see also* strategies

Adam, Barry 12

Adorno, Theodor 87

Airaksinen, Timo 13

Allen, Amy 12

Althusser, Louis 87

Arbitrariness: defined 95–8; as a condition of domination 95, 98, 100–1, 112, 119–20, 134; and the rule of law 98–9; and social conventions 111; procedural vs. substantive interpretations of 112–19; modeling 243–9

Arendt, Hannah 30n5, 100–1

Aristocratic principle 175

Aristotle 30n6, 135, 225n52

Authority, defined 67–8

Barry, Brian 6, 69, 70n20, 210n34

Basic needs: and vulnerability to domination 194–6; public provisions for 197–200; and unconditional basic income 201–3

Basic structure: of society, defined 41–2; and social justice 158–9; of global society, defined 230

Battle of the sexes game 104–5

Bentham, Jeremy 152, 164

Berlin, Isaiah 152–3

Blackstone, William 8, 156, 216n41

Case method 27–8; *see also* reflective equilibrium

Ceausescu, Nicolae 94

Cicero 8, 236–7

Civic humanism 161, 170; vs. civic republicanism 8n9, 215n40

Civic republicanism *see* republicanism

Civic virtues 215–17

Coercion: defined 76; domination and 122, 241–3; *see also* power, social

Communitarianism 170

Consensual domination 147–51, 180–1, 196

Consent-based theories *see* justice, social

Constitutionalism 218–19

Constructivism 16–17

Criteria for a successful theory of domination: generality 4–6, 91–2, 120, 233; practical usefulness 4, 18–20, 38, 95, 99, 108–9, 111, 114–15, 120–1, 233; reasonable fit with existing intuitions 4–5, 27–30, 114, 117–19, 121, 168, 233

Critical Legal Studies 109

Critical theory 87

Democracy: deliberative 7, 219–20; and domination 210–20; defined 211; value of 213–17; forms of 217–19; *see also* domination, conceptions of

Deontological theories *see* justice, social

Dependency: defined, 38–9; and exit costs 39–40, 49–51; as a condition of domination 49–52, 83, 119–20, 134; and markets 53; impossibility of eliminating 53–4; modeling 249–53; *see also* exit costs

Difference principle 175, 178

Discrimination, institutionalized 117–19

Distributive justice *see* justice

Lightning Source UK Ltd.
Milton Keynes UK
UKOW032305141112

202164UK00002B/8/P